Community Schools in Action

—

Community Schools in Action

—

Lessons from a Decade of Practice

EDITED BY

JOY G. DRYFOOS

JANE QUINN

CAROL BARKIN

OXFORD
UNIVERSITY PRESS
2005

OXFORD
UNIVERSITY PRESS

Oxford University Press, Inc., publishes works that further
Oxford University's objective of excellence
in research, scholarship, and education.

Oxford   New York
Auckland   Cape Town   Dar es Salaam   Hong Kong   Karachi
Kuala Lumpur   Madrid   Melbourne   Mexico City   Nairobi
New Delhi   Shanghai   Taipei   Toronto

With offices in
Argentina   Austria   Brazil   Chile   Czech Republic   France   Greece
Guatemala   Hungary   Italy   Japan   Poland   Portugal   Singapore
South Korea   Switzerland   Thailand   Turkey   Ukraine   Vietnam

Library of Congress Cataloging-in-Publication Data
Community schools in action : lessons from a decade of practice /
edited by Joy G. Dryfoos, Jane Quinn, Carol Barkin.
p.   cm.
Includes bibliographical references and index.
ISBN-13 978-0-19-516959-1
ISBN 0-19-516959-X
1. Children's Aid Society (New York, N.Y.) 2. Community schools—
New York (State)—New York.
I. Dryfoos, Joy G.   II. Quinn, Jane.   III. Barkin, Carol.
LB2820.C654 2005
371.03′09747′1—dc22   2004012389

1 3 5 7 9 8 6 4 2

Printed in the United States of America
on acid-free paper

Preface

JOY G. DRYFOOS

I believe in serendipity. In 1992 a snowstorm shut down the planes from Washington, DC, to New York City, forcing Philip Coltoff, head of The Children's Aid Society (CAS), and me to return from a meeting by train. The four-hour trip gave us the rare opportunity to explore in depth a new project that CAS had recently undertaken—forming a partnership with the New York City school system for the development of two community schools in Washington Heights. By the time we arrived at Penn Station, I was convinced that CAS was embarking on a significant initiative, one that appeared to address complex social issues in a fresh and constructive way. This new knowledge changed my life.

In my own work as a researcher in the field of adolescent behavior, I had concluded that, in order for contemporary young people to succeed, they needed an array of coordinated and intensive health and social service interventions. But I had also concluded that these programs had to be connected to the most influential institution in our society, public schools. Community schools had the potential to bring together the necessary forces for simultaneously enhancing education and overcoming barriers to learning.

I observed that a variety of school-based health, social service, and academic enrichment programs were popping up all around the country. In Florida they were called full-service schools; in California, Healthy Start sites; in Kentucky, family resource centers and youth services centers; and in New Jersey, school-based youth services programs. Other models were launched by national organizations such as Communities in Schools (formerly Cities in Schools) and United Way's Bridges to Success. New York City initiated Beacons, through which community-based organizations open schools after hours, and the Center for Community Partnerships at the University of Penn-sylvania created the model for university-assisted community schools. All of this was building on the experience of the C. S. Mott Foundation in Flint, Michigan, which had begun supporting "lighted schoolhouses"—schools kept open after hours for recreation and continuing education—a half century earlier.

We all began to talk to each other, and in 1997 I invited C. Warren "Pete" Moses, then chief operating officer of CAS, and Ira Harkavy, vice president of the University of Pennsylvania, to join me in Memphis, where we would present our concepts of community schools to school reformers attending a New American Schools conference. But only four attendees came to our ses-sion. It was clear that we had no visibility in the educational establishment. So, under the auspices of Fordham University's National Center for Schools and Communities, we gathered all the interested parties together and or-ganized the Coalition for Community Schools, located at the Institute for Educational Leadership in Washington. Within a short time we had created a new "field" of full-service community schools, a big tent that encompassed a very wide array of educational and social-support practitioners.

By 2003 CAS had organized 10 community schools in New York City and set up a national technical assistance center to help schools and com-munity agencies from around the country establish partnerships and repli-cate or adapt the community school model. CAS conceptualizes the model as a "web of support," a triangle that incorporates three interconnected sup-port systems: a strong core instructional program, enrichment activities to expand learning opportunities, and a full range of health and mental health services.

This volume will explore in depth the CAS model and how it has been implemented. We hope it will add to the growing literature on school-based interventions and school-community partnerships a hands-on account from the people who are doing the work. Part I provides an overview of CAS's past history and current experience with community schools, of the relevance of this work to the organization, and of the role of the lead agency and coor-dinator. Part II presents detailed accounts of each of the six core program components: parent involvement, after-school and summer activities, early-childhood programs, health services, mental health services, and community and economic development. The authors of these chapters are all CAS staff members, people with experience and expertise in a specific field. Each chap-ter describes the particular service, challenges for implementation, and the roles of schools and community agencies.

Part III gets into leadership, management, and governance issues. First, a school principal "tells all." Principals are, of course, central to this model; they are the primary facilitators of the integration of community agency staff with the school staff. But the lead agency has a major role, not only in day-to-day management but also in sustainability. This part looks at differences

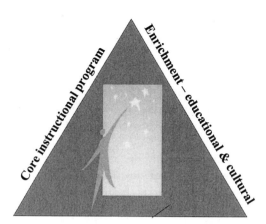

Removing barriers to learning & development

• Health   • Mental health
• Dental   • Social services

Developmental triangle for community schools. *Credit:* The Children's Aid Society.

and similarities among CAS's community schools in New York City and at the important questions of how to manage the expansion of the community schools initiative and how the schools are funded. The continuance of support may often depend on the program's ability to generate successful outcome data: chapter 13 provides an overview of evaluation of the CAS community schools initiative.

The final part, IV, moves to the national scene. First we learn about CAS's experience with adaptation of the model, not only in the United States but in other countries as well. Then, because we were interested in how educators view the prospect of community schools, we asked Thomas Payzant, superintendent of Boston Public Schools, to describe how these concepts fit into his ideas about school reform. We asked Steven Bingler, an architect, to present his ideas on what a community school should look like. We also invited Martin Blank to describe the work of the Coalition for Community Schools. The book closes with a look at what is ahead for community schools; Jane Quinn and I put our heads together and forecast a strong future for these models.

What is unique about community schools? In reading this volume, you should be looking out for certain issues. Although the word "model" is used a lot, in reality no two schools are alike; they are all different. The quality that is most compelling about community school philosophy is responsiveness to differences: in needs of populations to be served; in configurations of school staff; in capabilities of partner agencies; in capacity for change in community climate; and in availability of resources. These programs are always changing in response to changing conditions, turnover in staff, student mobility, access to new services and partners, and new knowledge about best practices from ongoing research and evaluation. They are also "aging." With their maturity, successful programs are replicated and programs without much promise are discarded.

Throughout this book you will encounter descriptions of what we consider to be successful community schools. Sometimes it is hard to capture the spirit of these places with words, and, although we include our best shots, photos do not always adequately pick up the unique climate and culture of a school building. Visits to community schools are the ideal way to observe the complexity of the effort, the dedication of the staff, the participation of the children, and the satisfaction of the parents.

Acknowledgments

Many individuals and organizations contributed to this work by providing information and responding to requests for materials. The editors particularly wish to acknowledge the help of Peter Johnson and Thomas Salvatore, Administrative Assistants at The Children's Aid Society, who communicated with the many authors and tracked down missing pieces. Philip Coltoff, Chief Executive Officer of The Children's Aid Society, and C. Warren "Pete" Moses, Executive Director, not only contributed chapters to this book but also encouraged staff members to actively participate in the process.

In addition, we would like to acknowledge the support of Joan Bossert, Vice President and Associate Publisher at Oxford University Press, whose enthusiasm for this project helped us get started, and the careful and consistent attention given to this work by Jennifer Rappaport, Associate Editor, and Heather Hartman, Production Editor, who helped us pull it all together. We are also indebted to Oxford University Press for its financial support through a small grant from the Oxford Foundation, and to the Citigroup Foundation for its generous support of The Children's Aid Society National Technical Assistance Center for Community Schools, including the development of much of this book.

Finally, we are grateful to the board of trustees of The Children's Aid Society for their vision, committed leadership, and financial support of community schools for more than "a decade of practice."

Contents

Contributors

Steven Bingler is founder and President of Concordia LLC, a community-based planning, policy, and architectural design firm with offices in New Orleans, Louisiana, and Los Angeles, California. Concordia's research and development alliances include the Massachusetts Institute of Technology's Media Lab, Harvard University's Project Zero, the University of New Mexico, NASA, the Thornburg Institute, the Appalachian Education Lab, and West Ed Lab. Bingler has published papers in the fields of urban planning, architectural design, education, public health, systems thinking, and smart-growth planning. He served as a special consultant to the Office of the Secretary of the U.S. Department of Education for policy related to the design of schools as the centers of the community. He is at work on a new book, *2076: A Democratic Revolution in Progress.*

Martin J. Blank is Director for School/Family/Community Connections at the Institute for Educational Leadership. In that role, he serves as the staff director for the Coalition for Community Schools. He has written numerous publications and articles on relationships between schools, government, and community agencies and institutions. He is a board member of DC VOICE (an education reform collaborative), chair of the DC Early Childhood Collaborative, and founding president of Yachad, the Jewish Community Housing Development Corporation. He lives with his wife, Helen, an early childhood advocate, and has two daughters, Liza and Molly.

Scott Bloom, of New York City, is Director of Mental Health for the School-Based Clinics for The Children's Aid Society. Bloom holds a master's degree in clinical social work and has been working with children and families for over 15 years. He is also an adjunct professor in human behavior for the graduate program at New York University School of Social Work. He is a founding member of the Relationships Lab, a not-for-profit organization created to further critical thinking and self-study in work, community, and personal lives. He has a private practice in New York City.

Janice Chu-Zhu is a community schools consultant with the Children's Aid Society (CAS) National Technical Assistance Center for Community Schools. In that capacity, she works with those interested in CAS's community school model. Her responsibilities include training, development, and consultation on such topics as youth development, program quality, organizational development, and parent involvement. A certified social worker, Chu-Zhu has worked in foster care and PINS Mediation and Diversion; for 10 years she worked on the national staff of Girl Scouts of the USA, consulting on pluralism strategies and quality recognition for its affiliates. She lives in Ossining, New York, with her husband, Xiang, and daughter, Jana.

Heléne Clark, Ph.D., is an environmental psychologist who works with organizations creating social change, using a participatory action research approach. She is the director and cofounder of ActKnowledge, Inc., whose purpose is to bring capacity for knowledge building, program evaluation, and research skills to not-for-profit organizations and collaborations. She has frequently taught in the areas of research methods and public policy and has authored numerous articles on social change. Currently, she is working to bring the "theory of change" approach to the field. Clark lives in New York City and serves on advisory boards to both community-based organizations and full-service school initiatives.

Beverly A. Colon, of New York City, is a physician assistant trained in family health, with subspecialty training in adolescent medicine. She is currently Director of Health Services for The Children's Aid Society (CAS) in New York City. During her career, Colon has worked for a community health center and served as Director of School-Based Clinics for Mount Sinai Hospital. As Director for Adolescent Health with the New York City Department of Health, she was responsible for securing funding to initiate school-based clinics operated by the NYCDOH. Prior to joining CAS, she was Deputy Director for Program Operations for Columbia Presbyterian Hospital and supervised several large ambulatory clinics. As a consultant to the federal government, she audits Title X family planning programs.

Philip Coltoff is Chief Executive Officer of The Children's Aid Society. He joined the organization in 1966 and, in 1981, was appointed Executive Director and Chief Executive Officer. Under his leadership, the society has achieved firsts in neighborhood Head Start classes, drug prevention, human sexuality and teen-pregnancy-prevention programs, mental health services, and services to homeless children in welfare hotels and transitional housing. He has presided over the opening of a medical foster care boarding-home program for boarder babies, and, in collaboration with the Department of Education, the city's first year-round community schools providing academic and full social services 15 hours a day. Coltoff lives with his wife, Lynn, in New York City.

Yvonne Green, of Fairfax County, Virginia, an independent consultant, is a senior consultant with the Children's Aid Society National Technical Assistance Center for Community Schools (NTACCS). Green provides technical support and consultations to NTACCS's clients and colleagues around the country. Before joining the CAS team, she was a school social worker for the New York City Public Schools and then was Director of the Safe Schools initiative for the District of Columbia Public Schools. Green has a master's degree in social work.

Clareann Grimaldi, of Brooklyn, New York, is an independent consultant providing technical solutions for nonprofit organizations. She supports the development, deployment, and operation of custom technology solutions that match the needs of organizations, their employees, and their clients. Her most recent work was the design and implementation of a Web management information system for over 1,000 youth programs, including after-school programs, community schools, and extended service schools; she has been technical advisor to community-based organizations that serve children through implementing networked technologies and has designed and implemented a suite of open-source Web tools. Grimaldi holds an Ed.D. in instructional technology and media from Teachers College, Columbia University.

Sarah Jonas is Director of Education Services at The Children's Aid Society in New York City. She has conducted staff development for youth workers through The After-School Corporation, the Partnership for After School Education, The Harlem Educational Activities Fund, and the Literacy Assistance Center. She is a certified teacher and taught for seven years in public elementary schools in Los Angeles (as a charter member of Teach for America) and New York City. She holds an Ed.M. in administration, planning, and social policy from the Harvard Graduate School of Education.

Hayin Kim, of Stanford, California, is a doctoral student in the Stanford University School of Education and Research Assistant at the John W. Gardner Center for Youth and Their Communities, working specifically on the Academy for Community Schools Development. Previously, she worked as Special Projects Coordinator for Community Schools at The Children's Aid Society, contributing to a public service advertising campaign, participating in data collection and analysis across 10 community schools, fundraising, engaging in parent and student advocacy efforts, and serving as part of the National Technical Assistance Center for Community Schools team.

Luis A. Malavé, M.S.Ed., of New York City, a former competitive gymnast and coach, decided to become an educator in 1980. After teaching in various capacities in the health and fitness area, he officially joined the New York City Board of Education in 1985. His work as an educator, curriculum developer, and teacher-trainer continued until his 1996 appointment as the assistant principal of the Math, Science and Technology Academy. Currently, he is the principal of The Children's Aid Society's full-service community school known as the Salomé Ureña de Henriquez Middle Academies at Intermediate School 218 in Manhattan.

Hersilia Méndez joined The Children's Aid Society (CAS) as the multimedia art instructor at Primary School 5 and Intermediate School 218 in 1993. Her formal training is in arts and communications; however, her work in the schools and a lifelong commitment to social justice led her to develop an expertise in the complexities of fostering partnerships in school settings. In 1995 she was invited to join CAS's National Technical Assistance Center for Community Schools as assistant director. She helps develop training, curricula, and consultation for hundreds of initiatives seeking guidance in adapting CAS's community school model. She is a published writer whose awards include the national Maggie Award from Planned Parenthood. She holds one master's degree in communications and one in fine arts.

C. Warren "Pete" Moses is Executive Director of The Children's Aid Society (CAS). As a social worker specializing in helping adolescents, Moses joined CAS in 1969, starting as Director of the Teen Program at the Rhinelander Center and going on to become Program Director and then Director of the center. He was promoted to Assistant Executive Director in 1984, Associate Executive Director in 1989, Chief Operating Officer and Associate Executive Director in 2000, and Executive Director in 2002. Moses has overseen strategic planning committees that focus on mental health, arts, sports, recreation services, camping, community schools, medical foster care, and foster-care-permanency planning. In 1992 he worked with the New York City Board of Education to open the first CAS community school in Washington Heights.

Richard Negrón is Director of Children's Aid Society (CAS) Community Schools, providing leadership and vision for CAS's community schools in New York City. He was a founding staff member of CAS's first community school, Intermediate School 218, and, as its director, was instrumental in creating the "full-service school" model that exists today. He also served as a staff member of the National Technical Assistance Center for Community Schools and was its director for two years, providing expertise in operations, policy, and partnership practices to individuals and organizations all over the United States and abroad. Negrón's involvement in public schools is also personal, as his son attends one. Negrón holds a master's degree in social work and is a certified parent-child and community mediator and trainer. He completed the Columbia School of Business Non-Profit Executive Management program.

Thomas W. Payzant has been Superintendent of the Boston Public Schools since October 1995. He has instituted new curricula in all subjects; high-stakes assessments for students, schools, and all staff; and a massive remediation initiative to bring the skills of all students up to high standards. Payzant came to Boston after serving as Assistant Secretary for Elementary and Secondary Education with the U.S. Department of Education. Earlier, he served as Superintendent for the San Diego City, Oklahoma City, and Eugene, Oregon, school districts. Payzant holds a doctorate in education.

Andrew Seltzer received a doctorate in counseling psychology from Rutgers University and a master's degree in early childhood education from Queens College. He has designed and implemented educational and social-service programs within New York City nonprofit organizations since 1973. He currently serves as The Children's Aid Society's Head Start Social Services Coordinator.

Editors

Carol Barkin, of Hastings-on-Hudson, New York, is a freelance editor with a particular interest in social sciences, psychology, and children. She was the editor of *Inside Full-Service Community Schools* by Joy Dryfoos and Sue Maguire. Barkin is also the author of more than 40 books for adults and children, including *When Your Kid Goes to College: A Parents' Survival Guide.*

Joy G. Dryfoos, of Brookline, Massachusetts, is an independent consultant and writer with a strong interest in full-service community schools. She has written five books and more than 100 articles on community schools and school-based health care as well as programs related to prevention of high-risk behavior in adolescents. Dryfoos has served on the National Academy of Science's panels on teen pregnancy, high-risk youth, and comprehensive school-based health. She is a founding member of the national Coalition for Community Schools and the Boston Roundtable for Full Service Schools and is a consultant to the Public Education Network's Schools and Community Initiative.

Jane Quinn is a social worker and youth worker with more than 30 years' experience, including direct service with children and families, program development, fundraising, grant making, research, and advocacy. She currently serves as Assistant Executive Director for Community Schools at The Children's Aid Society (CAS), where she leads and oversees local and national work to forge effective long-term partnerships between public schools and other community resources. Quinn came to CAS from the Wallace-Reader's Digest Funds, where she served as Program Director for seven years. Prior to that she directed a national study of community-based youth organizations for the Carnegie Corporation of New York, which resulted in a book entitled *A Matter of Time: Risk and Opportunity in the Nonschool Hours.*

Children's Aid Society Community Schools in New York City as of the 2002–2003 School Year

Washington Heights

Primary School (PS) 5, Ellen Lurie School
PS 8, Luis Belliard School
PS 152, Dyckman Valley School
Intermediate School (IS) 90, Mirabal Sisters School
IS 218, Salomé Ureña de Henriquez Middle Academies

East Harlem

PS 50, Vito Marcantonio School
Manhattan Center for Science and Mathematics (MCSM)

The Bronx

Community School (CS) 61, Francisco Oller School
IS 190, Environmental Science, Mathematics and Technology School
IS 98, Herman Ridder Intermediate School

Timeline of the Children's Aid Society Community Schools Initiative

1987	Planning starts
1990	New York City Board of Education passes resolution affirming partnership
1992	First community school (Intermediate School [IS] 218) opens
1993	Second community school (Primary School [PS] 5) opens
1993–1996	Formative evaluations conducted by Fordham University of IS 218 and PS 5
1994	Third community school (IS 90) opens
1994	Children's Aid Society (CAS) opens National Technical Assistance Center for Community Schools (NTACCS) with financial support from Carnegie Corporation of New York
1996	Fourth community school (PS 8) is launched
1996–1999	Three-year outcome evaluation conducted by Fordham University
1999	Five more schools open, with support from The After-School Corporation and other funders
1999	CAS and District 6 receive three-year federal grant from 21st Century Community Learning Centers for after-school programs
2001	CAS opens 10th community school

In 2003 CAS opened three more community schools; they are not included in this book's look at the first decade of the initiative. In 2004, CAS received a second 21st Century Community Learning Centers Grant.

To identify schools in your community, see www.communityschools.org.

PART ONE

Overview: Rationale, History, and Approach

—

Introduction

JOY G. DRYFOOS

A strong research base supports the rationale for community schools.[1] We have selected a few exemplary studies that document the impact of various community-school components on the problems children confront.

Early Intervention

Children come to school with an array of issues that limit their capacity to learn. They do better in school if they have access at very early ages to health and mental health services and family supports.

> Chicago's Child-Parent Centers provided sustained and comprehensive education, family and health services, and included half-day preschool at ages 3 to 4 years, half- or full-day kindergarten, and school-age services in linked elementary schools at ages 6 to 9 years. Relative to a preschool comparison group, children who participated in the preschool intervention for one or two years had a higher rate of high-school completion (49.7% versus 38.5%; $P = .01$); more years of completed education (10.6 versus 10.2; $P = .03$); and lower rates of juvenile arrest (16.9% versus 25.1%; $P = .003$) [and] violent arrests (9.0% versus 15.3%; $P = .002$). . . . Both preschool and school-age participation were significantly associated with lower rates of grade retention and special education services. The effects of preschool participation on educational attainment were greater for boys than girls, especially in reducing school dropout rates ($P = .03$).[2]

These findings are among the strongest evidence that established programs administered through public schools can promote children's long-term success.

3

Parent Involvement

Parents need help not only with parenting skills but also in many other aspects of their lives. Strong parent centers in schools can assist parents with many of the obstacles that stand in their way—for example, learning English as a Second Language (ESL), gaining employment, finding housing, and dealing with immigration problems. When parents are involved in their children's school experience, everyone benefits. Henderson and Mapp's review of 20 studies provides ample evidence that when families are engaged in their children's education, the results are better. No matter what the income or background, students with involved parents earned higher grades and test scores, were more frequently promoted, attended school regularly, had improved social skills and behavior, and tended to graduate and go on for further education.[3]

After-School Enrichment

Children need to be occupied during the after-school hours. Otherwise, if they are middle-schoolers and older, they are vulnerable to getting involved with well-documented high-risk behaviors related to sex, drugs, and violence. For younger children, after-school programs provide safe havens, protecting them from the temptations of the streets or the empty rooms and the ubiquitous TV set of a working-parent home. But after-school programs have been shown to do more than just keep children off the streets. These extended hours build on the school day and offer enrichment tied to classroom content.

> LA's BEST is one of the nation's largest after-school programs and most assiduously evaluated. Among the findings from six different research efforts are that children who participated: liked school more and were more engaged in school; were more likely to attend school; felt safer and their parents felt that their children were safer; enjoyed relationships with significant adults; had higher expectations about their futures; liked the program and had fun. The studies suggested that achievement was higher among after-school attendees, especially if they participated in the program over long periods of time (four years or more).[4]

Individual Attention

Children thrive in one-on-one relationships. Community schools offer close attachments between volunteer and paid mentors and the children. "Students who attended one of the three after-school sites of the Polk Bros. Full Service School Initiative in Chicago reported greater contact with supportive adults than did nonparticipants."[5]

Social Capital

Community schools, which are often located in very disadvantaged neighborhoods, have been shown to improve the social capital in their areas. Drug-ridden streets have been cleaned up; cultural events created, open to all; small businesses started; and the mobility rate reduced. "The analysis of the 20 school-based parenting programs also supported the strategies of community organizing that focused on building low-income families' power and political skills to hold schools accountable for results. This activism produced: upgraded school facilities; improved school leadership and staffing; higher-quality learning programs for students; and new resources and funding for after-school programs and family supports."[6]

Integration of Services

Fragmentation of services makes it difficult for low-income families to access the services they need. When these services are brought into the school and integrated with those provided by the school system, families can use them much more efficiently.

As you will read in the chapters that follow, the leaders of The Children's Aid Society were, from the beginning of their work, aware of the importance of building programs that were comprehensive and creative and that allowed for individual attention, started early, and involved parents. One way they described their emerging model was as a "settlement house in a school." But working directly in a school demanded a whole different orientation. The amount of time needed to bring all the necessary stakeholders together, plan this important initiative, and implement it cannot be overestimated. Even today, top-level staff members maintain continuing supervision and accountability for this large-scale effort.

NOTES

1. M. Blank, A. Melaville, and B. Shah, *Making the Difference: Research and Practice in Community Schools* (Washington, D.C.: Coalition for Community Schools, May 2003).
2. A. J. Reynolds, J. A. Temple, D. L. Robertson, and E. A. Mann, "Long-Term Effects of an Early Childhood Intervention on Educational Achievement and Juvenile Arrest: A 15-Year Follow-Up of Low-Income Children in Public Schools," *Journal of the American Medical Association* 285 (2001): 2339–46.
3. A. T. Henderson and K. L. Mapp, *A New Wave of Evidence: The Impact of School, Family and Community Connections on Student Achievement* (Austin, Tex.: National Center for Family and Community Connection with Schools, Southwest Educational Development Laboratory, 2002), www.sedl.org.
4. D. Huang, B. Gribbons, K. S. Kim, C. Lee, and E. I. Baker, *A Decade of Results: The Impact of the LA's BEST After School Enrichment Program on Subsequent Stu-*

dent Achievement and Performance (Los Angeles: UCLA Center for the Study of Evaluation, Graduate School of Education and Information Studies, June 2000), p. 61.

5. S. Whelan, *Report of the Evaluation of the Polk Bros. Foundation's Full Service School Initiative* (Chicago: Chapin Hall Center for Children, University of Chicago, 2002), p. 10.

6. Henderson and Mapp, p. 71.

Bill Foley

Why The Children's Aid Society
Is Involved in This Work

PHILIP COLTOFF
Chief Executive Officer, The Children's Aid Society

The Children's Aid Society (CAS), founded in 1853, is one of the largest and oldest child and family social-welfare agencies in the country. It serves 150,000 children and families through a continuum of services—adoption and foster care; medical, mental health, and dental services; summer and winter camps;

respite care for the disabled; group work and recreation in community centers and schools; homemaker services; counseling; and court mediation and conciliation programs. The agency's budget in 2003 was approximately $75 million, financed almost equally from public and private funds. In 1992, after several years of planning and negotiation, CAS opened its first community school in the Washington Heights neighborhood of New York City.

If you visit Intermediate School (IS) 218 or one of the many other community schools in New York City and around the country, it may seem very contemporary, like a "school of the future." Indeed, we at CAS feel that these schools are one of our most important efforts in the twentieth and twenty-first centuries. Yet community schools trace their roots back nearly 150 years, as previous generations tried to find ways to respond to children's and families' needs.

CAS's own commitment to public education is not new. When the organization was founded in the mid-nineteenth century by Charles Loring Brace, he sought not only to find shelter for homeless street children but to teach practical skills such as cobbling and hand-sewing while also creating free reading rooms for the enlightenment of young minds. Brace was actively involved in the campaign to abolish child labor, and he helped establish the nation's first compulsory education laws. He and his successors ultimately created New York City's first vocational schools, the first free kindergartens, and the first medical and dental clinics in public schools (the former to battle the perils of consumption, now known as tuberculosis).

Yet this historic commitment to education went only so far. Up until the late 1980s, CAS's role in the city's public schools was primarily that of a contracted provider of health, mental health, and dental services. The transformation of our role from tenant to partner and the establishment of our community schools program resulted from a number of interrelated factors.

Developing the CAS Community School Concept

The first deciding factor was our growing concern about the decline of public education, especially in inner cities. In New York City we were witnessing the failure of thousands of children to make it through the educational system—a system that was unable to respond to the growing problems of poverty, homelessness, physical and mental illness, and violence. The ever-increasing demands on our own social and health services provided daily indicators of the need for new approaches. Confronted by the evidence of the schools' failures and their lasting effects on the children and families we serve, our staff set out to determine what part an organization such as CAS might play in solving this problem. We wanted to learn how to address the social barriers to learning and how to establish firm relationships with the school system in order to carry out this goal.

The second important factor was our identification of a community that was ready for change. Our review of community-based services within the context of changing demographic and income patterns in New York City's neighborhoods clearly indicated that the Washington Heights section of Upper Manhattan, which is bounded by the Hudson and Harlem rivers, was an area of profound need. It also had the largest youth population in Manhattan and the most overcrowded schools in the city, with utilization at 116% even though more than 2,000 students were bused to other districts. In the course of a decade, between 1975 and 1985, the neighborhood had changed from a German/Irish/Jewish population to a predominantly Latino one made up almost entirely of new immigrants from the Dominican Republic. Most of the old institutions, such as churches, community centers, and youth-serving programs, had left as the community changed, and, while a new Latino infrastructure was starting to emerge, there was not yet a network of family and youth services available.

As we entered serious discussions with educators, health experts, community leaders, and others, we realized that if we truly wanted to make an impact on public education and address the barriers to learning, we would have to become involved on a broader scale and in a larger and more significant way than in the past. In order to get down to work on a project that would build on strong partnerships, we started communicating first with the central New York City Board of Education (now the Department of Education); second, with the district school board; and third, with the parent associations and other related groups.

We began to envision a different kind of connection with the city's public schools. We saw the many benefits that could come from clustering services and education in one place, right where the students and parents are, and we broadened our thinking to imagine a school that would fuse the best elements of a high-quality educational institution, a health clinic, a community center, and a social service organization. The school would not be open just from 9 A.M. to 3 P.M. for 10 months of the year; instead, it would open early, close late, and remain active throughout the summer, weekends, and holidays. Everyone from the principal to the teachers to the social workers, students, and parents would feel a sense of pride and ownership.

Our ideas were new—and shocking—to some traditional educators. Even those who thought such a relationship could be helpful and might address some of the social, mental health, and cultural needs of students nonetheless believed that the program we envisioned should be strictly separated from the school-day academics and operate only in after-school hours. However, we did meet with some exceptional educators (notably former Chancellor Joseph Fernandez and Deputy Chancellor Stanley Litow) who thought otherwise and who fully accepted our strategy as an appropriate and thoughtful response to the reality of the educational and social environment.

As a result, CAS was welcomed as a central stakeholder in the physical, educational, and social planning for a number of new schools in Washington Heights. We were permitted to meet with school architects and engineers, teachers, principals, local superintendents, and others, and we continued to refine our community school concept. A strong working partnership developed that allowed educators, social workers, and health professionals to function as a team with a common goal: to better serve the needs of each student and family.

To the best of our knowledge, CAS is the only organization that has presented its school-community collaboration plan to the New York City Board of Education. This relationship was formalized in 1990 with a legally binding resolution enabling CAS to be a partner for public school programs in the Washington Heights section of Manhattan (see appendix to this chapter).

Within a year of IS 218's opening in 1992, people began to make inquiries about what we were doing, and many educators, social workers, school district leaders, and elected board members wanted to visit. During the first two years of the partnership at IS 218 and, later, Primary School 5, many more visitors wanted to see what a community school looked and felt like. We hosted First Lady Hillary Clinton, Secretary of Health and Human Services Donna Shalala, Governor Mario Cuomo, Mayors David Dinkins and Rudolph Giuliani, United Federation of Teachers President Sandra Feldman, and scores of state legislators, members of Congress, public policy experts, and educators from all over the country. Representative Steny Hoyer of Maryland visited us in 2001; when he returned to Washington, he wrote the Full-Service Community Schools Act, which called for $200 million to support local consortia. Although the bill did not move forward then or when it was reintroduced in 2004, we hope for progress in the future.

Interest in our community school model was so great that we were able to establish a national technical assistance program to help others develop community schools, thanks to the initial help of the Carnegie Corporation of New York and later assistance from several other major foundations, including the Citigroup Foundation. Many documents were published, perhaps most importantly the "Building a Community School" workbook, which guides others through the community school philosophy and process. We were pleased to see programs spring up throughout the country.

As of 2003, we had 10 community schools in New York City and more than 150 adaptation sites throughout the country and around the world. I am gratified that our concept has been adapted to different needs and cultural settings in other countries such as the United Kingdom, the Netherlands, Colombia, and South Africa. As the momentum continues, we look forward to a significant further expansion here in New York City and far beyond.

Impact on Lead Agencies

As you can imagine, the community school program has had a significant impact on CAS. In a little more than a decade, it has grown to be one of our largest divisions, with a budget of $13 million and over 600 full- and part-time employees. We serve thousands of New York City children and their families and reach out across the nation and the world through our technical assistance center. We are an active participant in the Coalition for Community Schools and an advocate in New York State for full-service and after-school concepts and funding. Because we are such a large agency, our community school effort can call on every department for support. For example, our medical director can work with the clinics in the schools, our public relations director can escort visitors to the schools, and our fundraising department can help meet the growing budgetary requirements. Yet it is important to note that even if we were a small agency just starting out, we could still establish relationships with schools. We have worked with small YMCAs and Boys & Girls Clubs that have taken on the role of lead agency in school/community partnerships.

CAS's experience as a nonprofit organization acting as lead agency in a school/community partnership has resulted in some important lessons. First, it is crucial that the board of directors be part of the decision-making process. Our board members have been invaluable as innovators, sounding boards, cheerleaders, and contributors of financial support.

Second, all lead-agency staff members, whether they work on community schools or not, must understand the concepts and the practices. They need to learn how to communicate across turfs and domains, always keeping the best interests of the children and their families in focus. A key word here is *respect*, especially when entering schools. Principals are critical partners in all of our work and fundamental to the success of our efforts. The outcomes for the children are surely better when we all work together.

For me personally, CAS's community school work has been a challenging and exciting experience. I have seen my agency pick up the ball and run with it. Since our first discussions in Washington Heights about whether we would be allowed to establish a real partnership with the school system, the results have far exceeded my expectations. I am fortunate to be able to tour the schools frequently with visitors, and I delight in the vitality and creativity that have resulted from bringing social supports to a vigorous educational enterprise.

Of course, CAS could not have embraced the community school model without the talents and commitment of the staff. You will meet some of them in the chapters that follow. Believe me, they have worked long hours to produce high-quality programs for the children and families the CAS schools serve. They are all experts in their particular fields, but they also understand and appreciate the efforts of all the other players on our staff, in the schools, and in the community.

Looking to the Future

With our community school model, we are helping to change the national mind-set concerning public schools: education may succeed if every segment of the community makes its appropriate contribution. I know that to be on the cutting edge, you must take risks. When done right, risk taking is a responsible adventure in the area of social engineering, and it allows us to build on what we have learned. As we use our knowledge to expand and create programs, we are often questioned about why we do so many things in so many places. The answer is simple: we initiate and sustain those programs and services because they are what children and families need and want— and in the case of community schools, they make good sense.

Appendix: Statement of Support for the Children's Aid Society/ Community School District 6 Community School Partnership Plan

The following resolution was passed by the New York City Board of Education on September 26, 1990, in support of the community schools partnership between The Children's Aid Society and Community School District 6 in northern Manhattan, New York City.

WHEREAS, The Children's Aid Society wishes to provide community-based social services to the thousands of children and families in the Washington Heights/Inwood area who are in need and underserved; and

WHEREAS, The Children's Aid Society has a history of successfully providing social services, including health, dental, mental health, recreational, educational and camping services to children, teenagers and families; and

WHEREAS, The Children's Aid Society has had a long and distinguished history of working jointly with the New York City Public Schools in developing services for the city's children; and

WHEREAS, The New York City Schools invite and welcome collaborative partnerships with public and private agencies as a means of providing increased resources for children; and

WHEREAS, in partnership with Community School District 6 and in collaboration with other service providers and associations, The Children's Aid Society is willing to raise funds and provide coordination in establishing community-based services in one or more new schools currently being constructed in Washington Heights/ Inwood, to be used as full-service demonstration community schools open fourteen hours per day, six or seven days per week; now be it therefore

RESOLVED, that the New York City Board of Education welcomes this opportunity for a community school partnership with The Children's Aid Society and supports the establishment of this program in Community School District 6.

A similar resolution was subsequently passed by the Board of Community School District 6. This second resolution added that the local district "agrees to work in the spirit of cooperation in establishing such a program in the district and to so inform other appropriate officials with the district and the Central Board of Education."

Bill Foley

2

History of the Children's Aid Society Model

C. WARREN MOSES

Executive Director, The Children's Aid Society

The Children's Aid Society's concept of community schools came to life in February 1992 with the opening of the Salomé Ureña de Henriquez Middle Academies (Intermediate School [IS] 218) and the opening in March 1993 of the Ellen Lurie School (Primary School [PS] 5). These were the first community schools operated by The Children's Aid Society (CAS) in partnership with New York City's Board of Education. PS 5 is an elementary school whose students advance to middle school at IS 218. The model has evolved into a well-integrated, multidimensional community school involving CAS, the Board (now Department) of Education, and the parents and many other partners from the broader community.

Before the two schools opened, several years were spent in preparation and planning. Initially, CAS surveyed New York City communities to identify those that would benefit most from CAS's services. This was part of an ongoing effort on CAS's part to examine its current programs in order to modify them to meet current social and familial needs. The survey led to the selection of the Washington Heights community, which was characterized by a large influx of recent immigrants, substantial poverty, large families, and a dearth of services.

A more intensive study conducted by CAS in 1987 had documented the dramatic needs of families in this community and the shortage of services available to them. The school system ranked 32nd of 32 districts in nearly every category. The type of poverty that characterizes new immigrants was endemic: very low-wage jobs, two and three families sharing one apartment, and a reluctance to accept outside help. Washington Heights was the substance-abuse and drug-trafficking hub for the tri-state area and had the city's highest homicide rate. Teenage pregnancy rates were also among the city's highest. This community is not unlike those that CAS has traditionally served throughout its 150-year history. What was to be strikingly different was how CAS would address these problems.

In setting out to plan a service model, CAS drew on its long and rich history of operating community centers in low-income neighborhoods. This included its experience in providing health, dental, and mental health services; early childhood programs including Head Start, home-based Early Head Start, and day care; after-school and teen programs; summer camp programs; weekend and holiday programs; family-life and sex education; parent education; and an extensive array of parent-involvement opportunities and activities. In addition, CAS's community centers have traditionally offered a range of enriching and remedial supplemental educational programs.

CAS was also very much aware of the difficulties faced by the Board of Education in educating children in Washington Heights. Schools were overcrowded, understaffed, and failing dramatically, as demonstrated by the school district's ranking of last in the city. They had few resources with which to address the multitude of problems that limited the children's ability to learn.[1] Immigrant parents, though eager for their children to be educated, were largely disconnected from the schools.

It became increasingly clear that the children and families of Washington Heights would greatly benefit from the creation of community schools that would provide a one-stop shop for education, social services, and health services and that would maximize opportunities for parent participation leading to adult education and empowerment. It also became apparent that trying to do all of this with the limited Board of Education resources and within the short span of the school day and school year would be impossible; a significant, even dramatic, increase in capacity would be required. The hours of operation would need to be expanded into the evenings, weekends, and summers, and resources would have to be sought from every possible governmental, foundation, corporate, and individual source.

Using a community-building approach, we began to establish the foundation for the community schools.[2] The critical components of CAS's community school concept are:

- A three-way partnership among the Board of Education, CAS, and parents
- Full services—one-stop shopping
- Expanded school days, weeks, and year
- An integrated curriculum drawing all components into alignment
- Expansion and diversification of funding
- A durable commitment to the gradual transformation of the school into a community school

Forming a Strong Partnership

With a plan ready to implement, CAS's senior staff and board of trustees wholeheartedly committed themselves to creating community schools in Washington Heights. The initial step was to secure the maximum resources possible from diverse sources. First, CAS carefully looked at its own programs and budgets, including both private resources and public contracts. This intense internal examination of budgets and programs reflected CAS's desire to improve on past performance and practices. It involved careful assessment of existing programs and letting go of those that were no longer as relevant as they once were. These resources then could be redirected to meet emergent needs in Washington Heights.

Second, CAS targeted a few carefully selected foundations that had provided important support in the past and appealed to them to provide leadership support to the community school effort. While there was strong interest in the community school concept, there was also a serious question about whether it could be implemented. But CAS's long and successful record of program development in difficult areas gave some funders enough confidence to commit resources to the creation of the Children's Aid Society Community Schools. The Charles Hayden Foundation committed $2 million and the Clark Foundation committed $1 million. At this point, with resources in hand, it was time to present our idea to the New York City Board of Education.

In 1990 senior CAS staff members met with the New York City Chancellor's office, where the concept was very well received. The deputy chancellor arranged for additional meetings with the Division of School Facilities Planning Team and the other deputy chancellors. The Board of Education was planning to build a number of new schools in Washington Heights and welcomed the opportunity to have CAS join the design process so that selected schools could become community schools. Chancellor Joseph Fernandez described this collaboration as an "educator's dream come true" and a chance to meet the needs of the whole child with full community participation. Later that year, the New York City Board of Education unanimously approved a resolution (see the appendix at the end of Coltoff, ch. 1 in this volume) creating the Children's Aid Society/Board of Education Partnership, and Chancellor Fernandez announced the community schools program and partnership at a well-attended press conference.

The next step was to gain the support of the local community school district and its superintendent. Many meetings were held with the superintendent, the local school board (Community School Board 6), and the PTA Presidents Association, all of whom were enthusiastic about CAS's plans. Additional support was secured from many community-based organizations and other prominent Washington Heights institutions, including the Association of Progressive Dominicans, Alianza Dominicana, the Washington Heights/Inwood Coalition, and the Coalition for Neighborhood Improvement.

Building Community Support

The introduction of such a major change in the local schools and the dramatic expansion of CAS's activity in Washington Heights was a delicate process. CAS took time and great care to make sure residents, students, teachers, administrators, the teachers' union, other social agencies, and elected officials, including the mayor and the governor, understood the concept, the implementation plan, and CAS's commitment to services for the children and families of Washington Heights. As a demonstration of our willingness to use our resources and to act quickly, we bused 100 children from Washington Heights to the CAS day camp on Staten Island for eight weeks and assigned our mobile dental van to Washington Heights three days per week; the dental van served 50 children per week for several years, providing greatly needed care to immigrant children with serious dental needs.

We also worked with prominent community agencies to help expand their services and ability to work in local schools. A major collaboration was developed with Alianza Dominicana to create a substantial after-school program at IS 143, a school in considerable turmoil over allegations (later confirmed) of sexual abuse of students by a staff member. CAS provided the resources, expertise, and supervision, while Alianza provided the program design and selected the staff to operate the program. The program's name, "La Plaza," conveyed its centrality to community life in the neighborhood. As a direct result of this work, IS 143 became the first Beacon School in Washington Heights;[3] the program is still operated by Alianza.

In consultation with the superintendent of Community School District 6, we identified IS 218 as the first CAS community school, to be followed by PS 5 and IS 90. IS 218 was already under construction, which meant CAS could move quickly to create a community school without a long wait.

(From the initial idea through the planning, land acquisition, and construction, IS 218 took 10 years to complete. The School Construction Authority, created in 1989, promised a much quicker schedule; PS 5 was built in 2 1/2 years.) While IS 218 lacked several amenities that CAS would have included had it designed the school from the beginning—such as air conditioning, bleachers in the gymnasium and playground, a full-sized health and dental clinic, a mental health and counseling suite, and a family resource center—we decided to move ahead in the interest of demonstrating our desire to serve the community as quickly and completely as possible. This was, after all, the first new school to be built in Washington Heights in decades, and it had been designed to some degree for community use; its curved building, welcoming central rotunda, and large open playground were symbolic open arms to a community greatly in need of attention.

Creating Salomé Ureña de Henriquez Middle Academies (IS 218)

Beginning in 1991, one year before IS 218 opened, scores of meetings were held with parents, police officers, community representatives, social agency staff, mental health providers, housing advocates, hospital representatives, politicians, government officials, and others to help the community understand how this school would be different from others. Of special importance was an outreach to the natural leaders within the community, including parents, to secure their initial support for the concept and to ask for their help in establishing a community school with full parent partnership.

Approximately 10 months before the school opened, the assistant principals were freed from other responsibilities so that they could begin the planning process that would create New York City's first community school. They met with CAS staff members daily to design and plan the strongest program possible, drawing on the best of middle school philosophy as well as concepts of community education, community schools, and parent participation. Particularly important was the planning team's decision to adopt the middle school philosophy and approach recommended by the Carnegie Council on Adolescent Development's 1989 publication, *Turning Points: Preparing American Youth for the Twenty-First Century.*[4] Central to the Council's recommendations are ideas about middle school structure, including the creation of small learning communities (academies or schools-within-a-school). The IS 218 planning team fully embraced these concepts and organized the school around four academies, each with a thematic focus (arts, business, math/science/technology, and community service).

Early steps involved acquainting teacher applicants and others with the new school's mission and conducting aggressive outreach to locate a principal who was enthusiastic about implementing such a model. Additional preparation was provided for parents and prospective students to help them understand the special nature of this full-service, multidimensional, parent-friendly community school. It is fair to say that the initial response was largely one of hopefulness tempered with an understandable skepticism, based on previous experience with new programs launched by the Board of Education and others. CAS worked hard to secure the trust of the community and to engage participants sufficiently so that we could move forward together with the opening of the school.

Developing the Collaborative Process

An important part of the planning was to design, with the principal and the assistant principals, the day-to-day governance and operations of the schools. Essentially, in this design, the community school director is the right hand of the principal in supervising many of the school's operations. The principal oversees all of the educational activities, whether they occur during the regular school day or beyond; this includes curriculum supervision and instruction, special education, and school personnel. During after-school and summer programs, this responsibility is shared with the community school director, and all educational activities are jointly planned. The principal, as the Board of Education representative, is also responsible for determining which other community groups can use the school facility.

The community school director, on the other hand, oversees the health, dental, and mental health services, after-school program, evening teen program, parent programs, Saturday programs, holiday programs, and summer camp. The community school director also manages for the principal all other agencies and community groups who are approved to use the school. In short, the community school director manages the community part of the community school. At IS 218 Richard Negrón, a social worker with extensive experience with the Children's Aid Society Juvenile Justice programs, was selected to be the first community school director, and Dr. Mark Kavarsky, an educator with substantial middle school experience, strong educational leadership skills, and an uncommon commitment to partnering with the community, was selected as the first principal.

This collaboration requires day-to-day, shoulder-to-shoulder coordination between the principal and the community school director. Yet working in this way is no small challenge, as each group has different expectations of itself and of the others, and each group reports to a different authority. Earning respect and trust is absolutely crucial to the success of the program. Equally important are creating a common language that transcends individual professional jargon and establishing communication styles that work for teachers as well as all the other participants. All must share both responsibility and credit for outcomes (positive and negative) and see the education of our children as everyone's responsibility. These are not platitudes but critical operational challenges that have to be met if we are to succeed in this very different way of organizing the work of schools, communities, and parents in educating children.[5]

Some observers have thought that such collaboration requires an endless series of meetings, but in fact much of the communication occurs at ground level. Of course there are planning meetings and staff meetings and conferences and retreats; these are all essential to the smooth operation of the school. But much of the daily integrative work occurs in the hallways and by the front door and at dismissal and in the lunchroom as teachers, parents, and social workers collaborate, refer, redirect, and inform each other about the developments of the day so that they can modify their actions in ways that are in the best interest of the students.

Taking Action for Positive Change

It is very important, especially during the initial launching of a community school, to take action that quickly reinforces the positive changes and helps to create a "happy school" where both teachers and students wish to be.[6] To this end, at IS 218 a number of steps were taken, some small and symbolic, some larger and systemic. Respect was modeled constantly by the principal and the community school director and was the expected behavior for all; such modeling was especially important in handling conflicts and arguments between school personnel and students. The less dramatic demonstrations of respect also matter—the principal and the director always said "hello" in the morning and "goodbye" at dismissal to each student.

Special efforts were also made to treat teachers differently and more inclusively. Part of the planning for the first semester involved helping teachers and others design interesting after-school activities that they would like to teach. This planning exercise and the subsequent selection of activities for the first round of the after-school program greatly energized many teachers. They were excited by the prospect of having at least part of the week dedicated to fulfilling their own educational dreams and of not being hemmed in by the 40-minute period and curriculum requirements. Their enthusiasm has led to the development of dozens of stimulating after-school programs, including Recycle-a-Bicycle, the electric lab, the architecture shop, the dance studio, the track team, the theater group, the Latin band, the jazz band, the string orchestra, the school store, the entrepreneurship classes, the boys' knitting class, and much more.

Through one of the four academies (Community Service), more than 70 community service projects were initiated, each of which involved at least one partner in the community. Students fixed up a park, painted the subway station, assisted senior citizens, worked in Head Start programs, provided child care for mothers waiting in line at the local welfare center, advocated with elected officials, and painted murals.

Consistent with the *Turning Points* middle school philosophy, advisories were established as a vehicle for teachers to get to know students in a nonacademic way by administering to their special needs and helping connect them with services and activities that might allow them to grow and develop in ways beyond the normal classroom education. The school's four academies, each of which occupies one floor, are further divided into teams and then classes. Advisories are one-half the size of a class. Their purpose is to increase opportunities for students to feel noticed and cared for in small intimate settings. Respect for students, teachers, and all members of the community is seen as an active process, and the needs of the whole child, not just his or her cognitive process, are considered. The advisory exemplifies a high level of involvement, engagement, caring, and respect and helps to set the tone for an effective school climate.

"Town meetings" are special 90-minute periods serving 120 students. They are led by one licensed teacher and three community representatives selected by CAS. Seventeen town meetings are held each week, allowing nearly every student in the school an opportunity to speak his or her mind before the gathering, to participate in creating the curriculum for the meeting, and even to play a role in selecting the methodology of the teacher. The purpose is to provide creative ways for the students and community to come together on areas of common concern. Students have almost always opted for highly interactive educational forums on subjects as diverse as date rape, civil disturbances, gang involvement, and bereavement and loss.

The extension of the school's hours allowed IS 218 to expand in all sorts of ways. Within the first three months, an explosion of 50 different after-school and extended-day programs developed; in the second six months, "zero" and "double zero" periods (before-school programs) were developed in music, athletics, drama, and educational enrichment, as were evening programs for teenagers and a special Saturday program. Partnerships were formed with other organizations, including several in the arts such as Alvin Ailey American Dance Theater, Ballet Hispanico, the Joyce Theatre, and the Frick Museum. The typical school day began shortly after 7 A.M. and ended 12 hours later; the school then remained open in the evening for parents, college students, and teenagers, making a 15-hour day on more than 300 days a year.

Health and Mental Health Services

While the after-school programming was evolving, so were other elements of the community school. A health clinic staffed by nurses and a pediatrician and a dental clinic staffed by a fully trained dentist and assistant were created out of what had been designated in the construction drawings as a nurse's office and storeroom. These services, initially provided by CAS, were seen by the parents and the principal as among the most valuable. High-quality diagnostic and treatment services were provided at the school on a full-time basis; dental problems could be addressed without students having to miss school; and school staff could be assured that the daily occurrence of dozens of minor and major health problems could be properly attended to.

Over time this element has grown to include an optometry service, pediatric nurse practitioners, health educators (see Colon, ch. 7 in this volume), and a sophisticated mental health service (see Bloom, ch. 8 in this volume). Students who might otherwise be suspended can now remain in school while their behavioral and emotional problems are attended to and their education continues. Countless others, whose learning was interrupted by disruptive students, have a greatly improved learning environment.

Careful and sustained integration of a health service with the school's overall administration and its educational activities significantly increases its effectiveness; far too many school-based health clinics work in isolation and sometimes even have antagonistic relationships with school personnel. For the mental health clinic, this integration leads to higher utilization and much greater effect; its preventive strategies and the increase in student attendance alone are worth the effort. The overall impact of the health and mental health services on school culture and climate fosters an environment of wellness and health that uplifts everyone.

Parent Engagement

Community school directors often say to parents, "Please don't leave the education of your children to us alone. If you do, they will surely not do as well, and some will fail. We simply must do this together." At IS 218, it became everyone's business to do everything possible to engage parents and welcome them to the school: health clinic outreach, telephone contacts from teachers at every possible opportunity, social events, surveys of what parents would like to learn in school, and as many community-based activities inside the school as possible. Particular efforts were made, for example, to create performing arts programs with evening shows that parents and grandparents would enthusiastically attend and to create physical fitness and aerobic activities for parents, including weight training for the fathers. We worked constantly to counter the traditionally ambivalent way that schools invite parents to "come on in" while subtly and not so subtly discouraging their visits.

Seeing parents as learners in the school was an important factor. Many expressed a desire to learn to use computers, to learn English, or to study in preparation for citizenship. Through a local college, undergraduate-level classes were offered at the school in the evening, and special Saturday classes were offered by CAS in computers, English, cooking, arts and crafts, and entrepreneurship. Picnics and other community celebrations brought families together throughout the year and especially during holidays and in the summer. Importantly, in all of these engagement activities, virtually everyone from the school community participated together—students, teachers, parents, health professionals, safety officers, administrators. This contributed to a powerful sense of belonging and school spirit, which continues to this day.[7]

Launching the Ellen Lurie School (PS 5)

While the middle school was evolving, the first elementary school, PS 5, was in the planning stages, which followed many of the same principles described for IS 218. During 1991 and 1992 CAS was involved in the architectural design of this new school, which resulted in large areas for gathering in the auditorium, the dining area, the gym, and the substantial playground. We included air conditioning, medical and mental health facilities, a family resource center, and many other design details that made this school friendly and inviting to parents and the community.

The design also provided for significant levels of classroom intimacy. For example, in the lower grades, small groups can read, talk, and learn in intimate spaces located between every two classrooms. This shared space can also be used by parents, volunteers, and teachers who need to concentrate their attention on a few selected children at a time. The after-school program created a series of educational activities carefully integrated with the school's curriculum and often led by teachers, as well as an extensive array of student clubs. The Saturday program supplements these after-school activities, as does the summer and holiday programming. Special programs were created for grandparents who were raising children. In response to explosive immigration, classes in English as a second language and American history in preparation for the citizenship exam were offered at the school, along with legal representation for the many families who had complicated immigration situations. Services related to immigration were not just information and referral, but education and advocacy as well. The importance of the trust engendered by these activities between CAS, the school, and the community cannot be overstated.

On a parallel track, health, dental, and mental health services were also created and integrated carefully with the Board of Education–mandated pupil personnel services and special education activities. This integrated approach led to PS 5's assessment by the U.S. Department of Education's Civil Rights Division as the school that has the lowest rate of special education referrals as well as the highest rate of appropriate special education referrals of all the schools mentioned in their reviews.

Learning Starts before Birth at PS 5

A special accomplishment at PS 5 is the development of our early childhood programs (see Seltzer, ch. 6 in this volume). These include Early Head Start for pre-birth through age three and Head Start for ages three to five. Furthering the sense of continuity, Head Start graduates simply walk across the hall to attend their kindergarten class, eliminating 95% of the transitional problems experienced by graduates of early childhood programs that are outside the school. Consistency in the school and an integrated approach beginning at conception and going on through high school graduation simply makes sense. PS 5 is an excellent model of the first stage of this process.[8]

The Head Start program also provides the basis for substantial parental involvement in governance as well as in the program. Significantly, over the years parent leaders developed in the Head Start program go on to become leaders in the school Parent-Teacher Association (PTA) and then leaders in the middle school. Getting parents off to the right start pays dividends for decades to come.

By negotiating the local zoning so that graduates of PS 5 attend IS 218, CAS has been able to create a smooth transition from elementary school to middle school just as we do from Head Start to kindergarten. Shared summer programs, spring preparation activities for fifth graders that take place at both the middle school and the elementary school, and parent engagement in the process greatly improve this transition and help parents get through the often frightening changes as their children move on to another school.

Strategic Parent Engagement (Empowerment)

Parent engagement, leading to empowerment, is a cornerstone of CAS's community school concept. The story of PS 5's pedestrian bridge, told in chapter 4 in this volume, epitomizes this idea. Another example is the Peace Team, described in chapter 9, that was created at IS 218 in 1992 in response to riots after a police shooting. This program and the connections it fostered have been invaluable in improving relationships between the police and the community and in resolving conflicts.

Every school provides its own opportunities to demonstrate that we mean it when we invite our children's parents to be part of the process and part of the solution. If we help them engage in ways that they see are helpful, their success allows them to go on to new challenges that immeasurably strengthen our collective efforts.

Conclusion

At both IS 218 and PS 5, one of the most notable and observable outcomes was clear within the first three months: this was a school to which people wanted to come. Teachers, students, parents, and others were captivated and uplifted by the positive and enthusiastic environment that emanated from every corner of the building.

It is no small accomplishment that more than a decade later, outside observers still immediately comment on the positive culture and climate of these community schools and the inspiration provided by the breadth of the curriculum, the range of services, and the level of participation in all aspects of the school. The community school model demonstrates that by partnering with parents and community institutions in serious and professional collaborations, we are able not only to deliver effective programs and services but also to transform the institution formerly known as the school into one that is multidimensional, vibrant, and alive—the community school. Children's education does not take place in a vacuum, and without attention to their medical, emotional, and social needs, most children will continue to struggle in school. Without parental involvement, they will surely not do as well as they could with active parental engagement. By bringing the full range of the community under the schoolhouse roof, we have in effect created the learning community that is so often talked about in the literature and so rarely delivered in our society.

NOTES

1. Carnegie Corporation of New York, *Years of Promise* (New York: Carnegie Corporation, September 1996), pp. 45–47.
2. Marie O. Weil, "Community Building: Building Community Practice," *Social Work: Journal of the National Association of Social Workers* 41, no. 5 (1996): 481–99.
3. The Beacon Schools are public schools that partner with community-based organizations, with financial support from the New York City Department of Youth and Community Development. The community agencies can be awarded funds to operate after-school and other youth and community development programs in school-based sites.
4. Carnegie Council on Adolescent Development, *Turning Points: Preparing American Youth for the Twenty-First Century* (New York: Carnegie Council on Adolescent Development, June 1989).
5. Wayne Sailor and Thomas M. Skrtic, "School/Community Partnerships and Educational Reform," *Remedial and Special Education* 17 (1996): 267–70.
6. U.S. Department of Education, *Putting the Pieces Together: Comprehensive School-Linked Strategies for Children and Families* (Washington, D.C., 1996), pp. 68–82.
7. Thomas M. Skrtic and Wayne Sailor, "School-Linked Services Integration: Crisis and Opportunity in the Transition to Postmodern Society," *Remedial and Special Education* 17, no. 5 (1996): 271–83.
8. Joy G. Dryfoos, "Full-Service Schools," *Educational Leadership* 53, no. 7 (1996): 18–23.

3

Community Schools from a Lead Agency Administrator's Perspective

RICHARD NEGRÓN

Director, Community Schools, The Children's Aid Society

I first heard of the concept of community schools in 1987 while attending a briefing on a community assessment of the Washington Heights/Inwood neighborhood. The survey had been conducted to help The Children's Aid Society (CAS) determine what levels of services were needed in the community and whether it made sense for the agency to provide them. At this presentation I was immediately struck by the idea of working in a deep partnership with a public school to improve outcomes for children and their families; this concept of community schools seemed so simple, so fundamental, yet at the same time so powerful that I thought, How could anyone be against this? Armed with this belief, I arrived at Intermediate School (IS) 218 in the summer of 1992 as the community school director of CAS's first community school. Little did I know that my first full year as director would prove to be the most difficult, overwhelming, and at times downright humbling experience in my career.

Having survived those first few years, I now have the luxury of looking back and pinpointing some of the challenges—and there were many. First and foremost, CAS and the school knew that we needed somehow to put into practice the concept of collaboration and partnership, but no one understood what that involved. We all soon realized that we were defining what it meant to be a community school as we went along.

Another issue I faced was my relationship with the principal. How was I supposed to interact with him? Was he my boss? Did he have a final say on matters? Who was in charge? And what would happen when we disagreed? Still another challenge was posed by the multiple constituents in the school, from the custodian to the school safety officers, from kitchen personnel to the teachers, students, and their parents. What was my role with respect to them, and what credibility and authority did I have in dealing with all these different groups? In other words, who was I, and why should any of them listen to me?

While trying to cope with these questions, I also had to ensure the successful delivery of services to virtually the entire student population (approximately 1,400 students), their families, and neighborhood residents. As a colleague of mine is fond of saying, we were building the tracks while the train was running.

In this fluid and somewhat uncertain environment, it was essential that systems be put in place not only to share information and keep lines of communication open but also to ensure that realistic expectations were being developed and that there was support and understanding for our work. Yet creating systems meant much more than scheduling meetings to share information or solve problems. Successful implementation of the community school model required shared governance, leadership, and management, with all elements operating simultaneously. More important, it involved building strong relationships—getting to know people and talking to them about what we hoped to accomplish, how it would affect them, and how they could get involved. This element of human contact and interaction had to coexist with the development and implementation of systems. As the community school director, I had a responsibility to attend to both.

What Have We Learned?

Since the inception of the CAS community schools initiative, we have approached our work with the assumption that we are partners with the schools; their students, parents, teachers, and administrations; and the surrounding community. From the beginning, in working with the New York City Board of

Education and Community School District 6 School Board, we sought sanction for our work; we hoped to be viewed not as an outside organization parachuting in to save the schools but rather as a partner willing to work with, and on behalf of, students and their families. Our goal was to add value and, where possible, consistent with our organizational capacity, enhance the work.

This perspective applies at the school level as well. We work hard to keep principals informed and get their feedback, ever respectful of their role as the educational leaders who are ultimately responsible for what goes on in their school buildings. In reviewing how we evolved in the decade beginning in 1992, my first year as a community school director, we can point to several critical factors that allowed our vision for community schools to become a reality:

- Tending to relationships at multiple levels
- Establishing the concept of lead agency
- Creating a governance structure
- Strengthening the role of the community school director
- Building support for the community school director at the school level
- Building support for the community school director from the central office
- Working with, and on behalf of, children and their families

Tending to Relationships at Multiple Levels

From the very beginning, CAS sought to ensure that the community schools would have the buy-in necessary from a diverse group of partners, including the New York City Board of Education, the local community-school district (District 6), the principal, the teachers, and, of course, students, their families, and local community-based organizations. We felt that this buy-in was essential to ensuring that the community school model would be viewed not as an initiative that was imposed upon the community but rather as one that took into account all partners.

We set about establishing support and cooperation for the initiative by first approaching top school officials, school board members, leaders from community-based organizations, and parents. We conducted focus groups, attended school board and parent meetings, and made existing CAS services such as our medical van and summer camps available to neighborhood residents. All of this work proved invaluable when we opened IS 218 because it helped establish a foundation upon which to build. Today, we continue to tend to our relationships with the same constituents because we have learned that these efforts are not a one-time event.

Establishing the Concept of Lead Agency

Central to the implementation and management of the CAS community school model was the concept of lead agency. In our view, to successfully carry out the community school concept, it was essential to make a long-term commitment to the school. As an organization, we were prepared to do just that.

Equally important was to provide the principal and the superintendent with one point of contact rather than multiple organizations. The idea was not to exclude other community-based organizations as partners but to establish one organization with the responsibility for coordinating and facilitating the process. Given our organizational capacity as one of New York City's oldest and largest child welfare and youth development organizations, CAS was able to deliver core program services and provide the leadership for fundraising, staffing, and oversight.

Over the years other community-based organizations that had expertise in areas such as educational and recreational services were included, with the understanding that they would operate under the larger umbrella of the community school model. This unification was consistent with our goal of developing a comprehensive and integrated model that avoided duplication, which we believed was critical to the success of community schools. Even today, much effort is spent in ensuring that the principals and other school officials understand this concept, especially because they are often approached by other organizations about potential partnerships.

Creating a Governance Structure

Critical to our work was a governance structure that formalized interactions between the principal and the community school director. Regularly scheduled meetings to discuss such issues as how to coordinate and integrate our efforts around the development and implementation of an after-school program were extremely important. In fact, we insisted on these meetings because the nature of the work demanded that we set time aside to attend to the partnership. In a world of competing priorities, regular meetings also demonstrated symbolically the importance of the community schools initiative and its goals.

Interestingly, what began as one-on-one meetings with the principal at my instigation soon evolved into "cabinet meetings" that included the leadership of the school. For me, these meetings were a wonderful opportunity to learn about the inner workings of a public school, and they also allowed me to contribute my youth development and child welfare perspective to the discussion. Subsequently, my role in school-wide meetings grew until I became a fixture at every major school meeting. Today, our community school directors are valued members of school leadership teams, pupil personnel committees, school-performance review teams, and so on. In fact, the community school directors either lead or co-lead many of these meetings.

Strengthening the Role of the Community School Director

Recently, a community school director told me about a day when both the principal and the senior assistant principal were out of the building; the school staff members were overheard to say, "Not to worry, because the community school director is here." The director was a little put off by this added responsibility, but to my mind it spoke to the level of authority and credibility she had gained with staff, not because she has a title but because she is respected for her knowledge, problem-solving ability, and leadership. This incident shows how a community school director with experience, great interpersonal skills, and knowledge can have enormous influence and value in a public school. Yet this stature is something that must be earned, not only with the principal but also with all levels of school staff and with students and parents, and earning it is not easy to do.

As an organization, CAS felt it was critical to hire directors who were skilled, passionate about the work, and genuinely invested in working with people. Not unlike those who say that the most important factor in a school's success is the principal, we felt that we needed strong leadership at the community-school-director level—people who understood the importance of building relationships and developing trust. We also needed people who could comfortably work alongside a principal, confident in their own abilities and knowledge.

Several years ago a conscious effort was made to elevate the level of our community school directors by actively recruiting and retaining master's-level professionals in the area of social work or related fields, such as education, with at least five to seven years of post-master's experience. To CAS's credit, we were able to offer competitive salaries that allowed us to attract a talented and committed group of professionals. As a result, the principals felt that they had capable partners whom they could trust to look after the best interest of the school while also helping to implement the community school model.

Having identified a group of committed, experienced community school directors, CAS felt that these directors needed to build their capacity to effectively manage their sites. Consequently, a considerable amount of time was spent on skill building in such areas as budget development and management, supervision, and organization and time management. Community School Work Groups are monthly meetings that bring together all of the community school directors; they provide an opportunity for guidance, direction, and support, while also creating a sense of a unified team. We hold similar meetings for the program directors, office managers, and parent coordinators.

Building Support for the Community School Director at the School Level

Memories of my first year as a community school director include, among many others, working on medical and dental statistics, conducting workshops for parents, sweeping the playground during the Saturday program, and coaching the basketball team. I had two hardworking and committed colleagues, but clearly we were overwhelmed by the demands and the nature of the work. It was not enough to have a talented and committed community school staff; we needed help, and we needed a more effective infrastructure. Furthermore, given the comprehensiveness of the initiative—the school was open six days a week practically year round, often until 10 P.M.— we needed to more effectively distribute the work.

We learned early on that to deal successfully with the demands of the job and the huge investment of time on our parts, we had to add staff members not only to support the work but also to take responsibility for some of the day-to-day operations. The idea was that the community school director could devote significant time to building relationships, participating in governance opportunities such as School Leadership Team meetings, overseeing the initiative, and providing leadership without having to also be directly responsible for every aspect of the program. Examples of additional staff members include:

- A program director, who is responsible for the management and supervision of the extended-day program, summer camp, holiday program, and other special programs involving students in the community school
- An educational coordinator—a certified teacher (often a veteran teacher or an assistant principal)—who helps in the management and supervision of the educational component of the after-school program and other special programs
- A parental-involvement coordinator, who works with parents to ensure that they are full partners and participants in the community school
- A social worker, who provides case management, referral, and crisis intervention to students and their families
- An office manager, who provides back-office support and adds professionalism to our business practices

Figure 3.1 shows the community school staff at IS 218 as of 2003.

A core team of staff members most definitely allows the community school director to effectively manage and lead. Absent key staff, the task of fulfilling all of their roles will fall on the community school director.

Building Support for the Community School Director at the Central Office Level

Another critical factor was to surround the community school director with a team of seasoned administrators and supervisors who could provide guidance, support, and direction. By "seasoned administrators," I mean staff members who have experience working in community-school–like settings. During its initial stages, CAS's community schools initiative was driven from the executive level of the organization. Although our CEO and executive director remain intimately involved today, it was soon clear that if the initia-

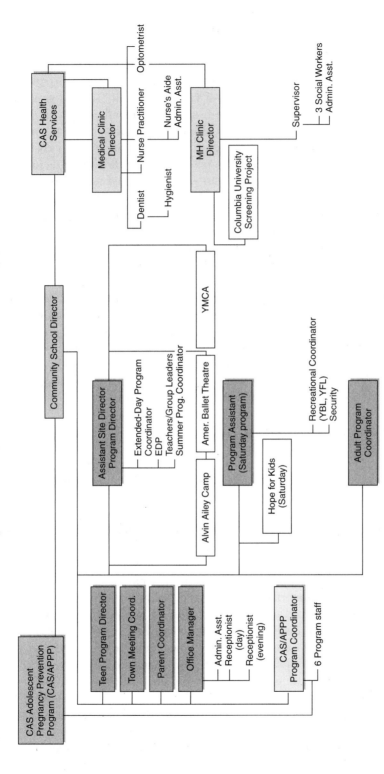

Figure 3.1. IS 218 organizational chart. YBL = Youth Basketball League, YFL = Youth Football League. *Credit:* The Children's Aid Society.

tive was to move from starting up to being part of the CAS institution, an internal structure would have to be created to support the work.

In order to facilitate this transition, a director was named to oversee all of the community schools. The community school directors reported directly to this person, but, as the number of CAS community schools grew, additional supervisory support was needed so two staff members were added. Reporting directly to the Director of Community Schools, they took over the responsibility for supervising the individual community school directors. As we continued to evolve, specialists, such as a budget director, director of education services, and payroll manager, were also added (see Figure 3.2).

During the period 2001–2003, CAS invested a lot of time and energy in assembling a team that could strengthen the community school directors' capacity to manage, and provide leadership to, a community school. Additionally, a considerable amount of time was spent in developing a vision for the work, in planning our path to fulfilling that vision, and then in finding the people who would help us get there. CAS's goal in assembling the team went beyond our desire to support the community school directors, although this was a major consideration; we also wanted to build a strategy that would allow us to manage our growth, improve program quality, and sustain our work for the CAS community schools initiative. The role of this team is to support the work at the local level, understanding that every school is different yet fostering a sense of one community school team with one philosophy, one mission, one vision, and a common set of goals and objectives.

Working with, and on Behalf of, Children and Their Families

When everything is said and done, CAS is a service-delivery organization. At our core our mission is to provide high-quality, cutting-edge services to children and families. We must keep this in mind because, during the daily grind of working in such an intimate way with public schools, we can easily lose sight of this basic goal. The demands on CAS and on the community school directors are enormous. After all, we bring significant financial and human resources into schools that would otherwise not have access to the services, opportunities, and materials thus provided for their students.

Within that context, it is easy to create the impression that we are the do-all-for-everyone provider; community school directors sometimes feel that they are treated like walking ATM machines and that what they are doing for the schools is not always appreciated or respected. It is easy to feel that we are not exactly getting a good return on our investment and that we are constantly being asked to do things for the principal, sometimes with little or no recognition. There's no question that the job can be thankless at times, but there is no doubt that we are in the right place. It is up to CAS to define our organizational expectations—for the school, for its children and families, and for us.

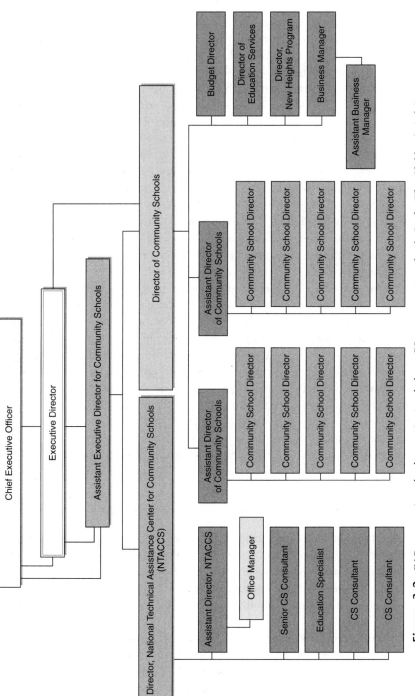

Figure 3.2. CAS community schools organizational chart. CS = community school. *Credit:* The Children's Aid Society.

Public schools need our support, and, more important, the children who attend the schools we work in need our support, encouragement, and, when necessary, a hand as they reach out to us. So, at its core, the community school is about working with and on behalf of children and their families. The challenges of working in public schools in the way we have chosen to do it are many, but they are worth facing as we reflect on the thousands of lives we touch every day and on our slow but sure progress toward redefining the relationship between a community and its public schools.

During my five years as director of IS 218, I worked with four different principals. But despite these abrupt changes, all too typical of public schools, CAS managed to maintain a level of consistency in presence and leadership. In a sea of change, we have been a stabilizing force in our schools. We have attempted to be responsive to the school but also to the children and families. As Lisbeth Schorr says, "In their responsiveness and willingness to hang in there, effective programs are more like families than bureaucracies."[1] We like to think that our commitment to the school and to its students and families is long-term.

We have worked hard at building a core program, consistent in our approach but flexible enough to respond to the changing needs of the communities we work in. When we realized that at one of our schools, Primary School 5, there were significant numbers of grandparents raising their grandchildren, we mobilized our social-work staff and, with considerable input from the grandparents, formed a support group called Abuelas en Acción (Grandmothers on the Move). Why did we do this? Because there was an unmet need that we were in the position to address and because, by supporting the grandparents, we help ensure that their grandchildren can attend school, and this helps the school itself. This strategy of being stable yet flexible has served us well, not only in working with students and their families but in the ever changing environment of public schools.

What Makes an Effective Community School Director?

When I first became a community school director, I never gave much thought to how to go about getting my job done. Certainly I believed deeply in what I was doing; I have always possessed the capacity to work hard; and of course I am one persistent individual; but during the first year and even part of year two, the job was, frankly, about doing what had to be done in whatever way possible.

However, as time went by and I had opportunities to reflect on our work, I became convinced that one of the most important requirements for success is the often uneventful yet meaningful exchanges with people. In day-to-day practice, success was about presence, about talking to people, about availability, about an open-door policy and access. It sometimes took me half an hour to get from the front entrance of the school to my office in the morning, because along the way I would stop to speak to anyone who needed to speak to me. Whether a student, a parent, a teacher, or a community resident, I made time to talk to the person.

Much has been written about emotional intelligence, and I am convinced that to be successful a community school director must possess a high degree of emotional intelligence and a commitment to communicating with, and engaging, individuals and groups on a personal level. The characteristics or competencies associated with emotional intelligence are foundations for building strong relationships and connections with people:

- Personal competencies, such as self-awareness; self-management, including adaptability, trustworthiness, and innovation; motivation, involving commitment, optimism, and initiative
- Interpersonal competencies, such as empathy, defined as understanding others and aiding their development; understanding group dynamics; and being responsive
- Social skills related to leadership, conflict management, communication, influence/persuasion, nurturance of relationships, collaboration and cooperation, and team spirit[2]

Community school directors need to be leaders and to care about people; I always look for that in candidates. I believe that they also need to be managers. However, given the choice between a leader who is responsive to children and families, genuine, willing to do whatever it takes, and equally comfortable talking to kids on the corner or officials in a boardroom and someone who is a strong manager, I will always go for the former. I believe that we can teach the nuts and bolts of management, but I am not so sure that crucial elements of leadership, such as personal connection with people, can be taught.

Some Final Thoughts

Across the street from IS 218 is a large, open playground. During our first year, we held numerous community events, picnics, parties, flea markets, basketball tournaments, and so on. It was a great way to meet people, to invite them into the school, to demonstrate that the school was something new, something different, something exciting. I first met Leo and Ralph and Lidia on the playground; they were neighborhood residents with kids scheduled to attend 218. We quickly developed a friendship. They were energetic, passionate about their kids, and eager to get involved. There were many others just like them—people with names like Maritza, Teresa, Luisa, Ernesto, and Reina. All of them wanted to get involved; they were waiting for an invitation. Many of them became part of our original core group of volunteers, and I believe all of them went on to work for CAS at IS 218. Many of them were still with us almost 12 years later.

Similarly, countless young people were touched and engaged in ways that made them feel like a part of something; they had a connection to IS 218 that was special. Our connections are still strong. We see former students in front of their buildings, out and about, walking to and fro. We bump into them at Frank's Pizzeria. We know their mothers, their boyfriends and girl-friends. The connection runs deep and it is hard to capture, but at its foundation it creates a sense of community.

I believe that all of these connections are related to management, leadership, and governance. Working in community schools does not permit remaining static. There are always new kids to meet and work with, parents to welcome, and principals and teachers to collaborate with, to disagree with, to make up with. From the perspective of a community-based organization like CAS, community schools offer a way to create an environment for mobilizing all the important domains in a child's life—family, community, institutions such as schools and youth-development and child-welfare organizations—and organizing them for the sole purpose of ensuring success for kids.

NOTES

1. Lisbeth Schorr, *Common Purpose: Strengthening Families and Neighborhoods to Rebuild America* (New York: Doubleday, 1997), p. 6.
2. Daniel Goleman, *Emotional Intelligence: Why It Can Matter More than IQ* (New York: Bantam, 1995).

PART TWO

Core Program Components

—

Introduction

JOY G. DRYFOOS

We have invited some practitioners who "do the work" to tell us what they do. Six program areas are covered here: parent involvement, after-school and summer programs, early childhood programs, primary health services, mental health services, and community development. These are the basic components of the community school model developed by The Children's Aid Society (CAS); most other models include some or all of these activities as well. We have asked our experts from CAS to provide the rationale for what they do in their components, describe a working example, discuss implementation issues and sources of financing for the component, and tell us about the challenges they faced and the lessons they have learned from their experiences.

Many of these components require space within the school—a designated area for parents to congregate, rooms for a primary health care clinic, private offices for mental health counseling, and classrooms and gyms for before- and after-school activities. Not every school can meet these space requirements, or at least many schools do not think that they have room for one more activity. I have observed, though, that more space becomes available in direct relationship to how essential the services become. One principal, reluctant to place a school-based clinic in his building, offered one very small room in a dark corner. Yet five years later, a full suite of rooms had been designated the "Health Place" with two examining rooms, a dental office, a meeting room, three private offices, and an attractive waiting room. The principal described the facility as "my clinic" when a newscaster came to do a story on the program.

Unquestionably, full-service community schools require delicate negotiations over many issues, especially space. The CAS schools make full use of classrooms for after-school activities and need access to the gymnasium, auditorium, band room, restrooms, cafeteria, and playground. The principal and the community school director must work out the arrangements for the use of facilities and for cleaning and maintaining them.

As you will see from these descriptions of the core components, this work is labor intensive. In every aspect of community school work, individual attention to students and their families is paramount. This quality reflects our best knowledge of what children need in order to succeed. Attachment to a caring adult is at the top of the list, and community schools have the capacity to ensure that this priority is met.

Core components are similar to "programs," but, unlike the way that most prevention and amelioration programs for young people are delivered, these components are not just dropped into the school. While we have presented them categorically, in reality the components are carefully integrated with each other and with what goes on in the school. This is a much different approach from that observed in the literally thousands of programs (mostly curricula) available for school-based delivery in the areas of substance-abuse and teen-pregnancy prevention; social and emotional learning and character education; suicide, violence, and bullying prevention—the list is very long. Those curricula are handed over to classroom teachers to teach. In community schools health professionals from collaborating agencies can take on this responsibility in conjunction with other health-related activities, either by coming into the classroom or by organizing groups before, during, and after school.

I believe that in the case of community schools, the sum is greater than the total of the individual parts. While each component, such as extended-day programs or health services, has a unique effect, the total effect is greater when children and families have access to all of the components knitted together. And, of course, when the lead-agency staff and the school staff are collaborators, everyone benefits. The CAS staff is expected to work as part of a school-wide team. You meet them in this part of the book as individuals. In the schools they must coordinate with each other, share information and space, and settle turf issues. CAS staff members learn quickly that in their work, the child must always be the center of attention.

Parent Involvement and Leadership in Action

HERSILIA MÉNDEZ

Assistant Director, National Technical Assistance Center
for Community Schools, The Children's Aid Society

From its founding in 1853, The Children's Aid Society (CAS) identified parent leadership and involvement as a win-win strategy and incorporated it as one of its core components. So naturally, when CAS entered into a partnership with the New York City Board of Education in 1990, parents were

41

invited to be central players from the planning phase onward. When CAS's first community school, Salomé Ureña de Henriquez Middle Academies (Intermediate School [IS] 218), opened in 1992, a red carpet was extended for parents by other parents and the staff; 11 years later it was still extended, not only at this school but also at nine others in Manhattan and the Bronx, as well as at many adaptation sites around the country and abroad.

In its work in community schools, CAS sees parents as assets and key allies, not as burdens; we aim not only to increase the number of parents involved in their children's education but also to deepen the intensity of their involvement and to encourage greater participation in their children's future. As we engage parents in skills workshops and advocacy events, we also create a critical link to the home, allowing us to serve and empower whole families and to foster effective leadership in their homes as well as their schools.

Most of the CAS community schools are located in low-income neighborhoods that have many recent immigrants; the challenges of meeting the numerous needs inherent in immigrant communities are added to the challenges of involving parents. However, after more than a decade, a number of evaluations and reports show that each year these schools see greater numbers of parents participating in events ranging from parenting training and advocacy events to holiday dinners.[1] This level of involvement represents a significant change in school culture; these parents are playing a greater role in their children's education and in the school as a whole. By 2003 leaders from both the New York City Department of Education and the New York State Department of Education, among others, had recognized the parent involvement strategy at CAS's community schools as a model to be emulated. Let us see how it all began and where it is going.

The CAS Strategy's History

From the beginning leaders at CAS saw the parent-community component as crucial to the long-term sustainability of the community schools and instilled in their staff the critical importance of making the schools truly accessible to parents and the community. The message was clear: CAS leaders were not saying, "They need us"; they were saying, "We need each other." They took a hands-on approach. Chief Executive Officer Philip Coltoff (Phil), then Chief Operating Officer C. Warren Moses (Pete), and Assistant Executive Director Herman Bagley were often seen waiting tables during family celebrations, participating at school board meetings, and cheering at community events. Their personal involvement motivated the staff and helped turn around the image in the community of "this 'white agency' that wants to take over our schools."

More than a decade later, many community activists and parents still feel that they can go straight to "Phil and Pete" if things are not going the way they believe they should. "The top Children's Aid Society leaders were always around—one or the other, or all at once. Our community, which is often distrustful (and rightfully so), got to know these guys, and it didn't take long for us to start trusting them. Time has proven that they came here to stay . . . that their commitment is real," observed Lidia Aguasanta, parent coordinator at IS 218.[2]

CAS wanted to erase the mixed invitation that schools often extend to parents—that parents should be involved in their children's schooling but only on the school's terms and often in rather menial ways. "We needed to convince the natural leaders (and they were not necessarily from the Parent-Teacher Association [PTA]) that we were doing something different; that we were there to offer respect and support, and that we really needed them if we were to succeed. We also made it clear that this was not another quick fix, that we were committed to stay around for a very long time. Little by little they saw that we were for real and began to trust us," said Pete Moses.[3]

Rosa Agosto, former director of the CAS community schools, said, "Naturally parents were going to gravitate toward locations that were so attractive and were offering them so many things. But it was also about offering them something they hadn't been offered before; beyond the services, we were offering them a relationship." Ms. Agosto explained that the active and visible role of CAS's senior leaders during the start-up years was critical in gaining credibility and support at many levels. "They were constantly around, and this was a very effective strategy. They were not only closely monitoring but also establishing presence and sending a very clear message about the importance of the project to the staff and to the community."[4]

Local leadership with cultural ties to the community (Ms. Agosto and Richard Negrón, then director of IS 218) helped parents feel comfortable with the people who worked in this new kind of school and allowed the parents to venture into unfamiliar territory. "We shouldn't forget that schools can be very intimidating places for adults, especially adults who are not highly educated and who are often treated by schools in very condescending ways," Ms. Agosto pointed out. "Not only because they don't speak English but because most parents don't speak the 'language of the educators,' they can't make the right questions or the right connections."[5] When you add in the cultural and economic challenges faced by most immigrants, the results can be paralyzing.

Parent Empowerment

My first encounter with the CAS community schools Parent Involvement Program and with parent empowerment in action was in 1993, when I started teaching art at the Ellen Lurie Elementary School (Primary School [PS] 5), then a beautiful, bright new building. To me, the parent outreach strategy provided by CAS was as new, as bright, and as welcoming as the building itself. As education writer Gene Maeroff observed, "It was almost impossible to walk through the front door of PS 5 and not encounter a parent. Some were volunteers, some were former volunteers who rose to part-time paid positions, and some came to the school for the sheer sake of companionship. When parents at PS 5 said 'This is my school,' they were talking about themselves, not their children."[6]

For an immigrant like me, whose children attended parent-unfriendly, not to mention immigrant-unfriendly, schools in Forest Hills (a section of Queens, New York City), PS 5's warm atmosphere was beyond belief. The beautifully furnished family room, the smell of fresh coffee, the presence of so many parents at all times, and, in particular, the friendly disposition of the staff were heartwarming; to me, it was an inconceivable atmosphere to find in any school, let alone a New York City public school. In contrast, the memory of my children's schools and what I went through as a young immigrant mother with language and cultural barriers becomes particularly bleak and even painful; I often wonder what impact a family- and immigrant-friendly school could have had on the bad choices that my husband and I—both young, isolated, and inexperienced—made in rearing our children, despite a relatively advantaged background compared to most immigrants.

One of my first memories of PS 5 is Chiqui (Enemencia "Chiqui" Diaz, then a parent volunteer, later the parent coordinator at PS 5 for many years) greeting everyone by the school door, many by name, often with hugs and kisses, always armed with the power of a smile as hearty and warm as herself and establishing a soulful connection not only with parents but also with children, teachers, and administrators. How could this image of accessibility not have had a positive impact on a parent rendered deaf-mute by a lack of English and startled by the intimidating, porcupine-like public school system? I have no doubt that a Chiqui could have had the positive influence on me and my family that I have witnessed with so many parents over the years. At the very least she would have gotten me to pass through the school's doorway, which I hardly did in all the years of my children's schooling.

The first tangible proof of the power of parents (immigrant or not) that I witnessed was the "PS 5 Bridge," as we still call it. There were two main challenges when PS 5 opened: it was opening in the middle of the school year and it was located at the exit of a busy highway where there was no pedestrian bridge. CAS, whose relationship with the school began long before it opened, got involved with both situations, first, by deploying key staff and parents from nearby IS 218, which had opened a few months before, to educate the parents of the feeder schools about PS 5's advantages and, second, by helping parents organize around the galvanizing bridge issue.

A footbridge had been part of the original design of PS 5. However, because of cost overruns on a footbridge at another school site, the Division of School Facilities decided not to build the PS 5 pedestrian bridge and to rely instead on crossing guards at this busy intersection. Regardless of the crossing guards, there was obvious danger, and parents were afraid to send their children to the school. After this need was identified, CAS encouraged and supported the parents' efforts. "We started by doing a human bridge. . . . I would stand in front of the school in the mornings, along with CAS staff, including top staff, and as parents arrived, we would approach them to help stop the traffic so our children could safely cross. We would do the same at dismissal," said Chiqui Diaz. "We went to local politicians and created traffic jams until we got the media's attention. . . . We took loads of parents to City Hall, in buses provided by CAS. . . . First we got the city to move the traffic lights and fix them so they could stop traffic longer, and then we got our bridge! It was a great feeling. . . . CAS supported us all along."[7]

Ms. Diaz believes that joining the school and the parents in their quest for the bridge not only gained CAS the support of many parents, teachers, and administrators but also helped spread the word about the school's services and, above all, established the family resource center (also known as the family room or parent resource center) as the magnet for families in the school. Parents were energized. "There are galvanizing issues in every school and every community, you just need to identify and act upon them. . . . Even if you don't succeed, trying is empowering." Ms. Diaz explained what parent empowerment means to her:

- Knowing and understanding your rights and the rights of your children so you can make appropriate choices and engage in negotiations to ensure that these rights are met
- Understanding your children's developmental processes
- Understanding the educational system and process and being able to differentiate good and bad instruction so as to have a true impact on your children's education
- Influencing school culture
- Educating yourself about resources that may expand your children's opportunities
- Building alliances to tap the power of other parents
- Becoming a lifelong learner to better your own and your children's opportunities[8]

The Parent Involvement Model

The Parent Involvement Program has a pivotal role within the larger context of CAS's partnership with the schools. It is based on the commonsense premise that students whose parents support, monitor, and advocate for their education are more successful in school—a premise substantiated by researchers such as Anne Henderson, Karen Mapp, and Joyce Epstein, whose comprehensive framework we follow (see Box 4.1).[9] The parent involvement model is culturally responsive and provides multiple entry points for meeting parents at their level as well as multiple opportunities to engage with, support, and strengthen the school. The following are key components of the parent involvement model: parent coordinator; family resource center; workshops, classes and trainings, adult education, support groups, clubs, and parent advisory councils; and parent advocacy efforts.

Box 4.1. Epstein's Keys of Parent Involvement

1. *Parenting:* Assist families with parenting skills, setting home conditions supportive of children as students, assist schools to understand families
2. *Communication:* Conduct effective communication from home to school and school to home about programs and children's progress
3. *Volunteering:* Organize volunteers and audiences to support the school and the students
4. *Learning at Home:* Involve families with their children in homework and other curriculum related activities and decisions
5. *Decision Making:* Include families as participants in school decisions and develop parent leaders and representatives
6. *Collaborating with the Community:* Coordinate resources and services from the community for families, students, and the school and provide services to the community

Source: "Epstein's Keys of Parent Involvement," in *Partnership 2000 Schools Manual* (Baltimore, Md.: Johns Hopkins University, 1996).

Parent Coordinator

The parent coordinator should have strong ties to the local community and links to the school and the parents. Usually a full-time employee, she or he may be a parent of a student or a graduate of the school. Good judgment, leadership ability, dependability, initiative, and energy are required; professional training is optional (experience in the community may be as important as professional training). Parent coordinators receive extensive training: the "train-the-trainer" program from EPIC (Every Person Influences Children) focuses on critical life skills such as communication both at school and in the home, successful single parenting, discipline, and study skills; ASPIRA Association, Inc., a grassroots organization that aims to empower the Latino community, provides the Parents for Educational Excellence training; and the Right Question Project, based at Suffolk University in Boston, prepares parents to engage in public-policy advocacy and to understand their local political climate. These trainings are combined with ongoing supervision by experienced social workers and educators employed by CAS.

One of the parent coordinator's primary responsibilities is to help the school create a welcoming atmosphere for parents. According to Phil Coltoff's mantra, you must put your best people in charge of parent involvement but always keep in mind that it is everybody's job. "Parents should be welcomed from every corner of the school," he says. The parent coordinator organizes workshops and other learning experiences, creates volunteer and leadership opportunities, seeks assistance for parents who need it, organizes opportunities for parents to educate decision-makers about their children's needs, does community outreach, and staffs the family resource center. The parent coordinator also works closely with the PTA and any other organization working with parents in the school.

But beyond the job description, the parent coordinator gets involved at many different levels, at times even acting as surrogate parent. Some years ago, parent coordinator Lidia Aguasanta, who was trained in marketing in her native Dominican Republic, was running an entrepreneurial program for parents at the school store. As part of the CAS–IS 218 Intensive Care Education program (ICE), it was decided to put some of the most troubled kids to work a few hours a week in the store under Ms. Aguasanta's and other mothers' supervision. Arquímides, an eighth grader prone to anger, perhaps the most challenging of the group, used to wear a tropical version of the "metal rocker" look (rings in his nose, ears, and on all fingers; bracelets, chains, ripped clothing, and so on) and often got in trouble for bringing weapons to school. Later, he reported, "Lidia put me to work in the school's store and became like a mother to me. Little by little, she convinced me that the way I was dressing was getting me in trouble, and I began to change. Now sometimes I even wear a suit and tie to school because she says that it is good for business to look good."[10] Arquímides went to a vocational graphic-design high school and has become a well-adjusted entrepreneur who volunteers at the school. He credits CAS and Ms. Aguasanta for changing the course of his life. There are many stories like his in the CAS schools.

The presence of the parent coordinator and of so many parents at all times, combined with the other support structures, had a positive impact on the CAS schools' climate and discipline from the start, as noted by hundreds of visitors and by evaluators early on. "There is higher attendance than at comparable middle schools. There is no graffiti, no truancy, and no destruction of property. Children who have been considered troublemakers in other schools were among the possible leaders here," reported Esther Robison, who conducted the first interim evaluation in 1993.[11]

We are pleased to report that this positive climate has been sustained. The 1999 Fordham University report by Ellen Brickman and Anthony Cancelli states, "The success of the schools is also evident in the sheer vibrancy and activity levels of PS 5 and IS 218. Hundreds of students participate in activities in the building before and after school, and dozens of adults attend programs in the evening. Perhaps more impressive is that, despite the sheer volume of adults and children in the school communities at all times, each school manages to retain an intimate feeling, with both CAS and Board of Education staff displaying real familiarity with both children and parents."[12] As of this writing, there has not yet been another formal evaluation; however, through self-assessment as well as observations from independent visitors, we can still brag about the climate of our schools.

The effects of our parent networks often transcend the schools' walls. The coordinators and their core leaders establish a relationship with parents that spills into the neighborhood, creating a sort of watchful guard to protect their children even on the streets. "We are like walking sponges around the school and the neighborhood . . . getting all sorts of information, always vigilant, always sharing. Just like in our country, we watch and even scold the neighbors' children as if they were our own. Most kids respond, it's something cultural," Ms. Aguasanta said.[13]

Another added value, and not a small one, is that effective parent coordinators provide leadership continuity, in contrast to the PTA's leadership, which usually changes every year.

Family Resource Center

The family resource center or family room is a magnetic, welcoming space with an open door policy. It is staffed by the parent coordinator and available year round all day and through the evening for parent interaction, trainings, and services. Ideally, this room should be located close to the entrance of the school, and it must show the school's respect for parents. Pete Moses, known for visiting the schools now and then to see not only what goes on but how they look, is emphatic about the importance of the appearance of these rooms; they should be spotless, and an effort must be made to maintain a homelike atmosphere, despite the challenges of conducting business and trainings there. "They shouldn't look like classrooms, offices, or storage spaces; they must show our respect for parents," he says.[14]

Live plants and a constant pot of fresh coffee can work wonders to achieve a homelike effect, but the atmosphere in the rooms is largely the result of a carefully maintained positive attitude and a clever mix of formal and informal structures. For instance, when IS 218 first opened, CAS built offices for the social workers inside the good-sized family room, not only because of lack of space elsewhere but also to allow the social workers to interact with parents in informal ways and to help destigmatize the need for mental health services, which is often taboo in Latin cultures. Another benefit was that the social workers were exposed to the family room's activities and could offer feedback (supervision) without being perceived as intruders.

The first evaluation of IS 218 in 1993 said, "The room was a bustle of activity, parents freely coming in, talking with helpful, outgoing, caring staff."[15] Ten years later, reports were equally enthusiastic: "Whether they are attending a workshop, meeting with the school's social worker or accompanying their child on a clinic visit, parent participation in our community schools is exceeding our outlined monthly goals. Site directors register an average of 800 visits per month with numbers occasionally soaring as high as 1,500."[16]

In a school that lacks space, as is often the case, a room used by the PTA can become the family resource center, which may facilitate the integration of the PTA leaders' and the parent coordinator's efforts toward the common goal of involving parents. With proper supervision and structure, turf issues and other challenges natural to sharing space may be overcome by the opportunities offered by interaction.

In fact, transforming an uninviting PTA room into a cozy family room can be a strategic and inexpensive win for community-based organizations (CBOs) starting a partnership with a school; this has become one of CAS's effective startup strategies. At the Vito Marcantonio Elementary School (PS 50), one of CAS's schools in East Harlem, New York City, there was a great deal of skepticism when we first got involved in 1999, and we needed some quick wins to convince people that change was possible. The PTA room was the obvious choice because of its strategic value; it would provide the opportunity to start a relationship with parents, and, because it was located at the entrance of the school, it would give us visibility, which is particularly important in the startup phase.

Doretta Headen, longtime leader and PTA president of the school, told me that when she saw what CAS had done with "our ugly PTA room, in no time," she started to believe that our promises could come true. The transformation of the room also helped convince teachers, other parents, the principal, and even the custodial staff, all of whom could not believe that the dingy, depressing, cluttered, storage-like space they had called a PTA room for 40 years could be transformed in less than a month (and for close to nothing) into an airy, colorful, spotless, inviting space. Also, in the process we identified and recruited parent and grandparent leaders who have remained involved for several years.

CAS Family Resource Center Characteristics

- Acts as a magnet space for parent interaction
- Staffed by the parent coordinator
- Maintains an open door policy
- Ideally located close to the school's entrance
- Has a welcoming atmosphere
- Offers both structured programs and informal gatherings
- Shows school's respect for parents
- Can double as PTA room
- Open year round from 8 A.M. to 9:30 P.M.

CAS Family Resource Center Activities

- Advocacy opportunities
- Volunteer and mentoring opportunities
- Strengthening of social networks
- Trainings
- Classes
- Ongoing assessment of needs and assets
- Informal gatherings and "hanging out"
- Celebrations and food
- Services and referrals

Workshops, Classes, Clubs, and Parent Advisory Councils

In its 2003 report to the Picower Foundation, longtime supporter of its Parent Involvement Program, CAS demonstrated that workshops and other programs for parents are thriving at all of the community schools. The schools work continuously to assess parent needs and determine workshop topics and content accordingly. As a result, both the number of enrichment workshops and the attendance (which has been historically high) have continued to increase. Topics have included domestic violence, understanding Child Health Plus (a New York State health insurance program open to children regardless of their immigration status), housing resources, single parenting, communicating with teachers, the impact of love, and reforms within the Department of Education. A number of stress management workshops have also been held to help parents and children manage growing concerns about security after September 11 and the war in Iraq. EPIC workshops continue on such topics as communicating with one's child, discipline, and behavioral challenges. Weekly classes include family life and holistic sexuality, "Growing Together" (a training offered to mothers and daughters), cooking, baking, catering, sewing, interior design, crafts, and painting. As part of our Adult Education Program, we offer English as a second language, preparation for the general equivalency diploma, basic computer training, and literacy, among others; classes run during the day and at night.

At some schools many classes run on Saturdays to increase accessibility and encourage participation. Access to vocational classes is especially important in these communities, where residents welcome opportunities to increase their income. Over the years a number of participants have started their own businesses or become trainers themselves.

In addition, several weekly support groups are held at all the schools. Approximately 500 parents and guardians attend parent and grandparent support groups, which address issues such as discipline and communication through role-playing and guided discussion. Some schools also have pregnancy clubs, grandparents' clubs, and literary circles.

At some of the schools, parent advisory councils have been established in which parents meet weekly to discuss the current state of parent programming and suggest future changes; there are plans to focus on after-school programming. Parent leaders also actively participate in School Leadership Teams (SLTs) with our schools' directors to help make curriculum and educational decisions along with teachers and administrators. Though SLTs are sometimes prone to being manipulated by school administrators (as frequently happens with PTAs), CAS is committed to helping strengthen these groups.

Parent coordinators meet monthly with the parent advisory councils to discuss program planning, parents' needs, and effective recruitment. At some schools the PTA Executive Board has been invited to become part of the advisory council, increasing the council's reach and improving coordination and communication between CAS and the school at large. Parent input is ongoing, with parents streaming in and out of the CAS offices at the schools each day. Some schools planned to distribute a survey at the end of 2003 to retrieve formal parent feedback on both the after-school and the parent initiatives.[17]

For five years PS 5 and IS 218 had a program aimed at fathers only. Julio Alvarado, the community organizer who ran the program for three years, describes it:

> We involved about 400 fathers a year through the Father's Club; we met four times a week, including Saturdays. Our weekend program usually drew about 30 fathers and their children. The 'club' culture is attractive to the Dominican community; therefore we decided on this model. We needed to use all our imagination and skills to attract them. Men, and in particular Latino men, don't believe that much in getting involved in their children's education—for most of them that's a thing for women, they focus more on being providers. . . . We were pretty successful, particularly considering the odds; funding was a big challenge and sometimes I felt we were not a priority, that we were an afterthought. The club eventually blended with the general program with some success. But I truly believe that you need a nontraditional strategy to involve fathers.[18]

Parent Advocacy Efforts

Advocacy has been at the center of the CAS parent involvement strategy. An example is the Immigration Center, which opened at PS 5 when immigration law changed in the mid-1990s. The center's purpose was to educate parents about their rights and to encourage them, whenever possible, to become U.S. citizens in order to have a voice and be able to count politically. The center, staffed by a lawyer, paralegals, and volunteers, served not only the parents but also the whole community.

Some parents from CAS schools have been elected to local school boards, where they actively participate in choosing or discarding principals and superintendents. For years CAS has taken hundreds of parents to Albany to lobby for after-school funding and other causes, and CAS joined with Citizen Action, a New York City group that advocated equity in education, to organize a parents' letter-writing campaign aimed at state legislators, the governor, and New York City's mayor in support of after-school funding.

From the beginning CAS has facilitated meetings between key public figures and parents on the parents' territory—the schools. For example, parents met with former Attorney General Janet Reno to discuss the importance of after-school programs in preventing crime; they have met with former Secretary of Education Richard Riley and Representative Steny Hoyer as well as with local leaders such as the city's mayor, mayoral candidates, and the head of the City Council. During critical budget sessions, Representative Steve Sanders, head of the Education Committee of the New York State Assembly, met with parents in the family resource center of IS 218 to hear their concerns about proposed cuts and their opinions about the value of school-community partnerships. Through such exposure our parents have refined their debating and advocating skills.

We continue to work on large-scale advocacy efforts that are not limited to our schools but in many cases include parents districtwide. CAS has developed a partnership with the current leadership of the New York City Department of Education, and CAS parents have participated in several key focus groups as part of the city's Children First initiative, a citywide strategic planning process. In 2003 a group of 25 parents was invited to discuss the value of school-CBO partnerships with Chancellor Joel Klein. Fourteen of the parents were from CAS community schools; they were the only minority participants (they were African American, Latino, and Indian) and the indisputable leaders of the meeting. Parent coordinator Lidia Aguasanta drew the only ovation of the night, led by Klein himself, when she offered to take as many parents as needed to Albany to protest budget cuts, saying "Come with us to show the governor that we won't stand for more cuts; we really want to help you get the appropriate funding for our kids."

Challenges

Resistance

The list of challenges to parental involvement in schools is long; it merits a book of its own. Resistance to the idea itself is one of the biggest challenges. "People pay a lot of lip service to the importance of parent involvement because it is politically correct, but most of them don't really want it because it interferes," said Negrón, CAS Director of Community Schools, who believes that this disconnect is one of the biggest challenges to meaningful parental involvement.[19] There is a general sense among politicians, principals, teachers, and even parents that when parents (poor parents in particular) start using their power, things can get messy. There is a "glass ceiling" that can prevent true parent empowerment. As a result, balancing parents' power and political risk is one of the main concerns for CBOs if they really want to keep the partnership long enough to effect comprehensive change.

The problem becomes even more difficult the closer it comes to "messing up the house." You can take hundreds of parents to Washington, Albany, or even City Hall rather safely, but what is a CBO partnering with a school to do about an inefficient principal, for instance? Does it help the parents organize around the issue, thus risking the partnership? Or what does a CBO do about an overcrowded school that is slated by the district to enroll 400 more students? There are no easy answers. Perhaps making advocacy the number one goal, helping to effectively build parents' political capacity, would strengthen natural networks of parents to the point that no catalyst is needed.

Negative Parent Involvement

The issues described above involve overt institutional resistance to a united front composed of the CBO and the parents. But there is another kind of resistance, one from both the school administration and cliques of parents who, for racial, political, or socioeconomic reasons, oppose the inclusion and empowerment of underprivileged parents. This negative parent involvement is damaging and extremely difficult to counteract; it can derail the best-intentioned initiative, and unfortunately it is not rare. "Fear kept them away from something that they knew was good for their children," said Janice Chu-Zhu, CAS Community Schools Consultant, about minority parents whose children were threatened at school in an interracial community where she was helping establish a community school; in the end, the initiative was aborted.[20] No partnership between a community and a school is immune to this kind of resistance.

Communication

Communication is often a major challenge. "Helping staff and other people (our partners, even the parents) to really understand the importance of meaningful parent involvement—it's very difficult," said Negrón.[21] He believes that getting the point across about parent involvement and building the capacity of the staff concerning this subject is crucial to sustaining and continuously improving the community school strategy. To create a parent-friendly atmosphere, schools must be aware that communication includes everything from staff attitudes to what is displayed on the walls. Getting the point across to everybody—parents, staff, and administration—is a herculean effort.

Funding

Lack of money is an obvious, ever-present challenge. For the most part, CAS has supported its Parent Involvement Programs with private funds. However, in 2003 CAS began to receive some public funding from New York City's Department of Education; it would be used to hire and supervise parent coordinators at selected schools.

Changing Leadership

In New York City chancellors often seem to be going through a revolving door; superintendents and principals move on rather frequently; and directors and parent leaders also leave. This is a major challenge, particularly in a field where building constituencies and alliances is not an easy task. The parent involvement strategy must adjust to every change, large or small; all changes remind us that parent involvement is a never-ending process, itself very challenging.

After Chancellor Klein took office in 2002, CAS successfully positioned our parent leaders and facilitated the meeting of hundreds of our parents with the new Department of Education leadership. Pete Moses, a perennial optimist, believes that leadership does matter, but that parent involvement, when done appropriately, snowballs and counteracts many challenges. "You must do constant outreach, whatever it takes. You must build a strong critical mass," he said.[22] I believe we must also build a critical mass of leaders; the broader the leadership base (parents, administrators, teachers, students), the better chance the schools have of excelling.

The list of challenges goes on and on. Since there is not much hope that the list will shrink any time soon, it is important to remember that tackling challenges fuels momentum, which is so vital to a healthy strategy.

Lessons Learned

CAS has built a critical mass, which is essential to community organizing, but we need to maintain it and also to keep deepening our parents' knowledge of curriculum and the process of teaching and learning. We will continue to closely watch the process of parent involvement, a policy we have followed from the beginning of the community schools initiative. A few years ago we slacked a bit, probably a sin of overconfidence, and paid with loss of momentum. We learned our lesson, however, and were able to correct our course.

By tracking research, adapting best practices, and building on the Epstein framework, at first intuitively and later purposefully, we have made the Parent Involvement Programs more structured and less dependent on individuals; the parents are much more empowered, expecting more and contributing more to the schools. The programs are now able to withstand leadership changes at different levels, whereas years ago a change would present a major challenge. Many of the positive outcomes can be measured; there are evaluations and reports to prove our success. Adaptation is now easier; as a result, CAS has been asked to provide technical assistance on the subject to key local and national organizations as well as to both New York City and New York State, which features our Parent Involvement Program as one of four outstanding programs in the state.[23]

Monitoring and modifying are crucial to progress, and we are committed to this process. We are determined to provide technical assistance to our sites, as we do to hundreds around the country and abroad, to develop their capacity to adapt the parent involvement model while maintaining its core philosophy. We need to make sure that parent involvement programs are less dependent on individuals and more cohesive across sites.

Conclusion

The Fordham University evaluation concluded the following:

> Parent involvement and engagement is one of the areas in which the [CAS] Community Schools have demonstrated their greatest success.

. . . Parents have heard and accepted the message that they are viewed as equal partners in the education of their children, and they take this responsibility seriously. . . . As parents have developed their sense of ownership, they have also made the schools their own, and use them as centers for both social activity and assistance with a broad range of needs. This, again, is a hallmark of CAS's success at engaging the population of families at PS 5 and IS 218.[24]

Over the long term, the guiding framework to measure our parents program is the six dimensions of parent involvement as proposed by Salinas, Epstein, and Sanders.[25] We cannot yet "scientifically" prove the direct positive impact of our parent involvement strategy on student achievement; but there is evidence that our parents are better prepared to advocate for their children and to understand their developmental and educational process, that they contribute to the climate and functioning of the school, and that we have established linkages between schools and parents. In their analysis of 56 studies to update *The Evidence Grows,* Karen Mapp and Anne Henderson support the conclusion that any form of parent involvement appears to produce measurable gains in student achievement: "The evidence is consistent, positive and convincing; families have a major influence on their children's achievement in school and through life. When schools build partnerships with families that respond to their contributions, they are successful in sustaining connections that are aimed at students' achievement."[26]

After years of sustained development, the CAS Parent Involvement Program has grown, become stronger, and gained respect among teachers, school administrators, funders, public institutions, and, in particular, parents. This complex and rewarding task of building strong partnerships among community, school, and parents has been accomplished by a combination of common sense, logic, and, most important, passion.

Our initial promise of long-term commitment is now unquestionable. We will continue helping schools develop their capacity to involve parents in meaningful ways. We will continue refining our methods to massively include parents in their children's educational process. More than ever, we want to unleash their power to advocate for significant roles in shaping what goes on in the school as well as for more parent and community accountability; to make sure that the role of parents is not reduced to rhetoric, parents need a clear mechanism of accountability from the system at all levels.

We must keep in mind that to be truly effective, parent involvement must be part of a wider social movement. "Middle and upper income communities make their schools work because they have the knowledge, the resources, and the time to go toe-to-toe with these systems. That's what we have to develop in low-income communities," says Otis Johnson.[27] Therefore empowerment and advocacy strategies must be at the forefront. We must keep the sense that we are doing something good, something new. We must maintain momentum. Involving parents has some similarities to missionary work; it is not only a job, it is a cause.

NOTES

1. Ellen Brickman and Anthony Cancelli, *Washington Heights Community School Evaluation Project: Third Year Evaluation Report* (New York: Graduate School of Social Service, Fordham University, 1999); Laura Jeffers, *New York City Community School District 6 and The Children's Aid Society 21st Century Community Learning Centers Evaluation Report* (New York: EDC's Center for Children and Technology, 2002); Children's Aid Society, *The Picower Foundation Report* (New York: Children's Aid Society, 2003).

2. Lidia Aguasanta, interview by author, March 3, 2003.

3. C. Warren "Pete" Moses, interview by author, March 4, 2003.

4. Rosa Agosto, interview by author, April 9, 2003.

5. Agosto, interview.

6. Gene Maeroff, *Altered Destinies* (New York: St. Martin's Press, 1998), p. 84.

7. Enemencia "Chiqui" Diaz, interview by author, April 9, 2003.

8. Ibid.

9. Anne T. Henderson and Karen L. Mapp, *A New Wave of Evidence: The Impact of School, Family and Community Connections on Student Achievement* (Austin, Tex.: National Center for Family and Community Connection with Schools, Southwest Educational Development Laboratory, 2002), p. 7; Joyce Epstein, *School, Family and Community Partnerships* (Thousand Oaks, Calif.: Corwin Press, 1997).

10. "A Voice from the School," *Community School News,* The Children's Aid Society, Fall 1996.

11. Esther Robison, *An Interim Evaluative Report Concerning a Collaboration between The Children's Aid Society and the New York City Board of Education, Community District Six and the IS 218 Salomé Ureña de Henriquez School* (New York: Graduate School of Social Service, Fordham University, 1993), p. 12.

12. Brickman and Cancelli, p. 8.

13. Aguasanta, interview.

14. Moses, interview.

15. Robison, p. 9.

16. Children's Aid Society, p. 3.

17. Ibid.

18. Julio Alvarado, interview by author, July 17, 2003.

19. Richard Negrón, interview by author, July 2, 2003.

20. Janice Chu-Zhu, interview by author, July 10, 2003.

21. Negrón, interview.

22. Moses, interview.

23. *Tools for School,* prod. Matt Guigno (Albany, N.Y.: New York State Department of Education, 2003), videocassette.

24. Brickman and Cancelli, p. 14.

25. Heléne Clark and Robert Engle, *Community Schools Evaluation Plan* (New York: ActKnowledge, Graduate School and University Center, City University of New York, 2001), p. 5.

26. Henderson and Mapp, p. 7.

27. Otis Johnson, interview by Joan Walsh, in *The Eye of the Storm: An Interview with Otis Johnson and Don Crary* (Baltimore, Md.: Annie E. Casey Foundation, 1999), p. 36.

Bill Foley

5

After-School and
Summer Enrichment Programs

SARAH JONAS
Director of Education Services, The Children's Aid Society

Research has demonstrated that nonschool hours provide a powerful opportunity for community-based organizations to help children and schools reach
their academic goals.[1] For example, Reginald Clark says, "Youngsters who
engage in constructive learning activities outside of school are more likely
to excel in school and in life than those who do not. By participating in a
well-rounded array of activities, they are able to practice and thoroughly learn
skills required for academic success."[2] Based on this knowledge, The Children's Aid Society (CAS) aims to integrate after-school and summer enrich-

57

ment programs with classroom instruction through a model that both supports the school's academic mission and promotes healthy youth development. The vast majority of students in CAS's 10 community schools, which are located in New York City, struggle with basic skills; in addition, more than half are Spanish speakers grappling with English as a second language. Their parents, teachers, and principals look to after-school and summer programs to help address their needs. The challenge for CAS is to answer this call in a way that is fun and engaging for children and achievable for program staff.

A crucial feature of high-quality after-school programs is balanced programming. In keeping with this concept, CAS after-school programs offer children an array of purely recreational activities (such as sports, dance, and visual and dramatic arts) along with academically enriching curricula that meet children's developmental needs and align with school standards. However, having strong curricula is only the first step. Critical to program quality has been the creation of a support system that incorporates key members of the school community and ensures that curricula are presented clearly so as to be accessible to a range of staff.

Simply being located in a community school does not guarantee that an after-school program will align with the school's academic goals for children. Rather, we have achieved this by partnering with the principal and lead teachers for program planning, by choosing curricula that support the school's academic goals for children, and by hiring a lead teacher or staff developer from the school to serve as the after-school education coordinator. This partnership begins at the level of the CAS community school director, who is responsible for all CAS programs in the school and who works with the principal to articulate their common goals for children. The day-to-day administration of the after-school and summer programs falls to the CAS program director, who works with the education coordinator to make sure the program is offering high-quality enrichment for children. Because our after-school programs and summer camps are staffed mainly by college students and smaller numbers of classroom teachers and high school students (except for our high school program, which is staffed entirely by classroom teachers), we have developed both curricula and training that allow staff with varying levels of experience and education to effectively support children's learning. We can also tie into other components of the CAS community school, helping children access school-based health care if it is in the building, encouraging their parents to use the family resource center, and working with other community agencies and businesses.

This combination of strong integrated curricula and effective staff support gives children the opportunity during nonschool hours to practice, and build on, the skills they need to meet academic standards; to develop positive social behaviors; to creatively express themselves as individuals; and to have fun.

After-School Enrichment

Each of the CAS after-school programs serves a target population of 250 to 400 children, or roughly one-quarter of the total school population. In keeping with the wide body of research showing that intensity of participation contributes to positive results, students who are registered are required to attend the program five days a week from 3 to 6 P.M. During this time they are involved in a range of activities, including daily homework help, sports, dance, and visual arts. We offer academic enrichment in science, mathematics, and reading. We have chosen, however, to make literacy the central focus, reflecting the needs of the children and the mission of our school partners.

The core literacy curricula in our after-school programs are Foundations and KidzLit.[3] Children in the elementary school programs participate in these curricula two to three times a week for 45-minute sessions; children in middle school programs participate in KidzLit twice a week for 45-minute sessions. Our adoption and implementation model for these programs provides a template for CAS's approach to all academic enrichment programs.

Choosing High-Quality Academic Enrichment Curricula

A number of important factors influenced our decision to use Foundations and KidzLit. Both curricula were specifically designed for use in after-school settings. They provide engaging, hands-on activities that help improve children's literacy, critical thinking, and social skills. Both are based on high-quality, high-interest fiction and nonfiction books that the children read, discuss, and respond to through art, drama, writing, and even music.

Both programs offer curriculum guides that provide everything the group leader needs to run the program, including questions to ask children about the books' themes and ideas for activities. Another benefit is that both programs are designed to be implemented by a range of staff, from experienced educators to college students to parent volunteers, all of whom are employed in the CAS programs. Finally, both programs are well researched and evaluated. Together, they offer a complementary range of experiences for different age groups and also provide variety for program staff, who may work with different age groups from year to year. The director of curriculum was trained in both programs in order to develop internal, centralized expertise that could be shared with staff at all sites.

By adopting existing curricula rather than spending time each year creating our own curricula from scratch, CAS was free to concentrate on implementation. The successful implementation process for KidzLit and Foundations was similar to that of all academic enrichment programs we adopt.

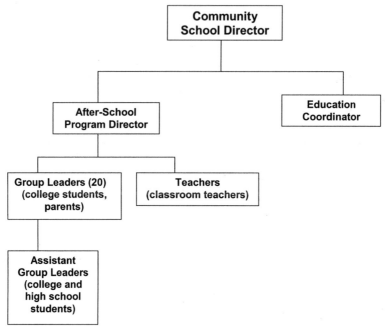

Figure 5.1. CAS extended-day program staff. *Credit*: The Children's Aid Society.

The Implementation Process

The first phase in implementing the curricula was to develop buy-in on the part of each CAS school's community school director. (See Figures 3.1 and 5.1.) We knew that a commitment to the curricula from the top would be crucial in ensuring that the rest of the partners and staff would come on board. A kick-off meeting was led by CAS's director of curriculum, who is responsible for researching, selecting, and designing high-quality enrichment curricula for our programs, for training staff, and for creating ongoing professional development opportunities.

At the meeting the director of curriculum asked the community school directors to share their literacy goals for children in the after-school programs. She then presented the curricula through hands-on activities, so that the directors could experience them as students would and see how these activities would build children's literacy skills. A handout summarizing state language-arts standards showed the directors how the curricula would address the standards and helped familiarize them with the educational language they would need to explain the curricula to the after-school staff, parents, and school partners.

At a second curriculum meeting, the directors worked together to create a new set of job descriptions to reflect the changes in the after-school program staff and an updated staff evaluation system tailored to the new job descriptions.

The Education Coordinator as Vital Link between Program and School

In addition to rewriting the job descriptions for after-school staff, the team of community school directors and the director of curriculum devised a new role, that of education coordinator. The education coordinator is a staff developer or lead teacher from the school who is hired by CAS during after-school hours to help after-school staff implement the academic enrichment programs.

An important goal of the after-school program is to create a very different feeling from the classroom setting—less formal and more active, creative, and project-based. The education coordinator is expected to visit the after-school groups regularly and provide the staff with ongoing feedback and support. For example, she might give a group leader ideas for structuring role-playing as a follow-up activity to reading a favorite book or share tips on reading aloud to children in a more engaging manner.

The education coordinator usually holds a position of leadership in the school; this sends a clear message to the principal, parents, and other school staff that CAS is committed to supporting learning during the hours from 3 to 6 P.M. Furthermore, having an education coordinator assures principals that after-school staff members who are not certified teachers will be trained and supported by someone who is; it strengthens principals' and teachers' confidence in the quality of our academic enrichment programs. In addition, the education coordinator can function as a kind of ambassador for our after-school program to the principal, teachers, and other key school personnel.

Working with the Principal and School Staff

Once our community school directors actively supported the adoption of the after-school curricula and an infrastructure for successful implementation had been created, the next step was securing buy-in among the school principals and classroom teachers. This was accomplished initially through meetings at each school between the community school director, the CAS director of curriculum, and the school principal. In many cases, the principals chose to invite their lead teachers, staff developers, and assistant principals as well. In these meetings CAS staff:

- Emphasized how our after-school program and curricula would complement and build on what children were learning during the regular school day
- Explained that the curricula we had chosen used quality children's literature and offered enjoyable activities that supported New York State standards
- Brought samples of the curricula (teacher's guides and children's books) for school staff to examine

- Shared our observations on how the curricula helped children develop new vocabulary and enjoy reading
- Emphasized the role of the education coordinator as a link between the after-school program and the school day

It was important to make clear to the school staff that while the program would support the school's mission, it would do so in a way designed for the after-school setting. Children would be active, have fun, and sometimes get messy! While we promised that the curriculum would enrich children's academic learning, we were careful not to make specific guarantees, such as bringing every student up to grade level in reading. We felt it was crucial not to promise anything we were not sure we could deliver; this could lead to mistrust and disillusionment on the school's part, undermining our partnership. Finally, we explained that program staff would receive thorough training on the new curricula at the start of the school year and ongoing support from the education coordinator throughout the year.

Our ability to speak knowledgeably about academic standards, connect them to our choice of curricula, and include structures for ongoing training was a key factor in securing the principals' support. Once that happened, the principals agreed to provide space for our program-materials storage bins in the classrooms, so after-school staff would not need to transport materials back and forth from the CAS office. Their support also translated fiscally when we coauthored a 21st Century Community Learning Centers grant with the school district and the district agreed to use a portion of these funds to pay for the new curricula. Further, the principals readily agreed with our proposal to give an overview of the after-school curriculum to day-school staff so they would understand how we were tackling the issue of academic enrichment; we met with these teachers during the "welcome back" meetings before school officially opened.

Participation by Program Staff and Parents

To create buy-in from the after-school program staff, three-hour curriculum-orientation sessions were held during the first few weeks of September. At these sessions staff could experience the curriculum activities hands-on and think about how they would adapt the program to meet their students' needs. To further strengthen our partnership with schools, we required that the education coordinators and program directors attend these sessions to learn about the curricula alongside those whom they would be expected to support.

To show parents how our program would support their children's school success, we included in our evening parent orientation a presentation on the new curricula. Conducted in English and Spanish, it emphasized how the curricula would support the school's academic standards and help children practice the literacy skills needed to successfully complete homework assignments. This was an important point to stress, as many parents were worried that the curricula would cut into the time children had traditionally spent on homework. Parents were invited to stop by our office and learn more about the curricula, visit the program, and consider volunteering with us. For parents unable to attend the orientation session, we sent home a letter in English and Spanish that covered the same information.

The Value of a Strong Infrastructure and Building Internal Capacity

The model we created for implementing KidzLit and Foundations has been key in successfully bringing new curricula to our programs. Our directors believe in the merits of academic enrichment in after-school programs, have high standards for the curricula we choose (namely, that they are fun and engaging while supporting the school's academic goals), and know how to successfully present these programs to our school partners and parents. We have created an infrastructure that supports the after-school staff's curriculum implementation and includes clear job descriptions and expectations; training; and ongoing professional development provided by the education coordinator. In the first year the CAS director of curriculum conducted curriculum orientation, but in subsequent years the education coordinators and veteran after-school teachers and group leaders have been instrumental in orienting new staff to the various enrichment programs.

In addition to the on-site support provided to after-school staff by the education coordinator, we have developed the Best Practices Workgroup, a support structure for the directors and program directors facilitated by the director of curriculum. In this group, which met monthly for the first two years that KidzLit and Foundations were used, the community school and program directors of the 10 schools came together to share the highlights and challenges of curriculum implementation at their sites. Besides providing an opportunity for the directors to get to know one another, the group fostered peer-to-peer problem solving and sharing of best practices across sites. For example, when one site was having trouble balancing academic enrichment with arts and recreational activities, another site described its program schedule that effectively met both needs. A secondary purpose of the meetings was to allow the director of curriculum as well as the sites to introduce new curriculum resources, such as a math game that would help children practice basic skills.

Since we began using KidzLit and Foundations in 1999, we have added additional curricula in the areas of math, science, technology, and literacy. For example, 24 Game and KidzMath reinforce basic skills through interactive games; we partnered with Girls Inc. to offer Operation SMART, a science program designed to empower girls in an arena generally dominated by boys; we developed a relationship with the Reid Foundation to offer a laptop program in which computer skills are taught as children are playing literacy and math games. Some of these are activities children can choose to participate in on

"Club Days" (generally Fridays), while others are worked into the schedule so that all children experience them over the course of the year. Still others are activities children can choose when they finish homework.

The After-School Program at Primary School (PS) 5

PS 5 community school provides an excellent example of high-quality after-school academic enrichment programming. Both the community school director, Myrna Torres, and the assistant community school director, Mayra Lopez, have a solid understanding of the design and benefits of the academic enrichment curricula used at their site. Along with their staff, they attend curriculum-orientation sessions and related professional development workshops. This sends a strong message to staff about the importance of this aspect of the program and also makes them feel respected and supported as educators.

The directors' commitment to the curriculum is communicated initially through the hiring process. Potential candidates are asked what kinds of entertaining projects they would do with children to go with different books; they are also asked to read aloud a children's book and to prepare questions they would ask children about the story. In the interview the directors clarify their expectations that staff implement the curriculum according to the program schedule and use their own creativity to actively engage children in the learning process.

To ensure that after-school staff have maximum support in implementing the various curricula, the directors of PS 5 chose a strong education coordinator, a reading specialist from the school who had worked in the after-school program. As an after-school teacher, Susan Mason was creative and dynamic, consistently creating a high level of engagement among her children. She and the students often used the KidzLit books as jumping-off points for extended literacy projects. For example, after reading *Diego*, a vibrant picture book chronicling the life of artist Diego Rivera, the class embarked on a study of other artists, which included reading biographies and creating their own pieces in the styles of the artists they were learning about.

Ms. Mason is also skilled at coaching others to develop their own strengths as educators. She regularly visits the after-school groups so that she knows the challenges facing each staff member with regard to both group management and curriculum implementation. She meets individually with staff to offer feedback and suggestions and also designs and implements professional development workshops for the entire staff. For example, to combat the winter slump many staff were experiencing, she offered a "Thinking Out of the Box" workshop in which staff could try out hands-on innovative project ideas, such as cooking, to use as literacy extensions.

The directors became aware of the need to share the after-school program's success beyond the program walls with school staff and parents, and they came up with a unique way to do this. As in many after-school programs, the children at PS 5 put on shows around the winter holidays and again at the close of the program year. Children from the dance, chorus, and drama clubs perform, and parents turn out in large numbers. However, the directors felt something was missing: They wanted a way to share the reading, writing, and related projects the children were doing in the academic enrichment curricula and decided to make the hallway outside the auditorium into a showcase for the children's work. Thus the Winter and Spring Expos were born.

As parents arrive to see their children perform, they are encouraged to stop and look at the work that covers the walls and tables. Each after-school group's staff and children take great pride in creating these elaborate displays, which include students' written descriptions of the work and even live student "explainers" who can answer questions and give more detail about the various projects. The principal and the entire school staff are also invited to the Expo so that they, too, can see what the children have been learning in the program.

To continue this kind of sharing between Expos, the directors of PS 5 worked with the principal to create a display in the hallway near the school's entrance. A bulletin board exhibits a rotating selection of children's curriculum work from the after-school program; each grade is responsible for a certain month. Staff and children choose the work they want to post, design the display, and put up the work themselves. The central location of the bulletin board ensures that school staff and parents will see it as they enter the school each day.

In addition to these lively displays, a bimonthly newsletter called *Sharing Our World* goes out to all school staff and parents. Written in English and Spanish, it offers each group in the after-school program the chance to write about what they are learning. Direct quotes from the children are included, as are images of the artwork and photos of students engaged in the projects. There is even a "Parents' Corner," in which a different parent each month writes about what her child is getting out of the after-school program.

Parent involvement in the academic enrichment program is further enhanced at PS 5 by the director's decision to require two parent visits per program year. Parents visit their children's after-school group and work side by side with the child on a project. For example, they might read a book to their child (or have their child read to them) and then together create a mask of a favorite character. This process acquaints the parents with the academic enrichment program and emphasizes the importance of parent involvement in children's academic outcomes.

Summer Enrichment

Academic enrichment in our summer day-camp programs differs somewhat from that in after-school programs. While it can be difficult to keep children engaged from 3 to 6 P.M. after they have been in school all day, summer provides its own set of challenges as temperatures soar and children want to celebrate being out of school. We have found what works best is to create our own summer camp enrichment curricula tied to trips in and around New York City. Often, our education coordinators help design the summer camp curricula, which are customized to a particular site. In the elementary schools, for example, we have created a curriculum based on weekly themes, such as oceans or animals; the children explore the theme through books and projects leading up to a trip to the aquarium or zoo.

The Summer Program at Intermediate School (IS) 90

Our IS 90 community school (grades 5–8) has developed an innovative model for summer enrichment called "Break-Aways," a six-week program of city and country academic day-camp that incorporates New York City Department of Education standards. The program, serving about 80 children, provides recreation along with a daily 3-hour academic instruction period that integrates four study areas—literacy/language arts, science, math, and expressive arts. Campers attend CAS's Wagon Road Camp, a fully licensed camp in Chappaqua, New York, twice a week; the other three days of the program weeks are held at IS 90.

IS 90's summer camp is a true partnership between CAS and the school. The after-school education coordinator, Mary Hemings, helps design the academic enrichment curriculum. Teachers from IS 90 are hired to teach in the Break-Aways program, where they build upon the school's literacy program and extend the 6th–8th grade science curriculum into the Wagon Road Camp setting. The curriculum integrates academic learning and activities into the natural environment by focusing on the theme of comparing city and country. Children choose from a reading list that relates to the New York City middle-school science frameworks and write responses to the books. They are also engaged in hands-on science and math projects, including animal and plant life studies, tree identification, flora and fungi collection and classification, solar experiments, local topography investigations, and weather station construction and monitoring.

The coordinated curriculum also integrates the CAS Adventures Learning programming, based on the Project Adventure curriculum. This includes orienteering, map-reading, mapmaking, and a variety of team-building exercises, such as ropes courses, which build cooperation, trust, and shared decision making. Children have the opportunity to work on arts and crafts projects that incorporate the science theme, such as finding and using materials from the natural environment to make leaf rubbings, collages, and weavings of grass, rushes, and sticks.

On days when they are not at Wagon Road, campers participate in day trips to destinations in and around New York City, including the American Museum of Natural History, the Hispanic Society Museum, and Fort Tryon Park. These trips are designed to complement lessons and activities related to the curricular theme. At the end of the summer, the children's written and visual-arts projects, as well as dramatic skits, songs, and dances, are shared on Parent's Day. Photographs of the children's projects, as well as their written work, are included in a summer portfolio.

During the regular school year, the education coordinator and teachers from the summer camp work together to create ongoing learning experiences for students who attended the summer camp. This includes follow-up overnight weekend trips back to Wagon Road Camp and after-school planting, gardening, and beautification projects in parks near IS 90 facilitated by our local parks partner, the New York Restoration Project. This additional learning time is designed to help students meet the academic standards by which they will be judged in order to move to the next grade.

Cost and Financing of CAS Enrichment Programs

Funding for the after-school and summer camp programs must cover the salaries of program staff, including the group leaders, teachers, and education coordinator, and must provide additional monies for time spent outside program hours on professional development and for the curricula materials themselves. CAS finances the programs through multiple funding streams, including government grants and contracts, legislative earmarks, money from private and corporate foundations and individuals, and in-kind gifts. Public sources include the federal 21st Century Community Learning Centers program, the Advantage After-School Program administered by the New York State Office of Children and Family Services, and the Extended-Day Violence Prevention program administered by the New York State Department of Education.

Major private funding sources include the Soros Foundation's After-School Corporation program (TASC), which provides major support for the after-school program in eight of our ten community schools. We also seek out partners who want to pilot their academic enrichment curricula—in return for giving them a setting in which to test their materials, we receive the curriculum and staff training free of charge. For example, we established a partnership with Columbia University Teachers College and Dark Horse Comics, who were piloting a literacy program called the Comic Book Project. Staff members from Teachers College trained several of our middle-school group leaders and provided us with the comic-book templates students use to practice literacy skills by producing their own comic books.

Challenges

Staff Turnover

Staff turnover is an ongoing obstacle to providing high-quality academic enrichment, particularly in after-school programs. In response, in addition to reaching out to classroom teachers from the school, CAS recruits staff through postings at the career and work-study offices of local colleges and high schools, job-search Web sites, and field publications such as the Partnership for After School Education (PASE) job newsletter. Once the staff has been hired, CAS program directors devote time and energy to creating a positive, supportive, and energizing work place; this is achieved through team-building activities incorporated into staff orientation and weekly staff meetings, through ongoing professional development in curriculum implementation, and through social activities such as holiday parties.

Despite these efforts, we lose several staff members over the course of each year due to everything from family problems to changes in college course schedules to offers of higher paying jobs. Although it is stressful for everyone when a staff member departs, our core curricula ensure a level of continuity. Often the assistant group leader can step up and teach the enrichment curriculum until a new group leader can be hired, thus keeping the group from falling behind. In addition, because the curricula are fairly easy to implement, new staff hired midyear can begin with a brief "mini" training offered by the education coordinator and can turn to more experienced staff for help since all are working with the same curricula.

Finding Good Education Coordinators

It can be challenging to find the right person to serve as education coordinator. Strong teachers sometimes lack the coaching skills to translate their knowledge for others' use. Or an education coordinator may be reluctant to observe after-school classrooms regularly because she is worried about being seen as merely a monitor rather than a positive resource for staff; hiring education coordinators with experience as peer educators or staff developers can help avert this problem. Some education coordinators have trouble moving away from a classroom teaching style to the informal after-school model, which is more active, flexible, and creative. In such cases the best approach is often a frank discussion between the program director and education coordinator, stressing the different needs of children in the nonschool hours and therefore the need for a different approach to curriculum implementation.

Our school and program directors have occasionally found themselves under pressure from the principal to hire an education coordinator whom they do not know well or whom they consider unsuitable for the position. However, in most cases where we have done a good job sharing the program goals and benefits with the principal, the principal's input is very helpful. Certainly, finding a person with whom the principal feels comfortable is a powerful tool in building a positive partnership with the school and legitimizing academic enrichment in the after-school program.

Assessment

The effectiveness and outcomes of the academic enrichment curricula in the CAS after-school and summer camp programs have been well researched and evaluated. We know the programs work when implemented correctly, and we therefore spend the bulk of our energy on building and maintaining structures that support high-quality implementation. However, we have come under increasing pressure from school leaders and funders to show that our enrichment programs raise children's grades and/or test scores. Certainly, we too would like to know if this is the case.

A report from Foundations summarizes the results of a 2001–2002 study of math and reading progress for students from 19 school sites who participated in the Foundations after-school program and a control group of students who did not participate.[4] Using results on the CTB/McGraw-Hill CAT-5 Mathematics and Reading Comprehension tests, the study found that the Foundations students' average score gains between the fall 2001 pretest and spring 2002 posttest were statistically significantly greater than those made by comparable students from the same schools and communities who were not in Foundations. While CAS was not one of the sites in this study, we are encouraged by these results.

In 2002 the Center for Children and Technology (CCT) carried out an evaluation of CAS's 21st Century Community Learning Centers programs in our five Washington Heights schools (PS 5, 8, and 152 and IS 218 and 90).[5] This evaluation consisted of feedback from program staff, children, and parents gathered through written surveys. One key finding was that the focus on academic enrichment and, in particular, implementation of the literacy curricula strengthened the partnership with the school in terms of continuity between classroom and after-school learning and improved relationships between classroom teachers and after-school staff. Another important finding was that the enrichment curricula supported communication among staff and helped to establish a sense of shared goals around academic achievement, a sense of efficacy, and an outlet for creativity. Further, the curricula provided needed structure for less skilled staff. Children enjoyed the books and related activities, and parents felt their children were better prepared for their in-school classes.

Although these findings from the Foundations and CCT evaluations are promising, CAS recognizes the need for a large-scale evaluation that would compare the grades and test scores of children in our after-school and summer camp programs with those of children who do not attend our programs and is engaged in raising funds for this purpose.

Time and Money for Training and Professional Development

In order for staff to get the support they need, time and money need to be allocated for professional development. Traditional program hours do not always provide this time, so CAS has held training in the early evening and occasionally on Saturdays, as well as during school holidays. Staff are paid their hourly rate for time spent in training—a consideration when designing program budgets. Sometimes, when time or budgets are tight, we have trained smaller groups of staff on a rotating basis during regular program hours by having several groups of children watch a video or play in the gym supervised by assistant group leaders or volunteer parents while their group leaders receive professional development.

Lessons Learned

Perhaps the most valuable lesson CAS has learned about quality academic enrichment in after-school and summer camp programs is the critical importance of building capacity at the site level. Choosing quality curricula that engage children and support academic standards is a crucial first step, yet it is not enough. Everyone, from the program directors to the school partners and the after-school staff, needs to buy in to the programs and commit fully to implementing them. The staff needs high-quality curriculum orientation, regular supervision, and ongoing professional development.

For these things to happen, sites need an education coordinator who is well regarded by the principal and classroom teachers, has a firm grasp of the school's academic goals for children, understands how after-school programs can support classroom learning without replicating a classroom environment, and is an able coach and mentor for the program staff.

Conclusion

While our core literacy curricula continue to give our sites a common language and infrastructure, sites have developed the enrichment aspect of their programs according to the individual needs of their community and youth populations. In this way each of our community-school after-school and summer camp programs has retained a distinct flavor and design while sharing a common commitment to academic enrichment and positive youth development.

Whereas, at first, sites required a great deal of contact with, and support from, the CAS director of curriculum, our oldest sites now manage their enrichment programs more or less independently with the on-site expertise of the education coordinators and program directors. Newer sites receive more intensive support until they, too, have reached a greater degree of comfort. This gradual process, in which sites build their own internal capacity and move toward full ownership of their programs, ensures that we can continue to add new community schools to our CAS family without sacrificing program quality.

Extending children's learning opportunities during the nonschool hours is crucial to raising academic achievement. Choosing high-quality curricula that meet students' needs and that allow them to have fun while building on what they learn in the classroom is a necessary first step. However, just as important is the creation of an infrastructure that will ensure effective implementation of the curricula by program staff. Successful academic enrichment programs must also harness the support of schools and provide a framework for ongoing program development.

Programs designed in this way require a significant investment of time and money, especially at the outset. Yet they are ultimately cost effective because, once the infrastructure and core curricula are in place, the program retains a strength, purpose, and identity that can withstand unforeseen scheduling changes, staff turnover, and even budget crises. Furthermore, the model provides a template within which program improvements, such as the addition of new curricula to meet participants' changing needs, can comfortably fit.

As the academic standards and accountability movement continues to gain favor with policy makers nationwide, successful after-school and summer programs will respond in a way that offers positive benefits for youth, families, and school partners.

NOTES

1. D. L. Vandell and L. Shumow, "After-School Child Care Programs," *The Future of Children: When School Is Out* 9, no. 2 (1999): 64–80.
2. R. M. Clark, *Critical Factors in Why Disadvantaged Children Succeed or Fail in School* (New York: Academy for Educational Development, 1988), p. 1.
3. Foundations was acquired from Foundations, Inc., Moorestown West Corp. Center, 2 Executive Drive, Suite 1, Moorestown, New Jersey. KidzLit was acquired from The Developmental Studies Center, 2000 Embarcadero, Suite 305, Oakland, California.
4. Stephen P. Klein and Roger Bolus, *Improvements in Math and Reading Scores of Students Who Did and Did Not Participate in the FOUNDATIONS After School Enrichment Program during the 2001–2002 School Year* (Santa Monica, Calif.: Gansk and Associates, 2002), p. 2.
5. Laura Jeffers, *New York City Community School District 6 and The Children's Aid Society 21st Century Community Learning Centers Evaluation Report* (New York: EDC's Center for Children and Technology, 2002), pp. 1–4.

Early Childhood Programs

ANDREW SELTZER

Head Start Social Services Coordinator,
The Children's Aid Society

The Children's Aid Society (CAS) early childhood initiative is located in two of our New York City community schools, Primary School (PS) 5 and PS 8, in the Washington Heights section of northern Manhattan. This initiative was conceived as a partnership between the New York City Board of Education and CAS. The collaboration brought newborns and their families into the schools in which the children would complete fifth grade. The initiative began in 1994 and has been in full operation since 1996. Since then, the need for such a project has been confirmed and experience has provided insights into how a program for pregnant women and children through age five (often called a Zero to Five Program) can be effectively implemented within a public school. The CAS Zero to Five model connects two federally funded programs—Early Head Start (birth to age three) and Head Start (ages three to five)—to provide comprehensive educational and social services to low-income families and their children.

The population attending the Zero to Five Program confronts the obstacles facing all new immigrant families living in poverty in an urban setting. In both schools more than 75% of the families are from the Dominican Republic; another 20% come from other Central and South American countries. The parents' language is Spanish, and language barriers and acculturation issues result in social isolation. In addition, because many residents lack legal documentation, they are reluctant to access health and social services.

The few early childhood programs in the neighborhood all have long waiting lists. A majority of the families share overcrowded apartments with other families or extended family; whole families often live in one bedroom where books and age-appropriate toys are scarce and there may be little child-centered language interaction. However, in spite of the difficulties, these parents have a drive to succeed and they understand the importance of education.

Program Model

By combining and linking Early Head Start and Head Start programs and integrating them into a community school, the CAS Zero to Five Program provides children and families with quality educational, health, and social services, after which the children transition into public school classes within the same building. Although both programs are funded by the federal government and are required to follow comprehensive performance standards, CAS has considerable flexibility in strengthening and enhancing the basic Early Head Start and Head Start models. Our work to link the two programs into one comprehensive model, and our work to help children transition from these early childhood experiences into regular kindergarten within the same building, are examples of such enhancements.

Parents entering Early Head Start during pregnancy know they must make a five-year commitment. In fact, children who maintain consistent attendance in Early Head Start are guaranteed placement in Head Start. Considering the waiting lists for both programs and the limited number of other early childhood programs in the community, admission to Early Head Start serves as motivation to maintain attendance and participation for the five-year duration of the program.

Early Head Start

The CAS Early Head Start program is the entry point for the family. The home-based model provides intensive intervention with the entire family. One-hour home visits are made biweekly throughout the year, and families attend two small age-specific groups lasting one and one-half hours each week. The same teachers conduct the home visits and lead the parent/child groups. This continuity of care provides a high level of interaction with each family and develops a sense of community and trust. There are up to 25 home visits and 100 interactions within a year; thus, over the three years of Early Head Start, families can have had 75 home visits and participated in 300 parent/child group interactions.

The home visit is a time for the family to focus on the child through age-appropriate, educationally stimulating activities. Music, language, early literacy activities, and parent/child games encourage the child's development and strengthen the parent-child bond. Through activities and role modeling, the teachers provide parents with an understanding of child development. During the home visits, parents learn songs with their children, read books, play with toys created from household items, and learn games that use their imagination. Home-based teachers and parents discuss how to make use of mealtime, bathtime, and bedtime routines to create parent-child interactions. The home visit also allows the parent to focus on interacting with the child without the distractions and stresses of everyday life.

The parent/child groups (eight children to a group) are held in a classroom in the community school. A playful, stimulating educational experience includes room exploration, songs, parent/child play, and snacks. Set up like an infant-toddler classroom, the space offers safe and inviting environments, such as a block area, early literacy area, make-believe kitchen, and a climbing area, for parents and children to try out activities together. There is room to explore and be comfortable. Parents learn the connection between play and learning while they create a closer bond with their children. In addition, parents find support from one another and from the staff; this social support creates a sense of community within the program.

The Early Head Start health coordinator ensures that all health care needs are met. The health coordinator accompanies parents and children on medical appointments as an advocate and, often, an interpreter and reviews children's physicals to see that health-related problems are being managed. She makes sure that children receive dental exams and checks to see that children and families are covered through health insurance; for undocumented families she finds low-cost medical care. The health coordinator also conducts CPR and first aid classes.

Pregnant women receive specialized services in Early Head Start. They attend a nine-week comprehensive course that includes a significant amount of time spent sharing personal experiences. The workshops educate the pregnant mothers about health, nutrition, stages of pregnancy, and issues during childbirth. They also include yoga and breathing exercises. The nine-week course creates strong bonds among the pregnant mothers and serves as an introduction to their involvement in Early Head Start. In addition, six Early Head Start program staff members have become credentialed as doulas who can provide physical, emotional, and informational support before birth, during labor, and in the perinatal period. As doulas, these members of the

Early Head Start staff participate in the birth process of program participants who want this kind of support. This significant and personal relationship creates a deep and trusting bond between parents and Early Head Start staff.

Making referrals for early intervention services provides an opportunity for children to receive special needs services; the special needs coordinator makes sure that early intervention services are consistently implemented and that parents remain involved.

Interventions such as obtaining necessities like furniture or food, ensuring proper medical care, advocating for legal services, and consistently responding to families in crisis are examples of what the CAS Zero to Five Program does; such interventions are especially frequent in Early Head Start because of the intimate level of contact provided by the home-based program.

Head Start

At the age of three, children move from the home-based Early Head Start program to the center-based Head Start classes. Their transition is facilitated by their previous educational experience in Early Head Start and by parent knowledge of child development learned in Early Head Start. Another plus is that the parents are familiar with the school environment; through the twice-weekly parent groups, they have developed a sense of belonging in the school. (Because the Head Start program is larger than the Early Head Start program at both sites, a number of Head Start spaces are available to other low-income families from the community; the criteria for entering Head Start include low income and greatest need.)

The three-year-old classes are the children's first experience in a center-based classroom in which parents are not present. In each community school, there is one classroom for three-year-olds, who attend half-days, either mornings or afternoons. The four-year-olds attend school from 8 A.M. to 3 P.M. At each school some of the children attend an extended-day program until 5:30 P.M. because of their parents' work schedule or a particular need for extended child care.

While there are differences in the curriculum and expectations for the three- and four-year-old classes, there are also many similarities. Each child is viewed individually with an emphasis on social, emotional, physical, cognitive, and language development. The educational component is organized around the Creative Curriculum.[1] The classroom learning environment combines structured areas with freedom of movement. Individual interest areas include such activities as blocks, dramatic play, writing, and sand and water. Children choose their activities within a classroom that has established schedules, routines, and codes of conduct. Content areas such as literacy, math, science, the arts, and technology are integrated through the daily life of the classroom.

A comprehensive assessment tool is used three times a year to focus on individual children; to understand their knowledge, skills, and temperament; and to assess their progress. The assessment process develops teachers' observational skills and assists in the planning for each child.

Every child in the program receives breakfast and a snack. The half-day afternoon classes and the full-day children get lunch, and those in the extended-day program get an additional snack later in the day. The food is nutritious, and meals are times for socialization, for gaining competence through serving and preparing food, and for developing positive attitudes toward food.

The list below shows the breakdown of participation in the Zero to Five Program:

- 75 children in Early Head Start:
  50 children at PS 5
  25 children at PS 8
- 75 children in PS 5 Head Start:
  35 children in half-day three-year-old classes
  40 children in two four-year-old full-day classes
  (20 children continue in extended-day class until 5:30 P.M.)
- 68 children in PS 8 Head Start:
  28 children in half-day three-year-old classes
  40 children in two four-year-old full-day classes
  (18 children continue in extended-day class until 5:30 P.M.)
- Total: 218 children in Zero to Five Program

The CAS community school is a resource-rich environment for the Zero to Five Program. The health clinic is housed in the school, as are programs for parent involvement and a family resource room. The facility itself meets all health and fire codes. The classrooms are designed to provide an educationally rich environment. The school building as a whole is a safe environment that reinforces a positive code of conduct.

Parent Involvement

The Zero to Five Program provides continuity, community, and enrichment for the parents as well as the children. From their initial contact with the program, parents become accustomed to a public school as an inviting educational environment. Within the program they find friends, as well as support from professionals. Advocacy is available to them in such areas as public assistance, housing, education, and the legal system. In a crisis the program is able to assist families with food, furniture, and clothing. Most important, parents feel supported in determining and reaching their own goals.

An important element of the Zero to Five Program is that its staff is representative of the community. In particular, this is demonstrated by the number of former parents from Early Head Start and Head Start who are now employed by the Zero to Five Program. With encouragement, training, and opportunities to volunteer, they have made the leap from parent to employee. Former parents work as teachers, assistant teachers, teacher aides, substitute teachers, custodians, family workers, and cooks.

Employment for parents is also found in the community schools, which are central parts of the communities they serve. Parents from the Zero to Five Program have been employed in the community schools as teachers, teacher aides, custodians, cafeteria aides, and after-school assistant teachers.

The organizational structure of the Zero to Five Program requires shared decision making with parents—this is both a requirement for federal funding and consistent with CAS's philosophy and approach in our community schools. We strongly believe that parent involvement is critical for a successful program. All parents are members of the Parents Committee, which elects a leadership group called the Policy Committee. The Policy Committee participates in decisions about the program. Through monthly classroom meetings held with each Head Start teacher, monthly Parents Committee meetings, and administrative meetings, parents become part of a collaborative leadership team.

The extensive parent involvement in the governance of the Zero to Five Program has served as a training ground for the Public School Parents Association at both PS 5 and PS 8. Consistently, upon graduating from the Zero to Five Program, parents serve as leaders in the community school, meeting regularly with the school administration and organizing parent groups.

Parent involvement in education within the home is fostered through the Home-School Connection Curriculum. The Home-School Connection Curriculum ensures that children's developing minds are engaged in questioning and discovery activities all day long, through conversation, artwork, and games. These activities are designed to engage parents in their children's education in the fullest sense and from the very start.

Every week, children take home a set of activities to be completed by the parent and child. A central component is a language-based activity that sparks conversation and seeks to kindle in-depth dialogue between parent and child. All Home-School Connection activities are distributed in both Spanish and English, allowing parents to choose the language in which they feel most comfortable interacting with their children. Parents record (in English or Spanish) their children's responses to the questions and write "adult reflection journals" that describe their personal experience of their child during the activity. These observations by parents are included as components of each child's assessment portfolio.

The home activities are unique in that they provide a set of questions for parents to ask their children while they engage them in activities. The conversation technique has a twofold goal: to build children's basic knowledge and vocabulary and to develop their higher-level thinking skills. For example, one week parents and children take a walk around the park, and parents ask their children the following set of questions:

1. What would you like to do in the park?
2. Do you think the park is a good place for children? Do you think it is a good place for grown-ups? Why?
3. What do we have at home that we don't have here?
4. What do we have here that we don't have at home?
5. Do you see any birds?
6. Where do you think the birds live?
7. What do you think birds do at night?

Parents record the child's answers to these questions. In their adult reflection journals, they answer the same three questions each week:

1. How did you feel about this activity?
2. What did you find out about your child?
3. What other questions did you ask your child?

An appendix to this chapter provides examples of responses to this home-school activity.

Staffing

Staffing is designed to provide comprehensive services to children and families. Staff members are bilingual and representative of the community; they have expertise in such specialized areas as education, special needs, health, nutrition, social service advocacy, and counseling. They receive ongoing training and supervision about their individual roles and responsibilities, and they find support in our team approach to addressing the needs of families. All staff members are familiar with the overall Head Start performance standards.

The CAS Zero to Five staff-development model places a high value on developing the strengths of individual staff members, providing support, and establishing teamwork. Staff members are encouraged to pursue higher education and are provided with financial aid. Staff members have completed infant-toddler certificate programs and family worker certificate programs. Teachers are pursuing higher education with the assistance of the Children's Aid Society scholarship fund. Staff members are also trained in first aid and CPR.

Funding

The Zero to Five Program is funded by separate grants from the federal government for Early Head Start and Head Start. Applications for funding must be made every year. The application requires a 20% in-kind contribution from

CAS; this includes services provided by CAS staff that are not funded through the federal Head Start grant. There is a close collaboration between CAS Head Start and the CAS Office of Public Policy and Client Advocacy, CAS Preventive Services, CAS Foster Care Services, CAS Family Wellness Program, CAS Mental Health Services, CAS Volunteer Services, and CAS Health Services. All of these CAS services are integrated into the Zero to Five Program, offering families access to comprehensive services within the same agency.

The Zero to Five Program also develops special projects through private funds. These funds are used to pilot projects that can be integrated into the program. The Home-School Connection Curriculum, Doula Project, and Pregnancy Curriculum all have been developed through private funds. Furthermore, a partnership with Albert Einstein College of Medicine has created a three-year research component that is funded by the federal government and implemented through the college.

Challenges and Lessons Learned

The major asset of the Zero to Five Program also presents its greatest challenge. Offering an early childhood program within a public school that is a community school offers tremendous opportunities to develop and implement comprehensive programs for children and families. Parents become part of their children's education from birth, and the education continues within the same building. Feelings of support from the staff are nourished from infancy. The potential for integration of services creates a comprehensive program for the whole family.

However, as with any situation where multiple constituencies share space, there are territorial issues. While these do not affect the actual supervision of the program, they do affect the availability of space in which to work as well as the relationships among programs that are needed in order to continuously provide integrated services. Privacy and space for staff meetings must be negotiated. Regular networking meetings need to be held for supervisory staffs of the different programs within the community school in order to defuse issues concerning space and program integration. Ultimately, the cooperation between programs makes each individual program more substantial. The lack of confidential space inhibits interactions with families. Files on families are appropriately locked, but there is extremely limited space for confidential interviews with families. Frequent informal conversations with families help develop a sense of trust and community; however, most confidential conversations are conducted during home visits.

For the Zero to Five Program, a major challenge is gaining the respect of the school administration and staff. Despite the volume of evidence on early brain development and the positive effects of Zero to Five education, educators still often feel that "real" education begins in kindergarten. This concept can have damaging effects on Zero to Five staff members and can create a hierarchy among the programs within the community school. Therefore, it becomes necessary to find ways to educate administration and community school staffs about the Zero to Five model. This educational process is ongoing. It depends upon the school administration's understanding the value of the model and making time to share the successes of the Zero to Five Program with the entire staff.

The principal of the community school is critical to the Zero to Five Program's success. She is ultimately in charge of education during the elementary school years and of the school plant. However, she has more than enough to do without managing the Zero to Five Program. Therefore, the program needs its own tight supervision and a sense of internal structure. There must be formal and informal modes of communication with the principal to ensure a healthy working relationship.

The Zero to Five Program also mandates that all parents be involved. This means that parents spend a lot of time volunteering and attending meetings and workshops at the school. Once they establish a relationship with the Zero to Five Program, they are likely to continue participating within the school. Thus, in embracing the Zero to Five parents, the community school is producing its future leaders.

Conclusion

The Zero to Five Program incorporates the intensive and integrated approach that epitomizes the community school philosophy. Services are not rendered in isolation. Rather, there is always coordination between education; programs for health, mental health, and special needs; and such concrete services as food assistance, legal assistance, and help in obtaining government services.

Low-income families vary in their ability to provide a stable environment for their children. Too often a crisis occurs that interrupts progress. Even with hard work and the best intentions, families suffer from unemployment, overcrowded housing, lack of food, and mental health issues. The Zero to Five Program creates a long-term relationship in which children are engaged daily in stimulating, safe, and educational activities and parents are supported in their struggle to maintain family stability.

A Zero to Five Program within a community school expands and strengthens the school's mission. Parents begin participating in the school during the mother's pregnancy. Families are offered comprehensive services from birth through the school years. Children in the Zero to Five Program learn to manage their emotions and interact with peers within a classroom environment. They are prepared for kindergarten. In addition, the Zero to Five Program offers high-quality care, well-trained and supervised teachers, and a curriculum that is developmentally and culturally appropriate.

The best way to determine the effectiveness of the program is through long-term research. A three-year study that followed Zero to Three families from birth through the age of three was recently completed by researchers from Albert Einstein College of Medicine. The study measured the impact of the Zero to Three Program on maternal depression, parent/child play, parent social support, children's attention, and children's cognitive development. Results of the study are expected in 2005.

The Zero to Five Program is part of a larger effort within the CAS community schools. Creating a long-term relationship with a low-income family that begins at birth and follows through to fifth grade may be viewed as an ideal; at PS 5 and PS 8 such a program is being implemented, and the long-term impact is worth researching. A critical issue to observe is how family involvement continues through the years. The first years of the program are obviously spent in a concerted effort to involve the entire family and implement a holistic approach. It is natural for parents to become less involved as children get older. However, programs that offer support for the entire family create a safety net so low-income families can continue to grow and succeed.

After six years CAS knows the need for Zero to Five programs and recognizes their potential. A 2003 article in the *New York Times* about a family attending the Zero to Five Program discussed how the program prepares children for kindergarten and described the extensive parent involvement. The mother interviewed explained, "I am more patient and now I try to find solutions instead of getting angry. . . . Sometimes I have a small problem and feel like my world is ending. But now I stay positive. Through communication and looking for assistance, I am moving toward my goals. . . . I want to wait until Egbert is in school before starting my own career. . . . Most importantly I want my children to have an excellent education. Education is the only thing I can give them after I am gone."[2]

NOTES

1. Diane Trister Dodge, Laura Colker, and Cate Hereman, *Creative Curriculum for Preschool* (Washington, D.C.: Teaching Strategies, 2002).
2. "Help with Rent for Exhausted Family," *New York Times*, January 28, 2003, sec. B.

Appendix: Sample Responses to Home-School Activity

1. Ask, "What would you like to do in the park?"
   Answer: Play on the slide and the swing.
2. Ask, "Do you think the park is a good place for children?" "Do you think it is a good place for grown-ups?" "Why?"
   Answer: Yes, 'cause you can be with your friends. No, 'cause the mommies can't play on the slide.
3. Ask, "What do we have at home that we don't have here?"
   Answer: Toys.
4. Ask, "What do we have here that we do not have at home?"
   Answer: Slides and swings.
5. Ask, "Do you see any birds?"
   Answer: Yes.
6. Ask, "Where do you think the birds live?"
   Answer: In a house where nobody lives.
7. Ask, "What do you think the birds do at night time?"
   Answer: Eat and go to sleep.

Sample Answers in Spanish with Translations

1. *A jugar, jugar en el parque y jugar con la bicicleta y corriendo, y bañando.*
   To play, to play in the park and to play with a bike, and running, and bathing.
2. *Si, si, entonce ellos ven a los niños jugando, porque ellos jugan con los columpio.*
   Yes, yes, then they (adults) can watch the children playing, because they play with the swings.
3. *No hay cama, cocina, cuarto, o juguetes en el parque.*
   There are no beds, kitchen, bedroom, toys in the park.
4. *Árboles y sillas y sillas y agua y un animales que sea un gato, un perrito.*
   Trees and benches and benches, and water and "an" animals that could be a cat, a doggy.
5. *Si, yo vi un pájarito en el árboles.*
   Yes, I saw a little bird on the trees.
6. *Viven en una casa chiquita como este dedito.*
   They live in a little house like this little finger.
7. *Comen en su casa y después se duermen en su cama y rezan con su mamí pájarita.*
   They get to eat in their house and then they go to sleep in their bed and they pray with their little mother bird.

A Parent's Responses in an Adult Reflection Journal (Translated from Spanish)

1. How did you feel about this activity?

   I was very happy because she behaved so well when we went to the park. Now she wants me to take her to the park all the time.

2. What did you find out about your child?

   That she is very intelligent and that she knows many things, but I am very proud of her because she changes her attitude when she misbehaves and I tell her, and she starts behaving better.

3. What other questions did you ask your child?

   What would you like to have in the park? The child answered, I would like to have a stove to cook because I want to cook outdoors to make a meal for you.

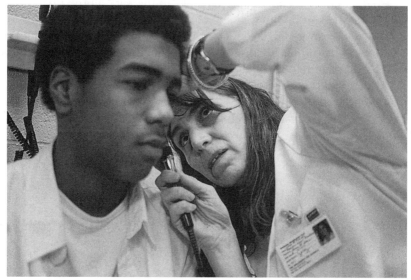

7

School-Based Health Services

BEVERLY A. COLON
Director of Health Services, The Children's Aid Society

In order to be successful in school, children must be able to see and hear and must be free of troubling health problems. Our experience with community schools confirms the idea that locating health services within a school provides easy access for students who are not receiving health care elsewhere. However, many problems, such as working with children who lack health insurance and typically end up in the emergency room for episodic care, have to be overcome. More and more of these children and their parents in our schools are recent undocumented immigrants who fear dealing with the health care system. An even larger number of children are simply from "working poor" families in which parents work off the books or for employers that do not or cannot provide health insurance. For those families

84

who are enrolled in public health insurance plans (most typically Medicaid), having that insurance card in hand does not necessarily provide access to care if the family does not know how to negotiate the health care system.

Adolescents raise another issue altogether. It has been well documented that adolescents are the largest group of uninsured children. They generally want help with issues they do not want anyone to know about, such as birth control, sexually transmitted diseases, and depression and suicidal thoughts. However, they can, and do, access school-based health centers (SBHCs) for these health needs. The goal of SBHCs is to improve the overall physical and emotional health of children and adolescents. They do this in two important ways—by providing prevention services and by providing direct health care.

The majority of school-based clinics are started by a health care provider who has approached a particular school and formed a relationship with the school's administrators. Such SBHCs are organizationally external to the school system, administered by local health care facilities such as hospitals and community health centers. Once the clinic is in the school, constant outreach to administrators, teachers, and parents must be maintained to remind them that the health center is on-site. The biggest challenge such providers face is the integration of the health services with the activities of the school.

In the Children's Aid Society (CAS) community schools, the implementation of health clinics is totally different from externally administered clinics. CAS is clearly the lead agency and a full partner with the principal of the school, so the health and mental health services become an integral part of the school's and the students' educational life.

CAS School-Based Health Centers

CAS provides on-site primary health care services at five of its New York City sites—three in elementary schools and two in middle schools. In addition, we are working with three schools in the Bronx on what we call a "school-linked" model; children from these schools can receive health and mental health services at CAS's Bronx Family Center, located near the schools.

In our community schools, we believe that it is most important to involve the student's family. Because the SBHCs are part of CAS's continuum of services, a host of opportunities arise to involve parents and siblings in the student's care. Parents are actively solicited to participate in their child's health care, and notification of availability of health services is made through several avenues: school registration materials, SBHC enrollment, facilitated insurance enrollment, CAS's family resource center, and the school's Parent-Teacher Association (PTA) organization. Family involvement begins at the time of enrollment in the SBHC, and year-round services and evening hours facilitate parents' participation in their children's care and preventive health education. For those parents unable to be present during their child's medical visit, a record of the treatment is sent home. Since the clinic is open long hours, we can accommodate children from the after-school programs.

CAS is an Article 28 Diagnosis and Treatment Center, fully licensed by the State of New York. This certification is required by the state, and it enables a clinic to become a Medicaid provider. We have formed affiliations and partnerships with several hospitals in New York City to assist us in providing referrals to specialty health care for students. All CAS doctors are pediatricians and faculty on staff at Mount Sinai Hospital and are assigned to work at CAS full time. This partnership is invaluable, because our doctors can admit and follow patients if they need hospitalization. The arrangement permits us full access to all of the hospital's continuing medical educational services. All other members of the medical staff are CAS employees.

CAS also has an affiliation with New York Presbyterian Hospital's Child and Adolescent Psychiatry Division, which makes available the services of a psychiatrist. This doctor carries out on-site school-based mental health evaluations and screenings, provides consultation services for our social workers, and serves as our connection for mental health service referrals to the hospital. The pediatricians from Mt. Sinai regularly confer with the psychiatrists on certain cases. Our other partnerships include Columbia University's College of Dental and Oral Surgery and the State University of New York College of Optometry.

Services Provided in School-Based Health Centers

A wide array of services is available at CAS's SBHCs:

- Comprehensive primary care, including physical exams, routine check-ups, immunizations, and tuberculosis testing in compliance with American Academy of Pediatrics (AAP) guidelines, American Medical Association (AMA) Guidelines for Adolescent Prevention Services, and New York State Child/Teen Health Program (C/THP) guidelines
- Anticipatory counseling: at first visit, elementary children and their parents are counseled about safety and appropriate health issues. Middle-school students, usually not accompanied by parents, are counseled on sexual activity, smoking, alcohol, violence, and other relevant issues.
- Emergency care and first aid treatment
- Diagnosis, monitoring, and management of chronic disease, such as asthma and diabetes
- Administration of prescribed medications
- Laboratory screening for anemia, sickle-cell diseases, cholesterol
- Treatment of minor and major acute illness
- Gynecological exams and family planning services, including pregnancy testing
- Mental health services, including individual and/or group counseling and family counseling
- Psychiatric evaluations for problems such as depression; monitoring of related medications

- Social services, including outreach and enrollment in Medicaid or Child Health Plus
- Case management
- Health education, both individual and classroom, and workshops for parents on various health issues
- Dental services, including preventive treatment, fillings, and routine extractions
- Optometry services, including disease prevention and early diagnosis and treatment of ocular disease and visual disorders
- Referrals for specialty services and clinics: students who require specialty clinic services are referred to the Mt. Sinai Medical Center, CAS's principal backup for all SBHC services in Manhattan. Up to the age of 18, children must be accompanied by parents.

Figure 7.1 shows the distribution of services used in each of the five SBHCs during the 2002–2003 school year. The most common presenting problems were colds, allergies, headaches, and earaches. Asthma was the next most frequent problem. Services at elementary schools differed slightly from those at middle schools, particularly in the area of reproductive health care, and older clinics saw more patients than newer ones.

The first CAS school-based clinic, the Student Wellness Center, is located at Intermediate School (IS) 218 and is typical of most of our clinics. Its medical, dental, optometry, and mental health services (see Bloom, ch. 8 in this volume, for a detailed description of the mental health component) are provided as part of CAS's community school model, which emphasizes parent involvement and offers a host of services to increase academic achievement and reduce health and social risks. Because all of CAS's school-based programs are totally integrated into the fabric of the schools, school staff and resources are involved in all aspects of the program components detailed below.

The Student Wellness Center is open five days a week from 8:30 A.M. to 7 P.M., on Saturdays by appointment, and through the summer. On-call 24-hour emergency medical coverage for students and parents is available seven days a week; if a child gets ill during the night or on a weekend, a call to the SBHC phone number reaches the answering service, which will contact the doctor on call. Once the medical issue is discussed, and depending on the severity of the problem, a plan is put in place and any needed follow-up is scheduled for the next day.

Components of the CAS SBHC Model

Enrollment and Outreach

Information about the medical and mental health services at the SBHC is available when parents register their children at school and throughout the calendar year. School staff members, including teachers, have firsthand knowledge

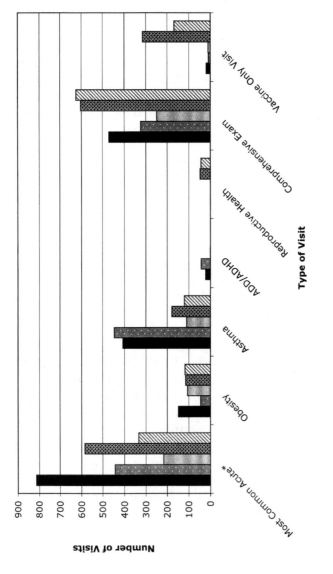

Figure 7.1. CAS school-based health clinic visits by purpose of visit, July 2002–June 2003. Asterisk indicates most common types of visits, including allergic rhinitis, conjunctivitis, headache, otitis media, pharyngitis, strep throat, upper respiratory infection (URI), and viral syndrome. *Credit:* The Children's Aid Society.

of the services and refer students and their parents to the SBHC. If families have access to no other health care, the siblings are served as well.

Parental Consent and Involvement

Parental consent for health services is sought as part of the SBHC's outreach and enrollment efforts. Parents are involved on an ongoing basis in planning and oversight committees for the SBHC and the after-school programs, some of which are exclusively for parents. Parents are invited and encouraged to participate in the care and treatment of their children. If they cannot be present, standing protocol dictates that they receive written notification of the health needs of their child and the type of treatment received.

New York State law allows adolescents to access certain clinical services without parental consent; these include confidential family planning services, emergency contraception, pregnancy testing, prenatal care, testing for and treatment of sexually transmitted diseases, HIV/AIDS testing and treatment, general emergency treatment, confidential alcohol and substance abuse counseling, and, in many cases, mental health services. In addition, minors can consent to their own care if they are pregnant, parents, married, or emancipated.[1] We always encourage teenagers to involve parents or another responsible adult in decisions regarding their health care. However, if a teenager chooses not to do so, we must honor his or her decision, with some exceptions; for example, if a student is homicidal, suicidal, or in danger, we must notify the parents or guardians.

Health Education

Health education is provided as part of screening and routine health services. To reinforce one-on-one health education, students and/or their parents are given educational brochures and other materials published by the AMA and the AAP. Health education is also provided in the classroom, where our health educators supplement the school's health curriculum with lessons that meet specific needs, such as family life and sexuality education, street safety, and HIV prevention. Health workshops are regularly provided for parents on such topics as asthma, attention-deficit/hyperactivity disorder (ADHD), and prevention of childhood obesity.

Screenings

All students enrolled in the SBHC receive hearing and vision screening at the clinic on an age-appropriate schedule. Health center staff members also assist in mass hearing and vision screenings in the classrooms, as required by New York City. If problems are identified, the children are referred to specialists for follow-up. Mental health assessments are also carried out for students who are enrolled in the SBHC.

Health Insurance Screening and Enrollment

The SBHC provides eligibility screening for Medicaid, Child Health Plus (CHP), and Family Health Plus insurance, as well as help with enrollment for qualified families; this service is open to all uninsured community residents, not just those with children enrolled in the community school. Federal money given to the states for providing health insurance to uninsured children is called Child Health Plus in New York State; the governor-initiated program called Family Health Plus insures the parents of some of the children we enroll in CHP.

Staffing

The advantage of having a fully integrated multidisciplinary health team on-site is that children receive almost all of the services they need right in the school. Clearly, not all SBHCs can assemble this kind of multidisciplinary staff, nor do all schools need full-time access to all of these services.

The following describes the staff at IS 218 and the staff's responsibilities as part of the health team.

Full-Time Staff, or Core Health Team, at the Student Wellness Center, IS 218

- *Nurse practitioner/physician assistant:* Provides comprehensive health care services and treatment of chronic and acute medical problems; can prescribe medications
- *Medical assistant:* Assists with screenings, obtaining vital signs, and first aid to students with minor injuries; performs duties according to established protocols when the practitioner is not on site
- *Medical receptionist:* Performs clerical duties, including entering data into computer, making appointments, billing, and following up on patients who need to be rescheduled
- *Student escort:* Assists the medical assistant by taking the younger children from the classroom to medical or dental appointments
- *Certified social workers (four full-time, one half-time):* Provide individual and group counseling to students experiencing psychosocial problems related to family stress, depression, peer relationships, and classroom behavioral problems; act as consultants in cases of suspected child abuse; assist in facilitating referrals in psychiatric emergencies

Part-Time Staff at the Student Wellness Center, IS 218

- *Consulting and precepting physician:* On-site three hours a week; provides ongoing medical consultation and supervision for the center's clinical staff; at the request of nurse practitioner/physician assistant, provides medical consultation for patients with difficult medical problems
- *Psychiatrist:* Provides psychiatric evaluations, consultations, and psychopharmacological prescriptions as needed

- *Dentist:* Provides dental screenings, exams, and diagnosis, as well as preventive services such as placement of sealants, oral prophylaxis, fluoride treatments, and restorative procedures
- *Dental hygienist:* Provides oral hygiene education and preventive services
- *Dental assistant:* Provides support to the dentist and prepares patients for procedures
- *Health educator:* Provides individual and group health counseling for students; provides classroom health presentations; works with the after-school program and parent groups to enhance healthy lifestyles
- *Health insurance enrollment facilitator:* Helps families who have no health insurance apply for Medicaid or CHP

Administrative Staff for All SBHCs

Overall responsibility for all CAS-provided health services is held by CAS's Health Services Division, including data collection, analysis, funding report submissions, fiscal and billing procedures, and facilitated insurance enrollment. This is the "central office" staff, members of which work not only with school-based clinics but with other health services provided by CAS in community centers, foster care programs, and summer camps. They provide overall guidance, direction, and administration of all clinical services and are responsible for policies and procedures for all patient care components.

- *Director of health administration:* For all CAS programs
- *School-based health center manager:* Responsible for day-to-day supervision of clinical staff at all five CAS SBHCs
- *Director of school-based mental health services:* Responsible for day-to-day supervision of mental health services at all five CAS SBHCs
- *Social work supervisor:* For all CAS programs
- *Medical director:* For all CAS programs
- *Dental director:* For all CAS programs
- *Dental administrator:* For all CAS programs

Space Requirements for the Student Wellness Center at IS 218

We felt that putting the health and mental health services in one location would be the most efficient and effective way to meet the medical and mental health needs of the more than 1,600 children who attend IS 218. The space needed to provide this type of full service is approximately 1,600 square feet. The center space includes:

- Two exam rooms
- One intake/processing room
- One small lab area for tests

- One bathroom
- One dental office equipped with dental chair and X-ray machine
- One waiting area with reception desk and 10 chairs for clients
- Three social worker counseling offices
- One supervising social worker office
- Storage capacity in each office

Finding space in overcrowded New York City schools can be a major implementation issue for providers planning to start SBHCs. We are fortunate to have a close partnership with the school, because it has enabled us to secure sufficient space to build our dream health center. Initially the health center was much smaller, but, in response to the demand for services, we were able to double its size in 2002.

Quality Assurance and Continuous Quality Improvement

CAS's medical director and dental director are responsible for maintenance of quality assurance and continuous quality improvement systems for all of the SBHCs. Monthly meetings of the Quality Assurance Committee, which consists of the SBHC manager, dental administrator, CAS's Director of Health Administration, and dental and medical directors, are held to review policies and procedures that need to be changed or created to conform with external and internal definitions of new practice standards. In addition, the committee analyzes the results of predefined audits and selected clinical and management indicators.

Such predefined audits are a part of the CAS health division's larger quality assurance systems, which comply with New York State Article 28 regulations regarding policies and procedures in various categories, including: administration (clinical and nonclinical personnel credentialing, continuing education and evaluation, confidentiality, medical records, quality assurance, and finance); infection control; medical services; laboratory services and Clinical Laboratory Improvement Amendment (CLIA) certification; safety management (security, fire, utilities, equipment, hazardous waste); and patient satisfaction. CLIA assures that health providers are in compliance with state regulations concerning which laboratory tests can be done on-site. Under these regulations we can provide urine tests, pregnancy tests, anemia tests, and others.

Cost and Financing

The cost of operating a school-based health center depends on the model that is chosen and the size of the school. Our Student Wellness Center in IS 218 costs approximately $450,000 a year to operate, or about $250 per student. Most of these funds support salaries; the remainder is used to purchase supplies and medical equipment.

In New York State, the city and state health departments use legislative and Maternal and Child Health block-grant dollars to fund these centers via a Request For Proposals (RFP) process. Federal funding is also available from such sources as Bureau of Primary Care, which funds Federally Qualified Health Centers (330 funded clinics). Many private foundations will also fund school-based health center activities.

In terms of revenue, most of New York City's SBHCs are allowed to bill Medicaid for health services provided. In New York State, as in other states, the advent of managed care created a shift in Medicaid policy; children were enrolled with a managed care provider that served as the "gatekeeper" to control costs. This was a threat to the viability of SBHCs because they were not considered eligible to be designated gatekeepers. There was no financial incentive for the managed care providers to contract with the school clinics, since they received the Medicaid capitated rate payment whether they provided services or not. A strong coalition of SBHC providers advocated in Albany and was able to create a "carve-out" for children enrolled in Medicaid managed care, meaning that the SBHC providers can bill Medicaid for services provided.

Another source of funding is the New York State Department of Health Bad Debt Pool; all health insurance companies in New York pay a "surcharge" to the state, which in turn is used to pay providers for health services given to uninsured patients. Some providers are able to tap into state education funding that is earmarked for specific school-based services, such as drug use prevention, attendance improvement, and dropout prevention. The Health Care Financing Administration tobacco-settlement monies that states receive are earmarked for health services.

In many cases, separate funding streams that support the provision of health-related services to school-age children lead to a patchwork rather than a stable pattern of services. The battle for steady funding and revenue sources is a continuing challenge for every SBHC provider. But as we in the SBHC world like to point out, the medical costs, welfare costs, and other costs to society of emergency room visits, unintended pregnancies, and high hospitalization rates for problems like asthma are far greater than the costs of these centers.

Observations

Every day we encounter situations that are stories in themselves. We have selected three cases that represent the thousands of young people who come to our clinics for help with a vast array of problems. We cannot solve all their problems, but we can alleviate certain chronic conditions, such as asthma, and find previously undiagnosed diseases. The parents of these children are invariably grateful for the services they receive.

Andre, Nine Years Old

Andre has many problems: a sleep disturbance, obesity, eczema, asthma, and allergies. Andre's mother is also sick, as is one of his sisters, who also has asthma. The family went to the emergency room for their care before they learned about the school-based clinic.

At the clinic Andre has received asthma treatments, as well as physical and dental exams. Although the family could not get a nebulizer from the hospital, the physician's assistant at the clinic was able to supply one. Andre reports that the clinic nurses help him feel better during the school day. Although other health problems remain, Andre's asthma is under control. The clinic is in the process of arranging for tonsil/adenoid surgery. His attendance record has improved along with his grades.

Roberto, Five Years Old

Roberto came into the clinic at the age of five with previously undiagnosed cystic fibrosis; his eventual diagnosis was made possible by the availability of the school-based clinic's personnel and resources. Because Roberto was in the school, the providers could monitor on a daily, weekly, and monthly basis certain key factors such as height/weight, anemia screenings, dental issues, nutritional status, and psychosocial dysfunction in the home. In conjunction with the medical clinic, dental examination provided evidence that an underlying chronic disease was causing severe tooth decay and gum disease beyond the usual baby-bottle tooth decay.

In this case, an extraordinary effort was made to acquire birth records, previous clinic records, and details of frequent hospitalizations for unidentified febrile illnesses. These records provided a much needed medical history, which was particularly important because the child's parent could not provide past records. This reconstructed medical history led to uncovering the underlying disease.

An effort to gain the family's trust and build a relationship, along with the clinic monitoring and thorough review of records, led to subspecialty referrals to both gastrointestinal medicine and pulmonology at Mount Sinai Hospital. Due to relationships between CAS's providers and the subspecialists, diagnostic testing was expedited and a diagnosis was soon made. This child will continue to receive careful monitoring as long as he remains in our system.

Tanya, Thirteen Years Old

Tanya has been diagnosed with bipolar disorder and is also asthmatic. The clinic staff members act as extra moms to Tanya. Tanya's mother can become overwhelmed and really appreciates the convenience of the school-based clinic, where all her children are registered. The clinic is especially helpful when Tanya has panic attacks during the school day; she can go to the clinic to calm down. The nurse practitioner is in contact with Tanya's doctors about her treatment in the clinic.

Concerning her asthma, the clinic has cut the number of emergency room visits the family must make and has reduced her fear by helping her learn about her illness. She says she feels safe and comfortable at the clinic. It has also opened doors for Tanya's mother to the school's ADHD and parenting groups, as well as to the health educator and social worker's one-on-one counseling.

Tanya was recently seen at the clinic for a pregnancy test, as she and her boyfriend had sex without using contraception. Tanya's pregnancy test was negative, and she is now seeing the clinic health educator who has counseled her on sexual decision making and reproductive health issues. Tanya has chosen not to continue to be sexually active at this time and is participating in a support group with other young teens that is co-led by the health educator and the social worker.

Lessons Learned

The challenges in the provision of health and mental health services in schools are many, but certainly not insurmountable. They include:

- Achieving financial viability
- Negotiating two radically different bureaucratic structures, a health provider with health mandates and regulations and an education department focused heavily on achievement and testing
- Dealing with possible community opposition to specific health services, such as family planning
- Securing adequate space in the school
- Providing security and maintenance for the facility
- Integrating health services with the "life" of the school

Unfortunately there will always be children and adolescents who come from economically disadvantaged families. We will continue to see many children of recent immigrants who may not have access to health insurance and who have never had access to highly trained health professionals before. There will always be adolescents with health issues that cannot be discussed with parents or other providers. SBHCs are a convenient and appropriate venue in which to reach these needy populations.

Not every school needs to set up a clinic, nor is there space in every school to set one up. When space is not available in the school, a provider can consider the school-linked model. Locating a health center adjacent to, or a few blocks away from, a school has the advantage of accessibility for students and for community children. It also allows the center to remain open when the school building is not, enabling a greater flexibility of hours and days of service. This may be particularly helpful if the school has a small population; the health center can also provide services to students from surrounding schools, creating a hub of services.

CAS has such a program operating out of our Bronx Family Center. Three CAS community schools surround this center. We have agreements in place

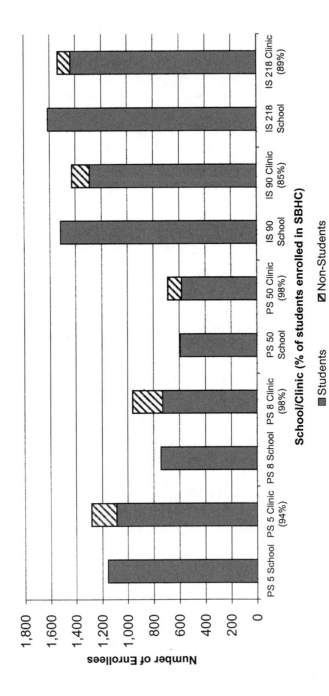

Figure 7.2. CAS school-based health clinic enrollment versus school enrollment, July 2002–June 2003. *Credit:* The Children's Aid Society.

with all of these schools to provide health and dental services to their students. To secure parental consent for medical services, our staff provides the same enrollment process, parent meetings, and classroom work as at IS 218. With cooperation from school staff, our escort brings children from school to the Bronx Family Center clinic for medical and dental services. As for mental health services, we have placed a team of social workers in the schools; their supervision is provided by a clinical supervisor also located at the center. Creating a "school-linked" clinic that serves several adjacent schools is also a cost-effective way of providing health services, because it entails operating only one set of health services as opposed to three or four.

Reliable evidence shows that SBHCs work.[2] The rapid proliferation of these health centers indicates that they are supported by many parents, students, politicians, and communities. CAS has made an effort to track statistics on SBHC utilization. Figure 7.2 shows that some 90% of the student body in each school is enrolled, a remarkably high rate. In the schools where the enrollment in the clinic exceeds the population of the school, the difference is made up by sibling use. Among all of these children, we have found many previously undetected health problems and are providing a wide range of health care that they might not otherwise be getting.

Clearly the CAS SBHCs are having an important impact on the children who attend the five schools where they are located. At IS 218 you can sit in the waiting room of the clinic and observe that there are always students lined up for diagnosis, treatment, counseling, or just a little tender loving care. Students feel no stigma; everyone in the school uses the center, and no one knows anyone else's reason for a visit, because all records and transactions are confidential.

It is difficult to envision a full-service community school that does not offer health services, either on-site or nearby. Our experience confirms the importance of striving toward two goals simultaneously: educational achievement and good health.

NOTES

1. Jessica Feierman et al., *Teenagers, Health Care and the Law: A Guide to the Law on Minors' Rights in New York State* (New York: New York Civil Liberties Union, July 2002).
2. "Center for Evaluation and Quality: National Data," *National Assembly on School-Based Health Care,* http://www.nasbhc.org/EQ/National_Data.htm.

Bill Foley

Mental Health Services

SCOTT BLOOM

Director of School-Based Mental Health, The Children's Aid Society

Mental health problems in children are a major deterrent to learning. Yet the President's New Freedom Commission on Mental Health in 2002 pointed out that mental health services for children are so fragmented as to be ineffective in major ways.[1] The commission's report emphasizes the importance of using the school system as the means of delivering such services.

The school-based approach to mental health helps accomplish several goals:

- Minimizing barriers to learning
- Overcoming stigma and inadequate access to care
- Providing comprehensive on-site counseling services
- Creating a school climate that promotes students' social and emotional functioning
- Promoting healthy psychological and social development

This chapter will describe the mental health services at the Children's Aid Society (CAS) community schools, focusing on staffing, structure, and strategies and describing the clinic at one school in greater detail. Questions of space, accountability, and funding will be explored, and some conclusions based on our work will be discussed.

Description of the Service

CAS's school-based clinics, located in elementary and middle schools, provide individual and family counseling, group therapy, in-depth assessments and re-ferrals, and crisis intervention for students and their family members. Referrals to the clinic are made by students, teachers, and parents. Assessment and in-tervention plans include the active participation of the child, his or her family, school staff, and anyone else who can help in understanding the child's needs.

Based on the assessment, the child and/or family are engaged in short- or long-term individual, group, or family counseling aimed at ameliorating the problems that precipitated the referral. An in-depth psychosocial as-sessment is the first step in developing a comprehensive treatment plan that includes short- and long-term goals. Psychological and psychiatric evalua-tions are scheduled as appropriate.

Clinicians (social workers with M.S.W. or C.S.W. degrees) generally have caseloads of 18–22 students, with enough room in their schedules to see walk-ins and emergencies. Problems that have been successfully treated in-clude suicide ideation, physical and sexual abuse, drug and alcohol use, dis-ruptive school behaviors, academic delays, hyperactivity, family and peer con-flicts, and depression.

These and other presenting problems usually serve as the child's and fam-ily's introduction to the mental health program. Staff members meet with fam-ilies to gain a more complete assessment, to work on resolving family conflicts, and to manage abuse and neglect issues in the home. As a result of this work with families, parents begin to see the school as a safe place to go for help; this often has the added benefits of involving the parents more closely in their children's education and encouraging them to take leadership roles within the school. Because of positive feelings in the community toward the mental health staff, these staff members are often the first to be approached by parents, even when the problem is not specifically a mental health issue.

Within the school clinic, staff members are integrated into the daily fabric through frequent consultation with teachers. This collaborative approach often provides opportunities to intervene before issues become more serious.

Staffing

At the CAS schools, mental health services are provided by social workers (master's-level or higher) in consultation with school administrators and teachers and under the overall supervision of the director of mental health (see Figure 8.1). Advanced training and continuing education are encouraged; special training is offered through monthly in-services as well as weekly and group supervision. Clinical supervision takes place during weekly clinic case conferences, convened by the social work supervisors. Staff members are bilingual (some of the schools are 90 percent Latino) and are expected to be sensitive to the diverse school population, which at various schools is a mix of African American, Latino, Russian, and other ethnic groups.

A consulting psychiatrist is available one or two days a week to provide psychiatric evaluations and diagnoses, prescriptions for medication, crisis evaluation, treatment review, clinician consultation, and teacher training.

Organization

The mental health services in the schools of Community School District 6 (now Regional District 10) in the Washington Heights neighborhood of New York City are provided through a collaborative partnership involving CAS, the school district, Columbia Presbyterian Hospital Psychiatric Center, Columbia University, and the Carmel Hill Fund. Additional psychiatric consultation and psychopharmacology management are available through the relationship with Columbia University and Columbia Presbyterian Hospital's Division of Child Psychiatry.

In 2002 the middle schools became participants in the School-Based Support Project III, a school-based mental health demonstration grant for Intermediate School (IS) 218 and IS 90 sponsored by the New York State Education Department and the State Office of Mental Health. This has led to new, and more consistent, protocols and procedures, as well as additional training for staff. Columbia's Center for the Advancement of Children's Mental Health (CACMH) is subcontracted by New York State to provide technical assistance for the grantees; they carry out monitoring and oversight of the project and conduct research on the assessments and short-term treatment modalities that the grantees are required to implement.

The mental health staff uses existing school structures (such as school cabinets, school leadership teams, and pupil personnel teams) to present new findings and recommendations and to facilitate discussion of documented

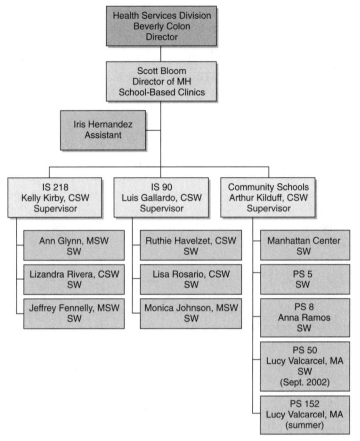

Figure 8.1. CAS mental health staff. *Credit:* The Children's Aid Society.

student needs so that Department of Education (DOE) and CAS resources will be appropriately allocated. Similar links and information sharing are used in assessments by the Committee on Special Education, so that intervention by mental health staff can help prevent out-of-school placements.

A unique example of the mental health staff's integration in the school is its involvement in the pupil personnel team (PPT), whose purpose is to provide preventive strategies and interventions for students in the school's general education population who are failing academically or whose chronic behavior problems interfere with their academic functioning. The PPT, made up of DOE special education counselors and school-based support staff (such as psychologists, counselors, and resource providers), facilitates enrollment in special education classes and makes referrals to support services such as resource room and occupational and speech therapy. Earlier, PPT members felt overwhelmed by the number and severity of referred cases and found it difficult to stay focused. Then the social work supervisor of the school-based clinic began to attend the meetings and to act as liaison between the PPT and the mental health clinic. Through her efforts the meetings were re-structured and streamlined, minutes are now taken and distributed, team members are required to follow up on actions agreed on at earlier meetings, duplication of services among the various entities is more easily prevented, and referrals to appropriate services are more efficient. Initiated at IS 218, this approach is now being used in other CAS schools.

Intervention Strategies

An array of intervention strategies is employed to help students, families, and staff effectively resolve problems, to reduce risky behaviors, to enhance cop-ing strategies, and to support appropriate behaviors. One-on-one counseling sessions are scheduled weekly when symptoms are most intense; later, they are held once every two weeks or once a month to sustain progress and con-solidate gains.

Groups

Groups are very effective in treating many of the students' presenting prob-lems. With their emphasis on mutual help and support, groups give students opportunities to solve problems and develop the socialization skills needed in the school setting. Groups have focused on such issues as adolescent sex-uality, social anxiety, depression, bereavement, behavior management, school problems, and immigration problems for newly arrived students.

Other groups begin when a student is hesitant to discuss personal issues or to disclose concerns to a clinician. The student brings two or three other students, usually friends, to the clinic; a group forms around a particular topic, such as puberty issues, socialization, parent-child conflicts, accultur-ation, or dating, and meets regularly. Guided by a clinician, group members begin to reveal very private feelings that other members identify with; the group structure neutralizes students' anxiety and offers a safe space, leading them to explore areas of their lives they had not expected to cover and to develop new insights. These naturally forming groups are effective largely because they are created and driven by the students.

Grandparents' support groups are composed primarily of grandparents who have had to assume full-time care of their grandchildren. The sharing and per-sonal support they receive from the group help strengthen their ability to keep the family going and to avoid relying on government spending programs. The groups may be organized around particular issues, such as helping a child who is failing in school or raising a child who has behavior problems.

Town Meetings

Town meetings are a very important part of the CAS approach in the middle schools. Every day three classes (about 60–65 students) meet for a full class period to discuss a wide variety of topics, such as dating, racism, cultural sensitivity, or test anxiety. A curriculum, such as "Overcoming Obstacles," is followed, and the meeting is run in a lively, engaging manner. A facilitator moves around the room with a microphone, gathering students' opinions and advice and stimulating discussion by challenging their beliefs, customs, and values. Guest speakers, role-playing, and game show techniques are some of the methods used to create a nonthreatening environment in which students can have fun and think out loud in ways that do not happen in the classroom.

A clinician's participation enhances the value of the town meeting. Often a clinician co-leads the meeting and offers an emotional or insight-oriented point of view on the topic of the day. The clinician is also ready to address intimate and emotionally charged issues with students who are deeply affected by the discussion, and he or she can intervene if necessary.

In one town meeting, the topic was family fighting (domestic violence). The facilitator asked how the students coped with the stress when parents argue or when arguments escalate into physical actions. Students volunteered various methods of withdrawal: going into their rooms, watching television, putting on their earphones to listen to CDs, reading, or calling a friend. The clinician noticed that a girl in the back row had her head down and was sniffling. Waiting until the meeting was over, the clinician approached the girl and asked if it would be okay for the two of them to talk. The girl agreed, and they went to the clinician's office for what amounted to a therapy session. Afterward they made follow-up appointments to continue processing the girl's sad feelings about her parents' frequent arguments.

New Arrival Groups

In 2003 more than 90% of the students at IS 218 were Dominican; 15% were newly arrived in the community and, frequently, in the United States. Such students need assistance in facing the challenges of adapting to a new culture, particularly because the system often does not address their emotional and psychological needs. Separation anxiety and issues of loss are prevalent in this group; acculturation issues often result in potentially debilitating problems, such as aggressive acting out or withdrawal from social activities; adjustment disorders, persistent anxiety, depression, and various maladaptive behaviors relating to home and family stressors can often be traced to adaptation issues.

The purpose of the new arrival groups is to orient students to their new culture, to mitigate the negative effects of the transition on their education, to empower them through peer modeling and support, to build on their strengths and resiliency, and to identify supportive resources from families and cultures of origin. Work in the groups emphasizes acculturation, reintegration, and facilitation of the grieving process.

Caregiver orientation is provided in collaboration with the school's parent coordinator, and the caregivers' involvement is ongoing, with individual meetings held when necessary. Such continuing participation by caregivers is an important component in reaching the groups' goals of decreasing mal-adaptive symptoms while increasing positive involvement in school.

Elementary School Programs

Elementary school social workers work closely with the after-school programs run by CAS. Students who would benefit from various groups or activities or who have problems with social skills are referred to the after-school program. The social workers also offer workshops and training for teachers and parents.

In each of the elementary schools, the mental health staff, in conjunction with the DOE and the after-school program, has created a safe zone. These structured after-school settings are designed for students who are disruptive and tardy. In the safe zone, children can take time to cool down, work with an adult to process their behavior, build skills to make other choices, and get assistance with conflict resolution if needed.

Rather than acting as a disciplinarian and suspending such students, the social worker works with other school support staff to offer them activities and counseling and to address the disruptive behavior. Half of the students referred to the safe zone are able to return to their after-school activities.

The clinicians in the elementary schools also meet weekly with the principal and other DOE counselors who may be working with special education students and/or with mainstream children. These counselors and the CAS mental health staff often work together to cover a particular grade level.

Interdisciplinary Cooperation

School-based mental health clinics see students whose stomachaches and asthma are triggered by test anxiety, trouble at home, and other emotionally related problems. The medical staff and mental health staff have always worked in a collaborative manner, and this integration of the mental health and medical programs carries out the holistic approach to serving the students. The student wellness center at each school provides a comprehensive range of services that specifically target the problems of students in the community, as well as providing general medical care. All students who receive health services also receive a mental health assessment; if a referral is needed, these students are given an appointment with a social worker.

Interdisciplinary meetings, held quarterly, bring together more than 25 mental health and medical program providers from the school clinics to review cases and make note of issues that have arisen. These meetings offer glimpses into each practice and suggest ways in which the same issue can be addressed from different angles. The medical and mental health providers at each school hold weekly team meetings to discuss shared patients. The medical and mental health records are included in one chart, which is kept in the school-based clinic, assuring confidentiality and enhancing the holistic approach.

A classic example of interdisciplinary collaboration is the case of 14-year-old Dora, who was known to the medical clinic because of her diabetes, obesity, and asthma. She came to the mental health clinic with a girlfriend and talked about her boredom in school and her many absences. The clinician ran a series of assessments and found that Dora was suffering from depression. When Dora began to miss both her medical and her mental health appointments, the two practitioners together made a plan with Dora. Though their efforts were thwarted by Dora's lack of compliance and by her mother, who did not help Dora follow through, in the end the two clinicians jointly recommended Dora's referral to a day treatment program where she could receive both medical and mental health services as well as school instruction.

When appropriate, staff members use home visits to engage families in treatment, work with resistant family members, broaden their assessments, and provide advocacy services to strengthen the therapeutic relationship. In 2003 plans were under way to further extend family support efforts through strengthening the role of the parent coordinator. Through the clinic's partnership with CACMH, the parent coordinator will receive training in mental health and in acting as a liaison with parents to guide them through the mental health system. The social work supervisor works with both the parent coordinator and the CAS community school director to create a comprehensive schedule and agenda for parent workshops.

IS 218

IS 218, Salomé Ureña de Henriquez Middle Academies, has more than 1,600 students and was CAS's first community school to have a school-based clinic. The school is divided into four academies (one per floor). Each social worker is assigned to an academy (or floor) and meets weekly with the academy team, which consists of an assistant principal, teachers, and other school personnel who provide services to that academy; this allows the social worker to receive referrals, discuss problems, and respond to the teachers' needs.

The social work supervisor facilitates discussions not only in the team meetings, which she attends on a rotating schedule, but throughout the school. She coordinates scheduled meetings and consultations with teachers and administrators to discuss student classroom problems, offering information on psychosocial issues related to the behavior and to teachers' responses to it.

Teacher training raises awareness of mental health issues and insures that proper referrals are made on a daily basis, informally as well as formally. The social work staff offers various kinds of training and workshops on topics such as making appropriate referrals, recognizing signs and symptoms of various mental illnesses, and classroom management, as well as on various clinical topics and treatment issues.

A good example of the mental health staff's integration into the school is the work with groups from the Academic Intervention Service (AIS) classes. AIS classes are designed to provide a small-class environment for students who are seen as needing smaller classes but who have not been designated for them through the special education system; there is one AIS class in three of the school's four academies. The social work supervisor is a resource for the administrative staff concerning the mental health needs of the students in these classes. The groups, consisting of students who have behavioral problems, are facilitated by the social workers; this frees the teachers to teach, provides them with informed feedback, and helps with classroom management.

Perhaps more important, work with these groups has made it clear that the AIS classes have some systemic problems that affect the students' academic needs. The social work supervisor has been actively involved with school personnel in developing ways to improve these classes. Through the school-based clinic's involvement, many of the AIS students have been connected to individual mental health services at the clinic;[2] when it was discovered that many of the AIS students were supposed to have been receiving counseling from one of the special education DOE social workers, this was brought to the attention of the administrative staff for follow-up. In addition, the severely disruptive behavior that is a daily occurrence in the AIS classes contributes to the frustration and burnout of the AIS teachers; in collaboration with the school leadership, the mental health staff is developing methods of providing ongoing support for these teachers.

Integration of the mental health staff into the school's daily life is also exemplified by the Positive Behavior in Schools campaign (PBIS), a school-wide program that reinforces positive behavior.[3] Driven by the principal and a select committee, the program is overseen by CACMH and the New York State Education Department.

PBIS is a systems approach to preventing and responding to school and classroom discipline problems. The theory is that by reducing behavioral problems, PBIS creates and maintains safe learning environments where teachers can teach and students can learn. The team consists of deans, teachers, the CAS site director, and the social work supervisor, who provides a psychological perspective; her participation also means that the mental health staff is involved in the planning stages of the program.

As of 2003, plans called for implementing PBIS floor by floor—introducing it in one academy at a time, working out the kinks, and evaluating the pros and cons before moving on to the next academy. Training and workshops are provided by the New York State Department of Education.

A diagnostic tool, the Diagnostic Interview Schedule for Children (DISC) screening, is used in the students' initial assessment. On a laptop the student answers questions that scan for depression, substance abuse/use, conduct disorders, and other diagnoses; the screening can usually be completed in one classroom period. Through a grant from the Carmel Hill Fund (supported by Bill Ruane), the school's consulting psychiatrist provides training for teachers; this includes recognizing general signs and symptoms of depression, anxiety, withdrawal, and other behavioral problems that should prompt teachers to refer a student for DISC screening.

The mental health clinic and the CAS parent coordinator together organize parent training. In one initiative parents of children who have oppositional defiant disorder, conduct disorder, or other behavioral problems are invited to participate in an ongoing group. The mental health staff works with the assistant principals to gather referrals for this group; this collaboration insures that outreach efforts are made to these families and that parents of these children are encouraged to attend the support group. Monthly workshops on topics concerning adolescent development issues are also offered to parents.

Space

A well-run mental health program needs safe, clean, appropriate space to deliver services and maintain confidentiality. Sometimes this requires some creativity—perhaps sharing space, rotating scheduling in various rooms, or working to find alternative spaces. The CAS schools' mental health services have sometimes used rooms with no windows, basement interiors, and even converted closet space. At one time, students had to wait outside the clinic in the school's entrance hall, on view for all passersby.

At the IS 218 clinic, medical and mental health space was combined to create the Student Wellness Center, turning two discrete rooms into a suite. Combining the clinics has helped diminish the stigma of receiving services, allowed better clerical coverage, and made the center a one-stop shopping place for services. In addition, it reflects the goal of viewing each child from a holistic point of view.

Visibility is an important key to the success of a school-based mental health clinic. In most clinical situations, patient and therapist meet once a week for a 45-minute session and then do not see one another until the next week. A school-based clinic, however, has a captive audience whose members are encountered regularly in hallways, lunchrooms, assemblies, and other school settings. Clinic staff members go to assemblies, after-school events, and holiday pageants; they hand out turkey dinners at Thanksgiving and Christmas. Students come to view the clinicians as a nonthreatening, ordinary part of the school scene and to look on them as some of the few reliable adults in their lives.

Some students even become clinic regulars or groupies. They stop by to say hello, to give a quick update on their lives, or just to offer a high five and thanks. The one-on-one relationship and the constant availability make all the difference.

The physical space contributes to this relaxed and reassuring atmosphere. Students expect that when they come into the clinic, they will be treated in a way that is different from other relationships in the school. They can speak their minds, knowing that confidentiality will be respected. The mental health clinic creates a zone of comfort and safety that nurtures students and facilitates the treatment process.

Accountability

Looking at outcomes helps clinicians evaluate effectiveness and steer programs in the right direction. Research shows that school-based clinic mental health programs contribute to improvement in attendance, in frequency of discipline referrals, and in student performance as evaluated by teachers.[4] The data collection system in the CAS schools can document enrollment in, and utilization of, mental health services, making it possible to assess mental health needs and trends and to facilitate research planning and protocols. Mental health encounter forms are the basis of the data, which is used to assess the type and severity of issues that arise, track the diagnosis and the level of intervention provided, and determine the need for follow-up.[5]

A variety of assessment tools are currently used to measure a range of behaviors. The Strengths Difficulty Questionnaire for pre- and post-testing provides a snapshot of the student at the beginning, middle, and end of treatment from the perspectives of the parent, teacher, and student. It looks at depression, hyperactivity, and conduct disorders as well as positive behavior and strengths, and it also helps track the student's behavior during the course of treatment. The Client Satisfaction Survey has forms in English and Spanish for both parent and student; it is administered at four-month intervals and when the treatment is terminated. This survey offers a glimpse into parents' and students' perceptions of the quality of treatment provided by the mental health service staff.

Other outcome assessments include a review of the turnaround period for referrals in order to track timeliness of referral procedures. Treatment plans for each case that is opened are also reviewed every three months for achievement of goals and objectives. Finally, questionnaires given to school staff, parents, and teachers at the end of workshops, group sessions, and training sessions provide feedback about the content and quality of the experience. (See the appendix to this chapter for examples of forms used by CAS community schools' mental health services.)

Overall feedback has been positive. Students feel "listened to" and respected. Parents feel engaged; they also feel they are given pertinent information that is personal yet useful in their relationships with their children. One parent said she "can't think of the school existing" without us. Many teachers find the clinicians approachable and accessible. They have gained knowledge that has changed their attitudes and approach to their students. And the administrative staff finds our work invaluable.

Funding

Mental health programs that are part of school-based clinics are usually funded through partnerships; funds may come from the state, school districts, hospital districts or catchment areas, community health centers, universities, special grants, and private fund-raising. Public and private grants, Medicaid billing, and fees collected for services generally pay for staffing costs and medical and office supplies; staff salaries and benefits account for the largest portion of the school-based clinic's and mental health center's budget. Clinic space, utilities, and janitorial services are usually in-kind contributions from the school district.

In the CAS schools in New York City, the school-based mental health services receive funds from, among others, the Ruane Foundation, the Robert Wood Johnson Foundation's Caring for Kids Program, the Mulago Foundation, New York State and New York City Offices of Mental Health, New York State Education Department, Medicaid, TANF Grants, and several Children's Aid Society trustees. Collaborations with Columbia Presbyterian Hospital Emergency Room and Pediatric Crisis Center and Columbia University's CACMH, as well as linkages with local agencies and organizations, afford a broader array of services to offer students and families.

While the school-based carve-out for Medicaid insurance claims has helped to support and sustain the school-based health and dental services, Medicaid cannot be claimed for the delivery of mental health services by clinical social workers under Article 28 (it may be used only for services provided by psychiatrists and psychologists). However, in January 2001 the two middle schools' mental health clinics received licenses under both Article 28 and Article 31; this permits them to bill Medicaid for social work services.

Lessons Learned

What we have learned at CAS's school-based mental health clinics is how deeply our work is interrelated with the various subsystems of the schools. In my presentations at the schools (approximately 24 each year), I often ask, If the first step in carrying out mental health services for a student is to do an assessment, why not do the same for a school? Just as we would with a client, we must learn the language of the school.

Such an assessment would include questions such as these:

- What is the culture of the school?
- How does the school's population see the mental health clinic?
- What is their definition of crisis?
- How do they respond to disciplinary efforts, to detention, and to suspension?
- What is it like to walk through the school's entrance?
- What is the atmosphere in the school?
- Who holds the power in the school?

Learning to understand the inner workings and language of a school is like working with a long-term case: it may take a few years, but once it is achieved we are able to plan interventions appropriately, to enhance strengths and shore up weaknesses, and, most important, to develop trust.

We engage with the school in the same way we engage in a therapeutic relationship with a student. We show up at meetings, presentations, and numerous student and family events. Our aim is to become part of the school's fabric so that, as in a positive therapeutic relationship, the school will begin to internalize the quality services we provide.

The school-based mental health clinics are works in progress. Meeting funding, programming, and staffing challenges requires ongoing attention and constant educating of the educators. Any greeting or hello in the halls is an opportunity to reinforce our mental health initiatives. The transactional nature of the school system and the mental health program offers a unique opportunity to put a plan in place based on a school-wide analysis: gather the history, identify the strengths and weaknesses, and devise a plan whereby the mental health center can become fully integrated while offering the services and care that the particular school needs.

The daily work necessary to keep the clinic operating requires of clinicians and school staff a mature partnership that evolves into a true working relationship. This is indeed critical when working with students who have histories of serious emotional disturbance. Dealing with these students can evoke strong feelings in the educational and mental health staff. For many such students, gaining insight and growth from their work with clinical staff represents their last chance to stay at home and in the community.

Numerous kinds of statistics are used to measure the effectiveness of evidence-based treatment. Yet none can truly measure what it means for students to have a positive relationship with an adult at this stage of their lives. At the end of the day, this trusting relationship provided by the school-based mental health clinic is what matters most.

NOTES

1. M. Hogan, *President's New Freedom Commission on Mental Health* (Washington, D.C.: National Academy Press, 2002).
2. G. Sugai et al., "Applying Positive Behavioral Support and Functional Behavioral Assessment in Schools," *Journal of Positive Behavior Intervention* 2, no. 3 (2000).
3. Ibid.
4. H. S. Adelman and L. Taylor, *A Resource Aid: Responding to Crisis at a School* (Los Angeles: UCLA Center for Mental Health in Schools, September 2000); Jonathan Fast, "An In-Law Comes to Stay: Examination of Interdisciplinary Conflict in a School-Based Health Center," *Social Work* 48, no. 1 (2003): 45–50.
5. J. Langford, *Mental Health Yearly Report* (New York: Children's Aid Society, 2000).

Appendix: Forms Used in Mental Health Services at CAS Community Schools

The Children's Aid Society—Health Services Division

Student Wellness Center: Referral/Intake Evaluation

Name: _____ Date: _____ OSIS No: _____

Address: _____ Apt. No.: _____

_____ Zip: _____ Phone: _____

D.O.B. _____ Age: _____ Gender: _____ Ethnicity: _____ Religion: _____

Primary Language Child: _____ Family: _____ English Fluent: ☐ Yes ☐ No

Known to CAS: ☐ Yes ☐ No   ☐ Medical ☐ MH   Chart No.: _____

Medicaid: ☐ Yes ☐ No Medicaid No.: _____   Social Security No.: _____

Referral Source: SELF: ☐   PARENT: ☐   TEACHER: ☐   OTHER: ☐

School: _____ Grade: _____ Spec. Ed.: ☐ Yes ☐ No Level: _____

Parents/Guardian Names:

_____

Address (if different than above): _____

Apt. No.: _____ Zip: _____ Phone: _____

Relevant Phone #'s: _____

Emergency Contact/Rel: _____ Phone: _____

Instructions to Contact: _____ Can We Call Home? ☐ Yes ☐ No

Please describe the reason(s) for referral (Presenting Problem):

_____

_____

For Clinic Use Only: HOUSEHOLD MEMBERS:

Name	Age	Relationship

Significant Others Not Living in the Home:

Name/Relationship	Age	Relationship

Agencies Involved:

Agency Name	Contact Person	Phone

How long has problem existed? _____

Other agencies involved with client/family? _____

_____

Other collaterals interviewed? _____

_____

What has been done previously to handle problem? _____

_____

_____

Child's needs and services: _____

_____

_____

Check if client had annual physical: _____ Referral to medical date: _____

Diagnosis:

Axis I:

(_____)_____

Axis II:

(_____)_____

Axis III:

(_____)_____

Check if client admitted: _____ Admission date: _____

Document reason client was not admitted: _____

_____

_____

If client was referred elsewhere, name and address of referral source: _____

_____

_____

Social Worker: _____

Date: _____

Client Satisfaction Survey
(For Parent or Guardian of Child in Treatment)

In our efforts to continually improve the quality of our clinic we would like your feedback about the services you have received. Please take a moment to complete the following questions. All answers will be kept private. Your social worker will not see them.

1. Social worker explained things in a way that was easily understood?	☐ YES ☐ NO
2. Social worker answered any questions you had?	☐ YES ☐ NO
3. Social worker thought what you had to say was important?	☐ YES ☐ NO
4. Social worker answered your questions as well as possible?	☐ YES ☐ NO
5. Privacy was respected?	☐ YES ☐ NO
6. Social worker was on time for your appointments?	☐ YES ☐ NO
7. You felt comfortable with the social worker?	☐ YES ☐ NO
8. Social worker had information that you found helpful?	☐ YES ☐ NO
9. You felt your social worker really listened to you and your child?	☐ YES ☐ NO
10. Social worker was rude or disrespectful?	☐ YES ☐ NO
11. You and social worker acted like a team to solve your problems?	☐ YES ☐ NO
12. You feel you and your child were helped by this social worker?	☐ YES ☐ NO
13. Social worker was aware and sensitive to your culture?	☐ YES ☐ NO
14. You were treated respectfully by other clinic professionals?	☐ YES ☐ NO
15. Have you recommended the clinic services to any other families?	☐ YES ☐ NO
16. Would you come back again if your child had another problem?	☐ YES ☐ NO

What benefits have you and your child experienced from working with our social work staff?

_____

_____

Do you feel that our social worker has helped your child succeed in school in any way? If yes, what has happened or what has changed?

_____

_____

Bill Foley

9

Promoting Community and
Economic Development

YVONNE GREEN
Senior Consultant, National Technical Assistance Center for
Community Schools, The Children's Aid Society

The previous five chapters describe major program components of Children's
Aid Society (CAS) community schools, all designed to contribute to the learning and healthy development of individual children and their families. This
chapter describes a different kind of programmatic focus—one that moves
beyond individual child and family well-being to influence the health and
welfare of the entire community. The central questions to be addressed in

this chapter are: How do community schools contribute to community and economic development? How is the community schools strategy both intentional and responsive in making these broader kinds of contributions? How has CAS's community and economic development work evolved over the past decade in response to changing needs and opportunities?

Community and Economic Development in the CAS Model

According to John P. Kretzmann, a leading scholar and advocate of community development, schools are ideal partners for community development because they have tremendous assets.[1] They have facilities for meetings and neighborhood celebrations and space for incubating small businesses; they have materials and equipment, purchasing power, the ability to raise funds, employment power, learning opportunities, skilled staff, energetic young people with ideas, and the capacity to attract adult involvement. This analysis is consistent with CAS's original vision about the potential of community schools to achieve broader outcomes and also consistent with our experience over the past decade in implementing a wide variety of community and economic development strategies, first in the Washington Heights area and more recently in the South Bronx.

The central idea of contributing to community and economic development in specific neighborhoods requires a long-term vision and commitment. Just as the early Progressive Era reformers understood the importance of "settling" into neighborhoods to achieve maximum impact, CAS's leadership perceived the value of committing the organization's resources to specific neighborhoods over a long term. In another similarity to the Progressive Era, CAS understood the importance of working on several levels or dimensions of activity at the same time. It is true that the original vision of community schools focused on improving outcomes for children and youth by addressing nonacademic needs in the context of schools, families, and communities. But it also included a vision of schools as places of learning, sharing information, acquiring skills, and networking for adults, with the school becoming a community hub and a center of community activity. Here, newly arrived immigrants would have opportunities to participate firsthand in democracy through parent engagement, families would get support in their acculturation process, and parents and community members would find encouragement to start small businesses as a result of access to entrepreneurial training.

To make all this happen, CAS would work in partnership with local community-based organizations in mutually beneficial ways, at times depending on them for advice and relationship brokering and at other times building their capacity to support their work and the well-being of the community. In other words, part of the original vision of the CAS community schools strategy was to develop public schools that would become engines of change, a means of creating and increasing social capital in the community and a mechanism for creating strong and resilient youth, families, and community.

This vision resonated powerfully with community members, elected officials, and young people—all of whom wanted to work with committed partners to help give life to their hopes for the future. The affirmation from the community, along with the readiness of many hands and hearts to do the necessary work, transformed the vision of school and community working together into a powerful reality.

Translating Vision into Practice

In creating the community schools, our work was anchored in some core practices. The first, long-term commitment, has already been mentioned. For CAS this meant that we planned to make human and financial resources available for the work in Washington Heights for a multiyear, indefinite period (not just for as long as grant dollars lasted). Other core practices include:

- An asset-based orientation—building on the community's strengths, particularly its entrepreneurial spirit and its deep commitment to its children
- Responsiveness to identified needs—using community-generated and city-generated data as the basis for decision making
- Encouragement of lifelong learning—creating an opportunity structure for residents of all ages to continue their education and to acquire new and relevant skills of their own choosing
- Empowerment for personal and community change—recognizing the reciprocal nature of change, in which individual learning and development feed and support neighborhood betterment and a strengthened neighborhood contributes to the welfare of individuals
- A commitment to the process of change itself—understanding that the work of community and economic development is never done
- Embedding economic and community development into the fabric of our community schools work—instead of having a designated staff and financial resources for this work, having many people address these issues as part of their overall responsibilities

Although community and economic development are closely interrelated, for purposes of description and analysis we will separate them and begin with economic development. CAS has employed several specific strategies over the past decade, and real-life examples can help to illustrate how each strategy works at the ground level.

Economic Development: Strategies and Examples

Hiring Community Residents

CAS, one of the biggest employers in Washington Heights, has used its employment power to hire hundreds of community residents over the years, including eligible youths and many parents from the elementary and middle schools. Parents are employed in a wide variety of roles, including parent coordinator, group leader, hallway monitor, and athletic coach. Several parents and youths have had their first employment experiences with CAS and then moved into full-time positions with the New York City Department of Education as classroom aides and teachers.

Entrepreneurial Education

Since its involvement in community schools, CAS has conducted a variety of classes at several of our Washington Heights schools that have taught entrepreneurial skills, including computer repair, catering (including cake decorating and baking), arts and crafts, and sewing. Many parents who were recent arrivals to the United States have found both fellowship and inspiration in entrepreneurship classes and have gone on to start their own small businesses in the community. One parent made exquisite floral arrangements using regular glue; another made beautiful three-dimensional framed crafts from old greeting cards. Today, many use their sewing skills to make wonderful drapes and household decorations. Often these products are sold through informal networks and word of mouth, resulting in additional income to help support families. Such efforts meet local demand for desirable products and also bolster the local economy by keeping dollars circulating in the community.

Adult Basic Education and English as a Second Language

Educating adults—parents and other community residents—is a core part of our community schools work. Decisions about what kinds of programs and courses to offer are based on needs identified in the community. Classes typically include adult basic education and English as a Second Language (ESL); these courses are offered by CAS staff or by Department of Education colleagues.

College Courses

Many community residents seek advanced education, and over the years CAS has developed partnerships with several colleges, including Mercy College, Touro College, and the Universidad Autonoma de Santo Domingo, that involve having satellite campuses at CAS community schools.

Partnering with Financial Institutions

Credit Where Credit Is Due (CWCID), founded in 1994, established the Neighborhood Trust Federal Credit Union; it is the only community-owned and community-controlled financial institution to serve Upper Manhattan, including Washington Heights. CWCID offers programs in financial literacy and runs the School Banking program, through which children in fourth and fifth grades can open bank accounts. When CAS was approached to open its schools to this program, we readily did so, both because CWCID's vision and mission for the community was aligned with ours and because effective community development involves partnering with organizations and initiatives that advance the larger vision of improved outcomes for children and families. Mark Levine, founder of CWCID, says that since the program's inception, students have collectively saved over $50,000.

Supporting Community Businesses

CAS purchasing power is used in the community. As a regular sponsor of celebrations and host for site visits, we are a major purchaser of catering services from local businesses and also of supplies for some programming.

Community Development: Strategies and Examples

At its core community development is about connection, collaboration, empowerment, economic development, learning, and democracy. These are interdependent processes that peak in effectiveness when they operate in concert.

In a thriving, resilient community, strong relationships abound and there are powerful feelings of connection and belonging. In analyzing CAS's engagement in community development, we can see that our community schools place a high value on developing strong relationships—with schools, residents, institutions, and the community at large. In addition to valuing the development of strong interpersonal relationships, we also ascribe significant value to fostering strong relationships between the community and its institutions; such connections allow participants to make decisions that are mutually beneficial.

Robert Putnam and Eva Cox describe this process of facilitating mutually beneficial relationships as developing social capital.[2] Communities with high levels of social capital have higher levels of civic engagement, greater self-determination, and greater hope about the future. Social capital becomes the fuel for change. CAS uses several strategies to build social capital and to contribute to a strong sense of community in Washington Heights.

Hosting Community Events

Our schools regularly host community events such as the annual Dominican Heritage Celebration, as well as civic and school board meetings. The Dominican Heritage Celebration, usually held at Intermediate School (IS) 218, draws several hundred children, youth, and adults from across the Washington Heights community. Local politicians participate regularly because they want to be associated with this positive, spirited event.

Encouraging Adult Political and Civic Activism

Each year CAS joins forces with the Coalition for After-School Funding to organize an advocacy trip to Albany, our state capital. The size of the Washington Heights delegation grew from about 15 parents the first year to 75 by the third year. The group leaves early in the morning, and during the long bus ride many new friendships are formed as pictures of loved ones are circulated and stories told. When they face the legislators, these parents speak passionately and compellingly not just for their children or community, but for all New York children. After the hearings they head back to the city, proud of participating in the democratic process and helping to create change instead of being victims of change. They have a greater awareness of their interdependence, of the impact they can have on one another's lives, and of their collective power to influence the course of their children's lives.

Through our community schools, we create opportunities for residents and parents to act on issues they feel strongly about, to advocate for themselves, and to successfully engage in democratic practices. Often in these contexts new relationships and connections are formed that later support other community or education issues. Such opportunities empower parents to speak up, both inside and outside their children's schools, about things they are pleased with as well as about their concerns. As parents participate in this fashion, they encourage greater accountability from their schools and from themselves; they become advocates for children and models for other parents.

Encouraging Student Activism and Community Involvement

Powerful transformations have occurred as the schools become more connected with the community and students have opportunities to contribute to improving their communities. In the early 1990s, IS 218 was divided into four academies. Students in the community service academy identified community issues they felt should be addressed, and out of these issues emerged a variety of service-learning activities. The 190th Street subway station used by the community had a long, dank, poorly lit tunnel that invited crime. Students felt the community deserved better, and so they began a process that involved writing letters to the city's department of transportation and police and to community organizations seeking support to transform the station. Students sought and received permission to paint a mural in the subway tunnel; they organized clean-up days to remove trash and litter; and they got better lighting installed. In a more recent example, IS 218 students created a colorful mural on the large outside wall of their local Pioneer supermarket, generating goodwill among community residents and publicizing their own talent and positive spirit.

This is what CAS envisioned—for learning to become relevant to community life and for the community to become an extension of the classroom for students. Lack of participation in the civic process has contributed to the demise of many communities. Through such service-learning experiences, CAS and our Department of Education colleagues are helping to build the civic capacity of the next generation.

Partnering with Existing Community Resources

Just as CAS has helped to broker relationships in the community, some community organizations have done that for us. When CAS came to Washington Heights, it was seen as a large, influential, white organization from "downtown." Organizations with this profile are not always welcomed in poor communities because they are frequently experienced as paternalistic and seen as maintaining the status quo and encouraging dependency instead of empowering people. It was therefore appropriate for some in the Washington Heights community to express misgivings about CAS. At the same time, others were sufficiently curious, hopeful, and open to give us a chance.

During the planning phase (1987–1991), CAS staff members spent almost two years listening to every sector of the community. As a result, community support was extended by a trusted local organization, the Association of Progressive Dominicans, which helped to open doors to key audiences and people in the community. Another important local organization, throughout the planning phase and still today, is Alianza Dominicana. In the early years, Alianza was committed to serving and supporting youth in the schools but did not have the resources or experience to do so. In 1990 CAS and Alianza approached the school district to jointly open a community school at IS 143. Together they established La Plaza at this school as the place where the community's education, business, and celebrations would take place. Alianza selected the staff for the programs and CAS provided supervision and operating funds.

CAS supported Alianza as La Plaza became known by city and state officials and began to respond to requests for proposals. Early in the partnership with the community organizations, CAS promised not to compete with them for funds; this promise is a significant demonstration of our commitment to community development and local institutions.

In subsequent years Alianza received several large grants to operate a Beacon school.[3] As their capacity to partner with local schools increased, CAS's involvement in their staff supervision and programming guidance decreased, but in 2003 we were still involved in collaborative advocacy, arts, and community-building efforts with Alianza and others.

CAS's core work with individuals, families, and communities involves supporting their efforts to reach their potential. When they feel strong and able to be on their own, we support their next level of development in the ways they identify. Our support of Alianza in bringing new dollars to the community is one of many ways we have contributed to community and economic development in Washington Heights. An important, though unintended, consequence of this activity occurred within a few years of CAS's initial implementation of community schools: when families heard about the services available in the Washington Heights community schools, many wanted to transfer their children from schools all over Manhattan and the Bronx, and local realtors began to report increases in real estate prices and occupancy rates.

Responding to Community Crises

Although much of CAS's economic and community development work is planned and ongoing, another facet has to do with responding to community issues and crises. An early example occurred in 1992–1993 when riots erupted in Washington Heights in response to the shooting of a drug dealer by the local police. The incident, perceived by many residents as another example of unbridled police brutality, pushed the community beyond its tolerance. Many buildings were burned, businesses were looted, and street protests were organized as the community's frustration and hostility toward the police turned, sadly, on itself.

Because CAS had invested in building relationships with both the police and the community, it was able to join with other community leaders and police to broker a resolution acceptable to all. CAS recognized that in order for the police and community to receive the respect they wanted from each other, relationship building was needed to make them more sensitive to, and appreciative of, each other's strengths. We established a program in which students taught the police Spanish and informed them about Dominican culture, while the police taught the students English and informed them about the law. This reciprocal relationship allowed both police and residents, especially the youths, to be perceived and experienced in a more humanized way and contributed significantly to healing in the community.

This interfacing between police and community was consistent with the community policing being practiced by the police department. After the program began, it was not unusual to find officers making friendly visits to the schools and being greeted warmly by the kids. Our work in strengthening the connection between police and the community occurred in both the school and the community. As a result, the relationship between police and community was less adversarial, and the community has learned more effective, less self-destructive ways to express its frustration and be heard.

In the fall of 2001 Washington Heights experienced two devastating crises. First, many residents lost family or extended-family members in the September 11 World Trade Center tragedy. CAS responded in several ways— by calling a community meeting, by deploying social workers to the community schools from other parts of the agency, and by consulting with teachers and other key Department of Education staff members, not only in the five Washington Heights community schools but across the whole school district. Just as the community was beginning to recover, a more localized tragedy occurred when American Airlines flight 587, bound for the Dominican Republic, crashed near the airport in New York City. At least half the passengers on that flight, all of whom died, were residents of Washington Heights. Almost every person in Washington Heights knew someone who had been on the plane, so many community school students and families suffered personal losses. Again, CAS responded immediately with grief counselors, financial assistance, and consultation with educators. We continue to remember these losses and honor the memory of the deceased through annual community events such as peace gatherings; a play about flight 587 was performed at IS 218 by a theatrical troupe from Alianza Dominicana, one of our long-term community partners.

Lessons Learned

This work of community building is about renegotiating relationships, facilitating opportunities for changed behaviors, creating the environment for everyone to be heard and understood, increasing the sense of connection and acceptance, and embracing each other's strengths. We know that such work costs money.

CAS leaders estimate that, through a combination of private and public funds, CAS has invested over $125 million in the first 10 years of the Washington Heights community schools. These funds have allowed many of our students to complete high school and college, find meaningful employment, stay connected to the community, work in our schools, and serve as role models to their peers. They have contributed to the development of a community that has become more optimistic about the future because it sees more kids graduating from high school and college, more kids staying out of trouble and off the streets, and more kids avoiding high-risk behaviors and making a difference in the community.

Other clear lessons emerge from CAS's rich history in community and economic development in Washington Heights. Most important is the recognition that within people and communities is a vision of something greater for themselves. When organizations or entities such as CAS join them as partners, whether as facilitators, advocates, or capacity builders, a process of sustainable transformation begins. The skills and knowledge gained from the partnership are transferable to other areas of their lives.

Another key lesson is the transformative power of trusting relationships. Services are helpful, but services offered in an environment of mutual trust are transformative. Researcher Bonnie Benard, in exploring the role of programs and relationships in nurturing resilience, noted that it is relationships that have the power to transform and effect change, not specific programs or approaches by themselves.[4]

Dennis Reina and Michelle Reina have identified three types of trust that CAS has engaged in and that have contributed to valuable development in the community.[5] First is competence trust—helping others acquire skills, involving others and seeking their input, and valuing and acknowledging people's skills and abilities. Second is communication trust—speaking constructively, sharing information, and being able to give and receive useful feedback. Third is contractual trust—encouraging mutuality, being consistent, and keeping agreements. All three kinds of trust are essential in building community over the long term.

A final important lesson is the interconnectedness of "development." As we seek to affect educational and familial outcomes, we naturally affect the economic and civic development of the community. Through a process that is intentional and responsive, as well as intuitive, the desired transformation can occur.

A Look to the Future

As we look to the next 10 years in Washington Heights, we see positive opportunities for building on some of our earlier practices—for example, returning to a business and entrepreneurial focus that includes a financial-literacy component. Economic development requires entrepreneurial activity and innovation; for some of our parents, it may mean learning how to market their skills and products to a larger, more intimidating market. Financial literacy is a life skill that all of our students need if they are to move from being simply consumers to being people who know how to make money work for them. The school banking program and a newer financial-literacy program that have been available to some of our students could become available across all of the community schools and perhaps the district, thus helping students develop the ability to envision, and plan for, their future and to delay gratification.

Although service-learning opportunities exist in our after-school programs, we need to bring more intentionality to the linking of school and community. Maybe our next step in this direction is to provide more exposure to the political process for our students. Communities like Washington Heights need to develop the next wave of leaders to go to Albany and Washington and become advocates and agents of change; we can be part of that experience.

NOTES

1. John P. Kretzmann, "Community-Based Development and Local Schools: A Promising Partnership," 1992, http://www.northwestern.edu/ipr/publications/papers/promising. pdf (accessed September 2003).
2. Robert Putnam, *Making Democracy Work: Civic Traditions in Modern Italy* (Princeton, N.J.: Princeton University Press, 2002), and Eva Cox, The 1995 Boyer Lectures (Australian Broadcasting Corporation, 1995). Summarized in Paul Bullen and Jenny

Onyx, "Measuring Social Capital in Five Communities in NSW," 1998, http://www.mapl.com.au/A2.htm (accessed April 2003).

3. The Beacon Schools are public schools that partner with community-based organizations, with financial support from the New York City Department of Youth and Community Development. The community agencies apply for, and are awarded, funds to operate after-school and other youth and community development programs in school-based sites.

4. B. Benard, "Turning It Around for All Youth: From Risk to Resilience," *ERIC Digest*, 1997, http://resilnet.uiuc.edu/library/dig126.html (accessed April 2003).

5. Dennis Reina and Michelle Reina, *Trust and Betrayal in the Workplace* (San Francisco: Berrett-Koehler Publishers, 1999).

PART THREE

Leadership, Management, and Governance Issues

—

Introduction

JOY G. DRYFOOS

In addition to providing services, community schools need to be governed. In this part you will learn how one principal views the overall partnership and his role in a community school, Intermediate School 218. You will also learn more about other Children's Aid Society (CAS) schools and how they came into being. The all-pervasive subject of financing is treated by my coeditor, who believes that it is possible to sustain these efforts, but not without constant attention to seeking new funds. Finally, we learn about various attempts to evaluate the CAS schools.

As would be expected, the principal is in charge. A full-service community school cannot exist unless the principal is willing to facilitate the arrangement. At the same time, this model cannot be implemented without the presence of a full-time community school director or coordinator (see Negrón, ch. 3 in this volume). The principal works closely with the community school director to integrate new services with what is already there. In one such community school, the principal shares her office with the coordinator, ensuring regular communication.

The role of the lead agency, in this case CAS, is extremely important. Just as the principal and the school staff have to support the community school concepts, so do the lead agency and its personnel. CAS is a long-established social service agency that also operates homemaker services, adoption and foster care programs, medical and mental health services, and other similar services. When such an infrastructure is already in place to support community schools, the whole enterprise is enriched, and the transformation of the traditional school into a community school is expedited by back-up from the lead agency's "home office." Such matters as payroll, benefits, public relations, and, most important, resource development can be addressed by existing staff members.

The expansion of CAS's community schools initiative—from one community school to ten in a single decade—made it clearer than ever that one size does not fit all. Adapting the model to various populations and conditions and to a wide range of partners requires sensitivity and flexibility on everyone's part.

Money is, of course, an important subject. You cannot really start a community school without some funds to create an infrastructure, particularly to hire a community school director. Community school practitioners appear to have a talent for finding resources in obscure places and redirecting categorical funds into their pot.

One area of exploration that may go outside of both the school system and the lead agency is evaluation. CAS has obtained foundation support to contract with university think tanks to conduct a series of evaluations of its community school efforts. It is no easy task to scientifically evaluate school-based programs. The population is highly mobile—as many as 50% of the students can move in and out in a year. Thus, tracking individual students is difficult. Since almost every school has some kind of support services or after-school programs, finding a comparison school that has none of the core components is difficult too. Yet well-designed evaluation is crucial to finding out how, and how well, community schools are fulfilling their mission.

The Power of Two or More: Partnership from a School Administrator's Perspective

LUIS A. MALAVÉ
Principal, Salomé Ureña de Henriquez Middle Academies, IS 218

I always had a partnership; I have one now; and I always will. Because what we have at Intermediate School (IS) 218—our partnership with The Children's Aid Society (CAS)—is the right thing for children. And despite the challenges, doing the right thing is what is going to take precedence. We have a common mission and a clear sense that we have issues we have to tackle together.

What inspired me to call this chapter "The Power of Two or More" is a video about an inclusion program—an effort designed to take kids out of special education—that demonstrates the power of two teachers teaming in the classroom for the good of children. Their collaboration is unquestionably powerful, and it reminded me of what we (CAS and the Department of Education) do at IS 218 on a larger scale. Our partnership makes the school much stronger than one entity trying to do the work by itself. We often use the analogy of a marriage without the possibility of divorce, a long-term commitment that we must make work, whatever it takes, because it is best for children.

When I was thinking about writing this chapter, I wondered, What can I say to convince other principals and other leaders of the advantages of a partnership like ours? Why would it be in their best interest to do something like this? For me it makes a lot of sense to join forces with a community partner as lead agency, but to some other people it may look like simply more work. To those reluctant reformers I would say that a functional partnership builds value, in spite of the challenges. The person who relishes the position as principal of a community school really needs to believe in the partnership's potential, to believe that a collaborative effort can exponentially multiply the benefits to students.

This partnership has taken me to another level as administrator and leader. I am always learning how to do this job—I am constantly creating it. Even when I must deal with Department of Education regulations, which sometimes create roadblocks to the partnership, I do not see this as an impediment to progress. Instead, I focus on the results of the partnership rather than the challenges. If you are going to succeed as a school administrator and instructional leader, you need to be a risk taker.

Leadership

One of the big topics I want to address in this chapter is leadership, which is the force driving the community schools initiative. And from experience I can say that if you are going to talk about leadership in community schools, you need to talk about releasing control. You are talking about shared leadership. But when do you take control and when do you release control so that it becomes a partnership, a marriage? You need to find the proper balance. A collaboration means that both parties are working toward a common goal. You do not give all the work to the partner and then rest—that will not work. A collaboration has got to involve teamwork.

Sharing the Vision and the Power

As principals we need to have a very focused, deliberate, persistent plan of action all the time, and we need to involve our partners in this plan. We cannot have one person setting all the goals and objectives and asking the others just to follow. All the partners must be involved in the development of the plan so that they can own it, and the development of the vision and philosophy must involve a mutual perspective. The message has to be "we are in this together," because if people are doing their own thing, then that is not really contributing to what we want to see for children. In other words, the real issue is the sharing of power.

The Importance of Trust

What we do at our school is much bigger than what I can possibly handle by myself. For example, our school is open five days a week from 7:30 in the morning until 10:00 or 11:00 at night, as well as during weekends and the summer; I cannot possibly be there all the time. I need to trust that CAS, my partner, is going to do the right thing; it will not work otherwise. So a lot of trust is involved in the relationship.

At IS 218 the main partners are the parents, the school, and CAS—a three-legged stool. Sometimes when I have not been informed about something, I say, "Well, why didn't I know? Did I really need to know?" Many times the answer is, "No, I didn't need to know. I need to trust my partners to do what has to be done."

And I really believe that if you are ready to trust and to share power, you are at the same time sharing the burden, so to speak, and by doing this you can make things happen.

Taking Risks

You need to be a risk taker to enter into this type of partnership. I am going to use an analogy: The ship in the harbor is safe, but that is not what ships were made for; a ship was made to go out into the sea and face risks. I learned that in *Outbound,* which is one of my favorite readings.[1] You must think outside the box, think about possibilities that are not necessarily apparent or not advocated in the traditional way of running a school.

Governance

In a school, if you are in a partnership, the best way to make your partner feel truly part of the team, part of the action plan, and part of the ambition is to invite the partner to be part of the governance of the school. Without participation in governance, the partner will not really be part of the school's fabric. We have a team of doers, not doubters, at IS 218; CAS has been critical to our team because of its positive disposition and constant support.

I have great respect for Rosa Bautista (CAS community school director at IS 218) as a professional and as a person. She is a master at negotiating and compromising, and I have learned so much from her. I admire how she maintains a balance: she is not the principal, yet she is able to be a force in moving the school forward along with me.

The School Leadership Team

The School Leadership Team (SLT) is a cohort of teachers, school administrators, parents, and CAS staff, all working on the master plan of the school. SLTs were mandated in 1996 by the New York City Board (now Department) of Education (DOE). They are responsible for guiding the comprehensive education plan of the school, as well as its vision and mission; they also have a say in budget allocation.

The SLT must be composed of 50% educators and 50% parents. There are three mandated positions: the principal, the United Federation of Teachers (union) representative, and the Parent-Teacher Association (PTA) president. If CAS was not a part of this team, how could it possibly be part of and support the master plan? And how could you have a collaborative effort if you did not include all the constituents?

What is unique about our school is that when we started, both the parents and the school personnel agreed that our partner CAS, one of the main players in the school, needed to be part of the team as a neutral participant with voting privileges. CAS is neutral because it represents neither the parents nor the school. In 2003 our SLT had 13 members. Our governance structure works because all the players are at the table.

Administrative Cabinet

Another governance structure is the Administrative Cabinet (AC). The SLT meets once or twice a month, whereas the AC meets frequently (minimum once a week, but as often as three or four times a week if necessary). While the SLT's charge is school-wide planning, the AC is what drives the engine for daily operations and instruction. The participants in the AC include the school's four assistant principals, the CAS community school director, a teacher who represents newly arrived students, a teacher who represents children with special needs, and the school's parent coordinator. CAS must be part of the school's day-to-day governance, as well as the SLT, and their presence is key to the success of these meetings.

The Expanded Team

The Expanded Team is another part of our governance structure helping us to implement the school plan. This team includes the key personnel involved in the AC; in addition, the community school director invites other CAS staff members to be part of this team as needed. For example, the CAS director of mental health and the social work supervisor, who train our teachers on

Table 10.1 Governing Structures at IS 218

	Purpose	Membership	Frequency of Meetings
School Leadership Team	Prepare and oversee implementation of school's Comprehensive Education Plan	13 people (50% educators and 50% parents)[a]	Once or twice a month
Administrative Cabinet	Make day-to-day decisions about instructions and operations	9 people (principal, 4 assistant principals, CAS community school director, 2 teachers, parent coordinator)	At least once a week (more frequently as needed)
Expanded Team	Address program planning, DOE directives	6 people (principal, 4 assistant principals, CAS community school director)[b]	Twice a week (more frequently as needed)

[a]Membership includes three mandated positions (principal, UFT union representative, and PTA president) as well as CAS community school director as voting member.
[b]Includes core Administrative Cabinet members and additional CAS staff if requested by community school director.
Credit: The Children's Aid Society.

reforms in the referral process and many other issues, are part of these meetings. (Table 10.1 shows an overview of IS 218's governance structures.)

Other Collaborative Structures

As an outgrowth of these collaborative governance structures, our school has recently streamlined some other structures that are embedded within the school day. For example, CAS social workers no longer have to coordinate through me if they need to see a teacher; they can now go directly to the teachers' team meetings, which occur almost every day. In one case a CAS social worker was working with a student I was concerned about—Luigi, who had a chronic absence and lateness problem. The social worker did not have to come to me to learn about him; he knew that, during the week, there was time when he could talk not just to one of Luigi's teachers but to all of them. Having a regular schedule for these team meetings streamlines the collaborative process because it allows the social worker to talk to all the key players at once and provides a better way of addressing a child's issues. There is a case management team devising positive behavioral intervention strategies for a student who needs a lot of attention and extra help.

Working Together and Sharing Expertise

Working together and sharing expertise is also part of our way of doing business. I have never before worked in a school that has had a partner so integrated, not only in developing the philosophy but also in developing the goals and objectives for the school as a whole. Just the fact that you have a thinking partner can be powerful. I enjoy sitting down with Ms. Bautista to figure things out. For instance, one of our goals is to increase reading opportunities for our students; she found out about a "virtual reading club" and brought it to our attention.

She also makes members of her staff available to the whole school. For example, the CAS director of mental health and the social work supervisor have conducted teacher training on various issues and have consulted with teaching staff on classroom management, reinforcing positive behavior, motivating students, lessening their stress, and getting them to focus on being good people and being good students.

Another requirement of working together successfully is a willingness to learn. As I said earlier, I certainly do not know all the answers, but I am willing to find out. One big thing I have learned with CAS is to turn trepidation into triumph. Sometimes when you get worried, you start thinking of negative things; that is when it helps to have a partner who can help you snap out of negative trains of thought and offer a problem-solving outlook.

Sharing Best Practices

Another powerful lesson I have learned from partnering with CAS is that an effective leader needs to share best practices. I learned this through the work we have done together in creating our extended-day (after-school) program and in particular with the mental health program, which runs all day long. In my view these programs—especially the mental health program—are saving children's lives; they are my pride and joy. There are things that we educators are good at and there are things CAS is good at, such as providing the kind of mental health services that many of our kids need. When we join forces, we have a better shot at having a powerful impact on our kids.

Analyzing and Using Data

Another thing we do together is analyze the data produced both by CAS and by the DOE. For example, when the school was structured according to multigrade subject area academies, we saw that one academy had more participation in the extended-day program than others. Why was it that these students were participating more? Was it because the teachers and administration of one academy advised the kids to take advantage of the extended-day program? Was it that another academy's teachers just wanted to be out the door at 3 P.M. and the academy's administration was not really interested either? We took this into account when we thought about restructuring into grades instead of academies. The reorganization of the school by grades was an SLT decision; we looked at the data and decided it would be better to serve all the eighth graders on one floor than trying to get to them on four different floors. For instance, now the guidance counselor does not have to travel to find her target population; she can find them all on one floor.

The analysis of the data has allowed us to better target certain populations for intervention services. It also has allowed us to do strategic planning to achieve the seamlessness we are after in terms of integration of the programs; the community school director plays an important role in this integration.

Joint Planning and Integrated Budgeting

We sit down together to plan our service matrix. For example, I might have money to buy $60,000 worth of musical instruments for our music program, but there is nothing in my budget to support the CAS extended-day program directly; however, by making the instruments available for the extended-day music program, in a way my budget is also supporting it. We look at all the components and identify what each of us needs and can do. I identify all the pieces that I can legally target during the day and after school, and then Ms. Bautista starts filling in the puzzle with her monies as best she can. By starting with a joint plan and working together, we are able to allocate resources for maximum benefit overall.

The joint plan and agreed-upon priorities help us both avoid the trap that many schools fall into—having an array of nice projects that have nothing to do with the mission of the school. When we do integrated budgeting, we ensure cohesion and continuity and eliminate waste and redundancy. Decisions have to be justified on the basis of their really contributing to the plan. So she shows me her budget and I show her mine, and we work together to maximize their potential.

People often do not realize how deep our information sharing and mutual planning go. Not only do we integrate monies for programs, but we also integrate monies to hire staff. For example, sometimes I can pay for a person half of the day and CAS can pay for the other half.

Grant Writing

Another benefit for me as a principal is CAS's expertise in grant writing. Their team of fundraising experts is available to the school. For instance, CAS took the lead in preparing the application for our 21st Century Community Learning Centers grant, which, like many other great grants, requires that the school work in collaboration with a community-based organization. CAS is always looking for innovative ways of getting us more funding to serve children, and this is tremendously helpful to the school.

Pupil Personnel Committee

We combine our teams (school administrators, CAS counselor, and teachers) to assess how best to serve students who are at risk. If a child is not doing well academically, the team will look at the whole child to determine why this is happening and will then design a course of action. We include the family in this discussion. We identify triggers—for example, a child may respond better to one teacher than to another. The problem may lie with the teacher; in that case, we can help the teacher change behavior toward this child. CAS is an invaluable member of this team because it can provide concrete resources (such as beds, help with a family's rent, or other forms of financial assistance) and also because its staff of social workers has expertise in removing nonacademic barriers to children's learning and healthy development.

Professional Development

Professional development in community schools has to be different from that at traditional schools because there are different needs, different projects, and a different dynamic. Both groups—the school's educational staff and the lead agency's staff—must be considered. For example, teachers and school staff members need to learn what the partnership means and what it brings to the school; at the same time, the community-based organization's staff must be included in teachers' trainings so they will understand what the school's core instructional program is all about.

When I offer professional development, I make sure to invite Ms. Bautista to have some of her staff members attend, and when she offers professional development, some of our staff members join. CAS also provides professional development to our teachers and staff in child abuse prevention, classroom management, and other issues in which it has expertise. Similarly, when the school conducts training on balanced literacy, we invite CAS staff to participate. Joining forces in professional development serves the double purpose of developing a shared understanding of the work and creating a more collegial dynamic.

Feedback and Evaluation

A big issue for us is how we deal with feedback and evaluation. Periodically, we sit down and look at what we are doing, how it is going, and what we need to do to adjust. We usually do this in an AC meeting.

For example, we are constantly looking at our extended-day program, which must incorporate creative ways to support the school day curriculum without overwhelming or boring the students. They need a breather, and in the long run we need kids to be happy about coming to school. A good way to evaluate the program is to examine attendance rates. Ours is very high—

around 93–94%, while the citywide average is 89–90%.[2] So the data suggest we are fulfilling our goal in this area.

Health Services

Most schools do not have the type of medical services that CAS provides at its community schools. Yet providing on-site medical services makes perfect sense; the education process is disrupted as little as possible when services are on-site and students do not have to waste a day or more to go to appointments. At IS 218 the Student Wellness Center offers medical, dental, and mental health services. It has taken our joint planning team several years to develop and implement this model, and I am very proud of our collective action. All of our students are enrolled in the Student Wellness Center, and we have a totally integrated system, with one medical chart for all three services. CAS has also been successful in getting a dual license for health and mental health services from New York State, and we have attracted both public and private funding for our center.

Safety during and after School

Ms. Bautista and CAS are also involved in the Safety Committee, which consists of CAS, the kitchen staff, the school aides, the PTA, an assistant principal, and me. We look at the building's blueprint and identify concerns; then we decide who is going to tackle what and who is going to be responsible for following up. For instance, I prefer having the school safety officers outside the building before dismissal, instead of having one of them stay at the school's front desk; to me that is a waste of a school safety officer at a time when they are more needed outside. So Ms. Bautista has a member of her staff monitor the front desk, which releases that safety officer. This is just one simple but important example of how we collaborate at different levels.

At dismissal time CAS adds as many as seven staff members to monitor the perimeter; with our officers, plus school administrators, we have up to 15 people monitoring at this crucial time when many safety issues may arise. When there is a crisis, all of the CAS staff is made available for safety purposes.

Our school has had no problem with safety after school. It is in CAS's best interest, just as it is in mine, to secure the building and the people in the building. CAS has always managed the building in an excellent manner, and I have great confidence in Felix Matos, the building manager for CAS. He knows the school well; he has systematized "sweeping" the building for intruders and other problems in the same way that we do during the day, and he reports things very quickly.

Because safety is a major concern for any principal, it is important to establish a way of working together when there is a partner. You have to communicate very clearly your ideas on how the building should be maintained, but, more important, you need to trust that the partner will know how to carry out your recommendations and you must always have an open channel of communication. Both Ms. Bautista and Mr. Matos have my cell and home telephone numbers. Mr. Matos has called me on a number of occasions to report things that were just a bit out of the ordinary. Because he took the time to communicate even the small things, I am confident that he will definitely communicate anything major.

The biggest safety incident at our school, and one of my most difficult days as a principal, was September 11, 2001. On that day the CAS staff leaped into action and supported the school and me 300%. We were able to manage almost 1,400 parents who came running in panic to get their children because of the terrorist attacks. Believe it or not, we evacuated the school in just over an hour without a mishap. This was possible only because we combined our people. We created a corridor system in which, as parents entered, we directed them to the elevator and stairs zone; on every floor there were CAS and school staff with rosters and sign-outs so that we could allow parents to pick up their children as quickly as possible and leave the building in an orderly manner, without falling into the panic mode experienced all over the city. In the aftermath CAS helped affected families with cash and mental health support and also created grieving opportunities in the school, which contributed to the healing process.

Another horrible day was when one of our kids jumped from a third-floor bathroom window, trying to commit suicide. The CAS medical team (which included a nurse practitioner, a pediatrician, and a psychiatrist) were at the scene within seconds and were already treating her when the paramedics arrived minutes later. I am convinced that this saved her life; she came back to the school and graduated. This is a rare occurrence; in such a situation, parents usually move the child to another school to avoid the stigma and help everyone forget. Such a move may actually turn out to be counterproductive, because when a child is so fragile, coping with a new environment may add to the stress. In this case CAS already had a history with the child and from the very beginning were 100% behind her and her family. They also provided intensive counseling for the teachers and the students, particularly those close to the child, to help them cope with the incident as well as to help the child integrate back into the school.

A remarkable thing CAS did that day was to help keep the school on track; it deployed all its staff to help with the crisis and even called social workers from other CAS sites to help. It also helped turn the incident into a lesson for the other kids; the message was "When you think that you have lost all hope, just look for help. There's always someone who can help you." That was a positive concept for our students.

Challenges

There are always challenges, but in my opinion the advantages of a community school outweigh the problems. The DOE has regulations that sometimes get in the way not only of the partnership but also of the whole process. However, sometimes CAS has been able to navigate some regulations better than we have. For instance, Toni DeNicola, the CAS director of school clinics, managed to eliminate a wasteful, senseless practice that I had not been able to get rid of however hard I tried. The DOE was paying $300 a day to a nurse to do a particular procedure, once a day, for a handicapped child, instead of using our medical staff. This nurse did not know the child or our school culture, so after she performed that one duty, she was doing practically nothing for the rest of the day, which really troubled me. We are always reminded about minimizing wasteful spending, and this was a flagrant example of just that.

I called many people to try to address the problem but got no results until Ms. DeNicola, who's an expert, figured out how to go up the ladder and talk to the right people. She told them, "Look, we have a fully staffed clinic, with competent people who know the child and can provide him not only with one procedure but with a comprehensive package that even includes mental health." They finally agreed to use our clinic—but we were not rewarded, as they took the service and the money away.

Space is a huge challenge in most New York City schools, especially in our district; since Washington Heights is one of the city's most crowded areas, we are overflowing. Overcrowding is difficult for the partnership, because the school, which is operating well over capacity, was not conceived as a community school to begin with. So the space challenge is a constant stressor, which can sometimes affect interpersonal relations. Sometimes I must reclaim rooms, and that may be perceived as my being uncooperative or capricious. For instance, recently we had to get rid of the Recycle-a-Bicycle program, which was one of my dearest projects and one I helped create many years ago. I wished there was some way I could have kept it from being eliminated, but there was not. I know that this created some resentment because the program was a very dear one for CAS as well. (Fortunately, CAS was able to save this program by moving it to another school.)

Maintenance of the facility is another big challenge. A traditional school would be closed at 3:30 P.M., or by 5:30 or 6 P.M. if it had an after-school program, but our school stays open until 10:30 P.M., or to 11 P.M. or midnight when there are community events (which happens often). We also operate during weekends, school breaks, and summers. So even though our school opened in 1992, we have been using it double time—by 2003 that was the equivalent of 22 years instead of 11! The life of the lightbulbs is a good measure of excess use; a lot of the bulbs in our building that were designed to last 20 years were beginning to burn out after only 11 years, and replacing them all was a big expense. Cleaning is another example; we need many more supplies and more personnel. Our custodial staff and engineers have been very supportive and creative in working around the needs of the partnership; CAS is conscious of this challenge and nurtures the relationship, which is helpful. But this challenge has not been considered by the DOE, which needs to address the real maintenance needs of a building that is open and in use for so many additional hours.

Documentation is a challenge that we have overcome, but it took us a while to negotiate documents that would fit the needs of both entities (CAS and the DOE) and reduce redundancy. Now, with some exceptions, we use basically the same forms. In fact, when parents come to register their children, we give them the forms the students need in order to be seen at our school's Student Wellness Center.

Obviously the fiscal climate is another challenge, especially at a time of downsized budgets. Certain monies disappear from one year to the next, and CAS is facing the same issue. This means that Ms. Bautista and I are teaming and planning even more, so we do not compromise the quality of the programs.

Parent involvement is challenging. Although historically we have done a pretty good job, I prefer to see it as a continuing challenge so that we can always be at the cutting edge. We aim to make our parent involvement program even stronger, a true model.

Conclusion

The partnership at our community school is much bigger than any one person. It focuses on doing the right thing for children. I think this approach is both developmentally appropriate and timely. To people who are reluctant, I would say that the results of a strong partnership are worth the challenges, if you are truly focused on what is right for children. Long-term means long-term; it does not mean that when there is a bump in the road you say "the deal is off." This is something I learned from C. Warren "Pete" Moses of CAS; he is a master at applying conflict resolution skills to the partnership. He knows how to navigate the bumps and has helped me navigate them, because sometimes you need another pair of lenses to see the road a little differently from the way you are seeing it.

You must choose your partners carefully and weigh the value added against the challenges. When we combine our competencies, we have a greater shot at having a powerful impact on our kids.

NOTES

1. William Storandt, *Outbound* (Madison: University of Wisconsin Press, 2001).
2. New York City Department of Education, 2002–2003 Annual Report IS 218, http://nycenet.edu/daa/schoolreports/03asr/106218.pdf? (accessed August 17, 2004).

Managing the Growth of Community Schools

HAYIN KIM

Director of Special Projects, Community Schools Division,
The Children's Aid Society

Essential to a community school's success is a committed partnership among the school and school district, community organizations, and parents—a partnership that makes students' academic success a shared responsibility and a shared goal. These partners come together to provide three key sets of supports and opportunities: (1) a strong, coherent core instructional program during the regular school day; (2) supports and services that address and

141

seek to remove barriers to learning; and (3) enrichment opportunities during nonschool hours that build students' motivation and capacity to succeed in school. Table 11.1 illustrates this concept through a graphic representation of supports and opportunities offered by New York community schools.[1]

After the early success of the work at Intermediate School (IS) 218 and Primary School (PS) 5 in Washington Heights, The Children's Aid Society (CAS) received scores of requests from principals around New York City who wanted their schools to become CAS community schools. Deciding how to respond to these requests became a major issue for CAS, because our intention from the beginning was to enter into a long-term partnership with each school—which meant that the agency was committing itself to sustaining each partnership for multiple years, if not forever. The financial implications of each decision were clear: we needed to build slowly and carefully, with a view toward long-term sustainability. In our strategic plans and discussions with CAS trustees and funders, managing the growth of community schools was an explicit goal.

Furthermore, we recognized that implementation of the CAS community school model must focus on adaptation, not replication. This meant that, as we added schools (at the rate of roughly one per year), we would conduct a local needs and resource assessment and make a plan that was responsive to the unique assets and needs of each school and its surrounding community. From March 1992 through June 2003, CAS worked in close partnership with the New York City public schools to develop ten community schools—five in the Washington Heights neighborhood of northern Manhattan, two in East Harlem (also in Manhattan), and three in the South Bronx.

What these neighborhoods have in common are high levels of poverty and associated problems of child and family well-being. The ten schools include five elementary schools, four middle (or intermediate) schools, and one high school. This age variation is one of many factors that determine differences in the programs, services, supports, and opportunities that characterize each school (see Table 11.1). Other factors that determine the precise programmatic mix at each school include needs assessment results, resource availability and constraints, school district and principal priorities, and community strengths and resources. The following snapshots of our initiatives in East Harlem and the South Bronx serve to illustrate variations on the CAS community school model.

PS 50, Vito Marcantonio School (Grades Prekindergarten to 6)

In 2000, in partnership with Mount Sinai Children's Community Health (MSCCH) and the New York City Department of Education (DOE), CAS established a community school at PS 50 in East Harlem. A disproportionately large percentage of PS 50 students suffer from medical and emotional conditions inherent to living in a community marked by extreme poverty.

Table 11.1 The Children's Aid Society Community-School Matrix

CAS	Extended Day				Health Services			Youth Development				Family Services			Adult Program	
	After school	Saturday	Summer	Holiday	Medical	Dental	Mental Health	Youth Council/Town Meeting/Freshman Seminar	Recycle a Bicycle	Pregnancy Prevention	Teen Program	Early Head Start/Head Start	Family Room	Preventive Services	Parenting Class	Adult Ed. (ESL, GED)
PS 5	X		X	X	X	X	X					X	X	X	X	X
PS 8	X		X	X	X	X						X	X	X	X	
PS 152	X	X		X									X	X	X	
PS 50	X	X	X		X	X	X						X	X		
CS 61/ IS 190	X	X	X	X	X^a	X^a	X	X^a		X			X	X^a	X	X
IS 98	X	X	X	X	X^a	X^a	X	X^a						X^a		X
IS 90	X	X	X	X	X		X	X	X					X		X
IS 218	X	X	X	X	X	X	X	X			X		X	X	X	X
MCSM	X						X	X						X	X	X

^aSchool-linked
Credit: The Children's Aid Society.

In response to the serious needs of these children, CAS and its community partners—MSCCH, the READ Foundation, Cornell Cooperative Extension, and others—worked to transform PS 50 into a comprehensive community school with an overarching theme of health in four key areas: medical and dental care, including health education; social work services; after-school and summer enrichment programming; and parent involvement.

The most striking characteristic of the school is its location in the middle of the Metro North Housing Project, a large, self-contained concrete complex of low-income housing located next to a busy highway. The surrounding community faces a dire lack of health and educational services. High rates of poverty, homelessness, unemployment, crime, drug activity, teenage pregnancy, and premature death place the community's youth at great risk; figures for 2000 show more than 77.5% of children in East Harlem born into poverty, more than one-third of families receiving public assistance, and unemployment at 11.6%.[2] East Harlem has the highest rate of asthma hospitalization in all of New York City—23.3 hospitalizations per 1,000, compared to the citywide average of 6.8 per 1,000. In addition, East Harlem has extremely high rates of infant mortality (10 deaths out of 1,000 live births), low birth weight babies (11.7%), and teenage pregnancy (15.2% of babies are born to teen mothers). A large percentage of PS 50's student population is homeless and temporarily living in three nearby transitional housing facilities, one of which is specifically designated for survivors of domestic violence. Many students also suffer from emotional disorders, manifested in classroom disruptions, behavioral outbreaks, and school violence.[3]

When CAS staff members first visited PS 50 in early May 2000, its hallways were dark and colorless, parental involvement was conspicuously absent, and the community's apathy and distrust of the school were palpable. The learning environment was strictly regulated, administration was largely disciplinary, and emotional supports for children and faculty were scarce. Children did not know how to express their emotions and often fell into extremes of acting out behaviorally or shutting down emotionally. Teachers were frequently unable to meet students' needs, and the resulting frustrations led to quick burnout and increased stress.

To gain quick wins that would garner support from administration and parents, the CAS staff immediately focused on improving the aesthetic atmosphere of the school. Colorful murals were painted on the walls of the main entrance. A redecorated Parent-Teacher Association (PTA) room offered a welcoming, comfortable area for socializing, computers and desks for parent workshops and other adult learning opportunities, a kitchenette, and a small recreation and reading area for younger children.

Early focus groups with parents and faculty identified the main issues: endemic asthma, obesity, diabetes, and attention-deficit/hyperactivity disorder; emotional problems, including bereavement, suicidal ideation, and violence; lack of access to health education and insufficient mental health services; lack of recreational and enrichment services; low levels of parental and community involvement; lack of support for parents; family problems, such as substance abuse, poor parenting skills, and illiteracy; high numbers of children living in shelters and foster care; gangs and drug use and sale in the community; and an unfriendly school atmosphere. Participants voiced their support for long-term programs and services that would address the barriers that interfered with children's learning and development.

In response, CAS and community school partners worked to design a comprehensive medical, dental, and mental health program that would extend beyond traditional school-nurse treatment and provide a foundation for academic enrichment and parent and community programs. Through an onsite health clinic in which more than 90% of the students are enrolled, comprehensive medical care includes routine checkups and physicals, first aid, administration of medication, and acute care for chronic asthma and diabetes. Students are part of a Mount Sinai Hospital study, which provides asthma screening as a first step in developing intervention and treatment strategies. Dental care includes a full dental exam and preventive and restorative treatment as necessary. The mental health services, delivered through a family health educator and a social worker, focus on helping children and families learn more about health issues and their impact on parenting, family life, and learning. Through workshops and individual consultations, CAS staff members work with students and families on issues such as self-esteem, family life and sexuality, asthma, diabetes, nutrition, conflict resolution, healthy parenting skills, crisis management, and coping with behavioral disorders. More than 7,120 medical, dental, and mental health visits were recorded in the first three years of the programs. The family resource room provides an additional range of social services, including emergency assistance, family counseling, and health insurance consultation.

Despite the partnership's capacity to address the extreme medical and social needs facing the students and their families, the community school staff quickly found that the most pressing issue was the way these problems contributed to a depressed school atmosphere that affected the learning community for both students and staff. Compared to students at other city schools, PS 50 students demonstrate many more behavioral problems: in 2000, 7.8% of students were suspended, compared to the city average of 2.0% at the elementary school level. Academically, students at PS 50 score consistently lower than the city average on New York State tests, with fewer than 25% reading at or above grade level in 2002 compared to city averages of 46%.

Behavioral challenges and emotional outbreaks were commonplace among students. Elizabeth O'Flanagan, CAS community school director of PS 50, reported that children did not know how to express their anger and emotions except by shouting, resorting to violence, or cringing in anticipation of punishment. In response, she implemented the Safe Zone to help students cope with their problems and build up their emotional resiliency.

The Safe Zone is a designated room where children who are exhibiting emotional or behavioral problems can go, either by referral from a staff member or on their own, to talk to a trained professional about their specific concerns. Going beyond a "time out" or punitive model, the Safe Zone gives children space to apply a therapeutic and constructive process that can help them understand their emotions and their disruptive behaviors. This novel approach to working with elementary school students helps them analyze their own feelings and learn alternative behavioral strategies, allowing them to take responsibility for their actions. Staffed by the community school director, a social worker, and a community health educator, the Safe Zone allows children to join small therapeutic groups that meet regularly or to simply drop in on an as-needed basis.

The Safe Zone introduced parents to the mental health services at the school and helped them understand the underlying issues behind their children's behavior. Staff members often look to parents as resources in identifying problems and as partners in the healing process; this interaction provides an entrée for many parents and family members to seek mental health services and supports for themselves. This work, in combination with the efforts of the parent coordinator and health educator, has increased parental and community participation in health and education workshops, as well as in various recreational, cultural, and advocacy opportunities. Both symbolically and operationally, the Safe Zone is valuable for everyone in the CAS community school. Acknowledged as a shared and open space, it has become a useful tool in helping CAS staff members pool their experiences and resources in order to be more effective in helping students.

Although PS 50's health-oriented adaptation of a community school was designed to respond to the severe medical needs of the community, the greatest impact of the partnership was the full integration of health into every facet of the program. The theme of health care as a vehicle for community improvement underlies a multidisciplinary and collaborative approach that embodies the basic concept of shared responsibility.

Community School (CS) 61, Francisco Oller School/ IS 190, School of Environmental Science, Mathematics and Technology (Grades Prekindergarten to 8)

Fortunately, students at CS 61/IS 190 in the South Bronx did not lose any family members or friends in the World Trade Center tragedy on September 11, 2001. Many of the students' families worked and lived in or near the immediate school neighborhood; the insular nature of the South Bronx community was, in this case, a blessing. Geographically, however, students at CS 61/IS 190 were not so fortunate; the school sits atop a hill, so students had a clear view of lower Manhattan and of the smoke-filled skies that followed the destruction. The impact on these students, though not measured in terms of personal loss, was markedly evident.

The combined elementary and middle school CS 61/IS 90 is located in the Morrisania section of the South Bronx, which, like many New York City communities, is very cohesive, despite its extreme poverty and lack of en-gaging youth development opportunities. The community faces high rates of unemployment, crime and drug activity, teenage pregnancy, and premature death. Over 67.3% of families in the neighborhood are in poverty, 40.2% of children receive public assistance, unemployment rates are at 14.2%, and 20.6% of births are to teen mothers. In 2000 Morrisania was reported to have the highest rate of child abuse and neglect in the entire city.[4] Students here demonstrated a higher degree of behavioral problems and youth vio-lence than in other schools, and fewer than 29% of students met state and city academic standards in English language arts and mathematics in 2000. In spite of these statistics, school staff and parents are deeply committed to the children's education. However, limited resources within the community clearly demonstrate a need for enrichment—academic, social, cultural, recre-ational, and developmental.

At the time of the September 11 disaster, CAS had been exploring ser-vice expansion opportunities in the South Bronx in conjunction with the newly constructed CAS Bronx Family Center facility, which offered early childhood/day care, comprehensive health and dental services, and mental health and family wellness programs. The district superintendent (and for-mer principal of CS 61) suggested that CAS work with this high-need school whose principal had demonstrated a readiness and capacity to work in part-nership with a community-based organization. The principal had also rec-ognized the need for mental health services for students, many of whom were struggling with the aftermath of September 11. Accordingly, CAS established a community school partnership with CS 61 in spring 2002.

Naturally, the beginning of any community school partnership is complex with regard to building relationships and trust and to assessing capacity and need. In this case, the process was further complicated by significant ad-ministrative changes at CS 61, in the district, and in the New York City Board of Education. CS 61, with an enrollment of 750, had served grades prekinder-garten to 8. However, in line with district recommendations and based on re-search on smaller learning communities,[5] the school was divided in July 2002; there were now two administratively separate schools, with two principals and two governing bodies, physically sharing the same building. CS 61 would now serve grades prekindergarten to 5 (approximately 500 students), and IS 190, the School of Environmental Science, Mathematics and Technology, would serve grades 6 to 8 (approximately 250 students). The second through fourth floors of the school are now allocated to the elementary school, while the middle school is on the fifth floor, accessible by a specifically designated stair-case. CS 61 uses the former girls' gym, and IS 190 uses the boys' gym. The auditorium space is rotated between the schools. Patricia Quigley, principal of CS 61 since 1999, continued in that position; Diana Alvarez Santiago, for-merly a CS 61 assistant principal, became principal of IS 190.

In 2003 the New York City DOE also experienced major structural changes, with a new chancellor reporting directly to the mayor and the replacement of 32 local school districts with 10 regional instructional divisions. The new administration's blueprints included formalized structures to support a universal curriculum, intensive parent involvement strategies, and increased community engagement. The CAS community school strategy had to be responsive to all of these factors—student needs with regard to high rates of academic failure, youth violence, and teen pregnancy, as well as the administrative and structural changes at the school, district, and city levels.

Taking advantage of the close links to services offered at the CAS Bronx Family Center, the CAS strategy for CS 61/IS 190 was to create a greater sense of community, both as a neighborhood and as a school community, that could encompass a broad range of changes. At the same time, CAS had to assess and attend to the unique characteristics and developmental needs of two school communities—the elementary and middle school students and their families. Initial assessment of the school and the district reflected a very family-oriented environment and an enduring sense of community history "with generations of students and families having come through the school," according to Tisha Jermin, the CAS community school director at CS 61/IS 190. This meant that the school had already been established as an informal but important center of the community. Capitalizing on the strength of this community network would be integral to our work in building relationships and providing appropriate services and enrichment opportunities.

The strategy of creating and strengthening relationships and community is reflected in Jermin's work, carried out in partnership with both principals and schools. She names her priority as building relationships, continually mapping and responding to the changing leadership in administration and the concerns and needs of a strong parent community. This trust-building has involved constant communication with the principals, both informally and through formal meetings and structures such as the School Leadership Team (a mandatory governance structure consisting of parents, teachers, administrators, and school staff, with responsibility for educational planning, budgeting, and reviewing student progress) and the Pupil Personnel Committee (social workers, teachers, and guidance counselors who discuss students' emotional and behavioral problems and make recommendations for special education referrals).

Building relationships also involves keeping in touch with parents as representatives of the larger community. Translated into action, this has meant gaining trust from all parties and emphasizing that CAS is not trying to take over, intrude, or pry. It includes acting as mediator and facilitator in promoting productive communication, building on existing assets, and participating in joint planning of events and other service opportunities.

Prior to this Bronx expansion, CAS had had extensive experience in negotiating space, especially working in several severely overcrowded Washington Heights schools. However, beginning with a physically small school, the challenge at CS 61/IS 190 was to provide relevant and comprehensive programming that would create a sense of community while also building independence and coherence—physically and programmatically—at each of the two schools. At the beginning of the partnership, focus groups of teachers and staff identified youth development programming and teen pregnancy prevention as priorities for the school community and were prepared to think creatively to accommodate program needs. In trying to secure office and program space for the CAS-Carrera Adolescent Sexuality and Pregnancy Prevention Program, CAS worked with custodians, principals, and teachers.

The solution was to transform a classroom that had already been promised to one of the schools for a staff development lounge into a shared space for teachers in both schools and CAS program staff. By strategically sharing this space, CAS sought to emphasize the importance of informal integration for school-day and after-school staff. Teachers use half of the room for curriculum development, while CAS staff members use the other half. The proximity works to strengthen the integration and collaborative efforts of both groups, and convenient access for both day school teachers and CAS staff helps facilitate both formal and informal discussions.

Conversations in this room range from programmatic and curricular topics to student concerns and interventions, all with the goal of supporting students' learning and social development. Students, too, recognize the collaborative space linking day school and after-school, further demonstrating the seamlessness of the partnership.

In 2002–2003, the first full academic year of partnership, the program at CS 61/IS 190 provided academic support and enrichment, interwoven with a variety of age-appropriate youth development opportunities. The after-school, summer, and holiday programs provided nearly 300 students with academic support, health education, social development, and recreational and cultural opportunities. Aimed at enriching the schools' academic core instructional programs, the after-school curriculum incorporated reading, writing, math, and arts activities, using research-based methods aligned with city and state standards. In addition, the CAS-Carrera teen pregnancy prevention program worked with the entire sixth grade.

Parental involvement is an integral part of the CS 61/IS 190 program, which offers adult and parent education classes and hosts events for students, parents, and the surrounding community. Parents are encouraged to participate in advocacy events such as the annual After-School Lobby Day in Albany. Social services include emergency assistance, individual and family counseling, and health insurance consultation. Additional medical, dental, mental health, and family wellness programs are available through the Bronx Family Center, which also serves the larger community and promotes community-wide events.

The early lesson from the community school expansion was that change could be seen as either a threat or an opportunity. The multiple levels of administrative change at CS 61/IS 190 gave CAS the opportunity to demonstrate the benefits of multilateral collaboration in providing a comprehensive program to meet the needs of both schools and their developmentally distinct student bodies. CAS's main role in this time of transformation was to facilitate communication and maintain a wider sense of school community, thereby helping the administration and students through the transition process while also attending to the immediate needs of children and families through both school-based and school-linked services at the CAS Bronx Family Center.

IS 98, Herman Ridder Intermediate School (FLAGS), Grades 5–8

Only blocks away from both CS 61/IS 190 and the Bronx Family Center is IS 98, the Herman Ridder Intermediate School (the acronym FLAGS stands for Foreign Language Academy Global Studies). Being in the same South Bronx Morrisania community, IS 98 students faced many of the same troubling problems that are prevalent in the CS 61/IS 190 population, including high rates of family unemployment, crime and drug activity, and teenage pregnancy. Principal Alan Geller asked to partner with CAS primarily to provide mental health and social services to many of his students who, by virtue of living in the community and facing economic and social hardships, had "grown up too fast." Geller recognized that middle school is a developmentally challenging time for all students, but he observed that, in contrast to the students at IS 190, most of whom had grown up within the same school community (CS 61/IS 190) with consistent access to adult guidance and leadership, IS 98 students struggled more with the transition from elementary school and the peer expectations of the new school environment. An added challenge, according to Principal Geller, was the fact that his students come from many Bronx neighborhoods, not just from the surrounding community, which makes it more difficult to develop a strong sense of community within the school.

In comparison to the family-oriented atmosphere of CS 61/IS 190, a difference in the school climate was evident from the first CAS staff visit to IS 98. According to the Bronx Regional Director, Sandy Gutierrez,

> You could feel the rawness and resilience of the Bronx spirit. Here is this community facing severe social problems and depressive circumstances of poverty, single parent families, and substance abuse. On the other hand, you can feel an underlying urgency to survive and do something different, "no matter what." In this charged atmosphere, if you put the right resources in the right hands, these students and families will flourish. Members of the school staff recognized this, but they were so overwhelmed in fulfilling the basic needs of their students, they didn't even know where to begin to harness and channel this tough spirit.[6]

Statistically, students at IS 98 demonstrated a high level of behavioral problems and youth violence, with a suspension rate in 2000 of 10.7%, considerably higher than the city's average of 8.3% at the middle school level. As of the 2001–2002 academic year, this rate had decreased substantially to 4.5%, though it remained higher than the city average, which had gone down to 3.9%.[7] Not surprisingly, IS 98 students struggle academically to meet state and city standards, with 78% of general education students testing below grade level in both English language arts and mathematics.[8]

Corroborating our initial observations, focus groups and needs assessments revealed an overwhelming need for youth development and leadership programs. Beyond that, the CAS staff found that students had a sense of helplessness and isolation. The problems they faced daily made up the only world they knew, and this contributed to a perspective that saw few opportunities and possibilities outside of this environment. CAS planned to work in conjunction with the community resources of the South Bronx, as well as those throughout the New York metropolitan area, to broaden the students' horizons and demonstrate that they can be active agents of change in their own lives, as well as in their community.

A central component of this community school is a developmentally appropriate, academically enriching after-school program that keeps students interested, engaged, and invested. The program encompasses traditional academic support opportunities, including homework help and tutoring sessions, and also provides enrichment through a wide variety of other offerings. For example, IS 98 was selected as a pilot site for The After-School Corporation's (TASC) community justice program, which seeks to promote healthy relationships between adolescents and the law enforcement and justice community. As part of the program, students meet with attorneys, judges, and police officers to learn more about the justice system and about young people's role in promoting community development and safety. Culminating activities such as mock trials give students opportunities to work on research, writing, and public speaking skills.

Also through TASC, IS 98 was chosen to participate in the Madison Square Garden (MSG)/Cheering for Children Foundation initiative that provides sports and literacy programming to several TASC-funded after-school programs. In addition to seeing games and shows and meeting players and staff from the New York Knicks and other members of the MSG Networks and Radio City Entertainment, students participate in sports clinics and presentations on topics such as goal setting and job opportunities. The program objectives are aligned closely with the CAS community school strategy for IS 98: to expose students to diverse cultural experiences, to provide consistent access to positive adult role models, and to inspire young people to set significant goals for themselves and aim toward success.

IS 98 students also participate in the CAS-sponsored Youth Council, composed of IS 190 and IS 98 students. Together, these students have identified pressing community issues to research, analyze, and propose solutions for, while also working to raise awareness among other area young people through presentations and local youth conferences.

Other extended-day offerings encourage positive youth development. Boys & Girls Club programs, such as Passport to Manhood and Smart Girls, help build a sense of community among the student body and boost individual self-esteem. To facilitate transitions for incoming students, CAS staff members have conducted outreach to the feeder elementary schools through district-wide programs developed by the CAS Bronx special projects coordinator, such as big brother/big sister programs and school orientations with an emphasis on positive youth development. Partnerships with another CAS community school, the Manhattan Center for Science and Mathematics (MCSM, a specialized college preparatory high school), provide another means for IS 98 students to envision their future academic careers. Finally, IS 98 students have access to the full array of medical, dental, mental health, and family wellness programs that are available through the CAS Bronx Family Center, which is within walking distance of the school.

Bronx Regional Director Sandy Gutierrez described IS 98's mission as providing students with a wider environment; experiencing more than just their immediate surroundings will prompt youngsters to ask different questions, to gain differing perspectives, and to envision new scenarios for their lives and for the future of their community.

Manhattan Center for Science and Mathematics (Grades 9–12)

CAS defines the overarching goal of its community school model as promoting children's learning and development in ways that prepare them for productive adulthood. Though the majority of our community school initiatives are at the elementary and middle school level, in 1998 CAS had an opportunity to work in partnership with MCSM, a specialized high school. With offerings such as science and environmental research; mentoring programs with Mount Sinai Hospital, General Electric, New York University, and Columbia University; Advanced Placement (AP) courses in calculus, chemistry, biology, computer science, statistics, history, Spanish, and English; and language classes in Spanish, French, Latin, and Japanese, MCSM is not typical of our other community schools. This selective high school focuses on preparing its students for college with an intensive curriculum in mathematics and science and a required foreign language component.

This community school partnership reflects CAS's commitment to remaining responsive to the needs of all students and to preparing youth to serve as resources for each other and the wider community. Located in East Harlem and within walking distance of PS 50, MCSM draws a diverse student population from all five New York City boroughs. Reflective of the entire New York City public school system, the majority of MCSM students qualify for free school lunch. Early work with students and faculty demonstrated a need for mental health services in helping to guide students' transition to high school and through this important stage of adolescence and young adulthood.

Because there was no coherent after-school program that would help to enrich the school's strong core curriculum, students were often left to themselves to find enrichment or job opportunities after the regular school day. In partnership with TASC, the school's dynamic principal, Steve Askanazi, and other MCSM faculty, CAS developed a comprehensive after-school program that would offer academic, social, recreational, athletic, mentoring, and job-training opportunities for students.

Academic offerings in the MCSM extended-day program include peer tutoring and creative academic enrichment classes. Additionally, students can apply to participate in the General Electric Scholars Program, designed to prepare them for entrance into engineering programs at colleges around the country. The Columbia Mentoring Program matches MCSM students with students attending Columbia University, who offer guidance through the college application process. Clubs such as the policy debate program, math team, and math peer tutoring provide further academic enrichment and social development. Many students also take advantage of extended-day hours at the library, computer lab, and college office.

Social and career programs are organized under the direction of a school-to-career coordinator, with most activities focused on career development. Programs and workshops assist students in résumé writing, work readiness skills, volunteer and internship opportunities, career exploration, and researching colleges. The Mount Sinai Scholars Program helps those students who are interested in exploring careers in medicine or research sciences. MCSM, another TASC community justice pilot site, also provides students with the opportunity to interact with, be mentored by, and learn from members of the local justice and law enforcement community.

A core component of the community school is a required year-long class for all ninth graders called Freshman Seminar. This class provides an orientation to high school with a focus on life skills, including such topics as goal setting, time management, study skills, dating, domestic violence, conflict resolution, and drug and alcohol abuse. The informal atmosphere and interactive curricula create an environment that allows teachers to refer students exhibiting emotional or behavioral issues to a CAS social worker for individual or group counseling. Students also self-refer to seek help from CAS mental health staff for themselves or family members. Since the program began in 1999, the percentage of freshmen failing multiple classes has dropped from 38% in 1999 to 26% in 2002. The 2002–2003 academic year had a record number of enrolled freshmen and the lowest percentage of failures to date.[9]

The MCSM partnership is also responsive to the needs of our other community school initiatives in Washington Heights, East Harlem, and the Bronx. Many of the CAS middle schools have established peer and transition programs for students who are selected to attend MCSM. In providing this comprehensive and sequential academic and youth development track, CAS seeks to give students the opportunity to attend community schools from birth

(Early Head Start) through high school graduation and to go on to college with the support of CAS scholarships.

An important component of the MCSM community school strategy is integrating students into the lives of other students and encouraging them to take an active role in shaping the public education system around them. Whether this is through mentoring peers in math tutoring, chaperoning PS 50 students to an after-school rally, testifying on behalf of CAS before the Manhattan borough president in support of after-school funding, or speaking with elected officials in Albany, the goal is to help these students see their responsibility to make their lives an example of how community schools work.

In comparison to the bleak statistics faced by New York City public school students, students at MCSM are already ahead of the curve. For CAS, MCSM represents not only a unique high school adaptation but also an opportunity to partner with an already successful school, exploring ways to add value around the school's very specific mission of helping first generation college-bound students achieve their goals.

Lessons Learned

According to the national Coalition for Community Schools, "Because community schools typically arise as unique responses to the specific needs of their communities, no two are exactly alike. At the same time, each community school reflects a common set of principles that characterizes most national models and local implementation."[10] The variations on a theme described in this chapter demonstrate the importance of *responsiveness* as a core organizing principle for community schools. A second organizing principle is the use of school and community data as the basis for *joint planning* between the school and the lead agency. A third organizing principle is the use of evaluation data and program experience as the basis for *continuous improvement*. With specific regard to managing growth, CAS has learned several key lessons over the past decade:

- Decisions about how quickly to grow and how much to grow depend not only on resource availability but also on the partners' ability to ensure program quality. Although on average CAS added one school per year, in one year we added five, which severely strained our capacity. Over the next two years, we had to intensify our efforts to build internal capacity by adding key staff positions, such as Community Schools Budget Director and Director of Curriculum and Program Design. This of course required generating adequate resources to underwrite these positions over the long term.
- For CAS it made sense to develop new community school partnerships in neighborhoods of strategic interest to the organization—for example, in the South Bronx, where in 2001 we opened a community-based

multiservice center. The decision to focus our work in specific neighborhoods helped to manage our growth by limiting the number of
school districts we partnered with (since the CAS model involves maintaining solid working relationships not only at the building level but
also at the local districts and central DOE).

- Decisions about growth are guided by principal leadership. Although
  all of the schools we partner with are high-need schools (and that is
  an important prerequisite), CAS has learned that there are many more
  schools that need and want to partner with us than we can accommodate. We have also learned that there is no substitute for a ready,
  willing, and able principal—one who wants a long-term partner in the
  building, working alongside school faculty and sharing space. Not all
  principals want these kinds of partnerships, and there is no reason to
  force the issue.

- A related lesson is that some principals who think they want to partner find out that, in reality, they would rather go it alone. CAS has
  had to terminate three relationships over the past 10 years because
  principals or district superintendents were unable to change their practice in ways that would make the partnership work. From the point of
  view of managing growth, it makes sense to know when to terminate
  a relationship that is not going well and to use the available human
  and financial resources more productively at another site and with another set of partners. In two other situations, district superintendents
  decided to change principals in particular schools, because they believed this would be most effective in making the partnerships work.

- Another part of managing growth is making sure, on an ongoing basis,
  that all the key players share a common vision. It is not enough to offer orientation and training to staff at the newest community schools
  and to new CAS staff at current sites. We have learned that, with the
  high turnover of teachers and other DOE staff members, it is important also to conduct orientation meetings and staff development for
  our DOE partners on a regular basis. This lesson extends to school
  chancellors and political leaders as well—people whose support is essential if community schools are to survive and thrive. Sustaining current sites and adding new ones depends on fostering positive relationships and creating a shared vision at multiple levels of a complex system.

- Finally, managing growth depends to a great extent on maintaining
  commitment to, and passion for, the work. Again, this lesson applies
  to all levels of our practice—continually working in partnership with
  parents to help develop leadership opportunities; and continually ensuring that CAS and DOE staff members keep children at the center
  of our collective attention.

The case for community schools continues to grow stronger as evidence
of their effectiveness increases. The development of public funding streams

such as the 21st Century Community Learning Centers and citywide community school initiatives such as the Chicago Campaign to Expand Community Schools makes the issue of managing growth even more central to our collective work. CAS has learned how important it is to plan ahead, make and keep long-term commitments, and build needed infrastructure to ensure quality while also increasing in quantity.

NOTES

1. The New York City Department of Education's school identification system uses a number system, separate by borough and according to educational level. "PS" refers to primary or elementary schools, usually prekindergarten to grade 5. "IS" designates intermediate level schools, usually grades 6 to 8. "CS" refers to community schools, irrespective of grade level, that take their name from the 1960s movement when community members demanded more control of their neighborhood schools. The schools that were established during this period were referred to as "community schools," though they do not necessarily follow the theoretical components of what we consider to be a community school. MCSM stands for Manhattan Center for Science and Mathematics, a specialized college preparatory high school.

2. Citizens' Committee for the Children of New York, *Keeping Track of New York City's Children: The Millennium Edition* (New York: Citizens' Committee for the Children of New York, 2002), p. 197.

3. Elizabeth O'Flanagan, interview by author, March 2, 2003, and July 8, 2003.

4. Citizens' Committee for the Children of New York, *Keeping Track*, p. 212.

5. Joe Nathan and Karen Febey, *Smaller, Safer, Saner, Successful Schools* (Washington, D.C.: National Clearinghouse for Educational Facilities, 2001), pp. 10–22.

6. Sandy Gutierrez, interview by author, May 18, 2003.

7. New York City Department of Education, *I.S. 98 (FLAGS) School Report Card* (New York: New York City Department of Education, 2001–2002), p. 2.

8. Ibid., p. 4.

9. Kim Hensley, interview by author, July 8, 2003.

10. Martin J. Blank, Atelia Melaville, and Bela P. Shah, *Making the Difference: Research and Practice in Community Schools* (Washington, D.C.: Coalition for Community Schools, May 2003), p. 2.

12

Sustaining Community Schools: Learning from Children's Aid Society's Experience

JANE QUINN

Assistant Executive Director for Community Schools,
The Children's Aid Society

Before The Children's Aid Society (CAS) opened its first two community schools in Washington Heights (1992–1993), our staff and board had already begun to address the issue of sustainability—that is, how to plan for the long-term development, implementation, assessment, and institutionalization of this new line of work. Internal strategic planning led to decisions by CAS board and staff leadership to realign existing resources in support of this new work, while external planning resulted in explicit partnership agreements, forged in 1990, with the New York City Board of Education and Community School District 6 (see appendix to Coltoff, ch. 1 in this volume) that also set the stage for long-term sustainability. As CAS's assistant executive director for community schools, my responsibilities include planning and overseeing our sustainability efforts. This chapter describes CAS's experience in raising funds for its community schools and offers suggestions for how other practitioners might proceed.

Essential Components of Sustainability

CAS views sustainability as involving not only aggressive fundraising but also public relations, constituency building, and advocacy, using a conceptual framework developed by the Finance Project, a national research and policy organization.[1] These four components are interrelated; work in one area supports and complements efforts in the other three.

Fundraising

For fiscal year 2003–2004, the operating budget for CAS's 10 community schools totaled almost $13 million, which included approximately $8.6 million for the extended-day, summer camp, teen, parent, and adult education components and $2.8 million for health services (medical, dental, and mental health). In addition, two sites have Early Head Start and Head Start programs operated by CAS; the costs for these programs are covered entirely by federal grants totaling approximately $1.4 million. Because the programs differ, each school has a different budget, but the estimated additional cost per student per year of a fully developed community school is $1,000.

CAS generates support for its community schools from a wide variety of sources. During the initial years, core support came primarily from private sources, including foundations, corporations, and individuals; the exception was the health and mental health services, which were financed partially by Medicaid and Child Health Plus (federally supported children's health insurance), as well as by other public and private sources. Our long-term strategy has been to move toward a solid mix of public and private funding for our overall services.

Public Sources

A major success for the strategy of diversifying our funding sources and increasing public support occurred in 1999, when CAS and Community School District 6 were awarded a three-year federal 21st Century Community Learning Centers grant, which provided nearly $1 million per year for our five Washington Heights schools. Early in 2004 CAS received a second grant from this source, which is now administered by the state departments of education. The second grant, which supports work in six of our community schools, totals $4 million over four and a half years. The 21st Century Community Learning

Table 12.1 Public Funding Sources for CAS Community Schools

	PS 5	PS 8	PS 152	IS 218	IS 90	PS 50	MCSM	IS 98	CS 61/IS 190
21st Century CLC (1999–2001)	xxx	xxx	xxx	xxx	xxx				
21st Century CLC (2003–08)				xxx	xxx			xxx	xxx
NYS Advantage After-School		xxx		xxx	xxx				
NYS Extended-Day/ Violence Prevention						xxx			
Early Head Start	xxx	xxx							
Head Start	xxx	xxx							
Medicaid/Child Health Plus	xxx	xxx		xxx	xxx	xxx			
Workforce Investment Act							xxx		
TASC (Public/ Private Mix)	xxx	xxx	xxx		xxx	xxx	xxx	xxx	xxx

Manhattan Center for Science and Mathematics (MCSM); Community School (CS); Twenty-First Century Community Learning Centers (21st Century CLC); New York State (NYS); The After-School Corporation (TASC)
Credit: The Children's Aid Society, 2004.

Centers program—which CAS helped develop through its early and sustained advocacy efforts—is the single most important funding source for community schools because of two factors: (1) the size of the program (it was funded at $1 billion nationally in 2002 and again in 2003) and (2) the focus of the program (extending the hours and services of public schools and encouraging partnerships between schools and community agencies).

Another major step toward increasing public support was the award in 2000 of a five-year New York State Advantage grant of $145,000 per year for after-school programs in two of our community schools (Intermediate School [IS] 90 and Primary School [PS] 8), followed in 2002 by a five-year Advantage grant of $250,000 per year for IS 218's after-school program. Also in 2000, CAS received a five-year grant from another New York State source, the state Department of Education's Extended-Day/Violence Prevention program, of $140,000 per year for PS 50. Small state grants have underwritten specific additions to the core work, such as substance abuse prevention and mental health services. In addition, Medicaid partially supports our medical, dental, and mental health services. (Table 12.1 summarizes the major public funding sources for CAS community schools.)

Finally, the CAS community schools have benefited from public funding allocated by the Bureau of Justice Assistance (U.S. Department of Justice) to Boys & Girls Clubs of America (B&GCA). As a member of B&GCA, CAS was eligible to receive several pass-through grants to start or expand individual school-based sites.

Private Sources

Like many New York City nonprofits, CAS has benefited greatly from the philanthropy of George Soros, whose support of The After-School Corporation (TASC) program has resulted in partial underwriting of eight of our ten community school after-school programs. TASC has been very successful in using private philanthropic funds from George Soros to leverage a mix of public and private dollars. To effect such leverage, TASC partners with other private foundations to cofund selected after-school programs, and it also partners with government agencies to provide private matching funds for publicly supported programs, including the Advantage After-School Program.

In order to generate other private support for our community schools, CAS engages in aggressive fundraising. Community schools have turned out to be easy for donors to understand, and site visits to the schools have helped translate their conceptual understanding into actual financial commitments. CAS has enjoyed steady financial support from a wide variety of private foundations, large and small, local and national. Contrary to conventional wisdom, many of these foundations have provided multiyear and sustained support over the past decade, based on solid results and ongoing relationships with our staff and trustees. CAS has also been able to tap corporate and individual support, aided in no small measure by the considerable efforts of our own board of trustees. Consistent with advice from the Finance Project,[2] several of our trustees have become vocal champions for community schools and have solicited financial contributions from their circles of business colleagues, family members, and friends. For example, one CAS trustee, Judy Dimon, established an education committee that provides advice and financial contributions to our community schools.

Public Relations

CAS uses all of its regular channels of communication to generate visibility for its community schools work: annual reports, annual meetings, newsletters, annual *New York Times* Neediest Cases campaigns, speeches and presentations by CAS staff, board and advisory committee meetings, and the like. In addition, we have developed monographs (such as *Building a Community School*), videos, and other support materials that serve multiple purposes, including public relations. Because the community schools work is considered integral to the work of CAS, our director of public relations regularly promotes awareness of community schools among her key contacts.

We also partner with other organizations in concerted public relations efforts. For example, the George Lucas Educational Foundation substantially increased the visibility of our schools when its staff made a professional-quality video about IS 218's community school program and Web-cast the video on its popular Internet site. Another major partnership—which served as a public relations, constituency-building, and advocacy effort—was a three-year

Ad Council campaign focused on the theme *Community Schools for Excellence*. The campaign ran from mid-2000 to mid-2003, generating more than $80 million in donated electronic and print media and 12,000 telephone responses to an 800 telephone line (all callers received packets of information about community schools, tailored either to parents or professionals).

Constituency Building

CAS considers constituency building to include activities at all levels, from the city's major political leaders (mayor, city council, school superintendent, director of youth services) to its own board of directors to neighborhood leaders, parents, principals, teachers, and young people themselves. This is ongoing work, not a one-time event. Specific activities include: participating regularly in local school board meetings; making presentations about community schools at key events; inviting decision makers to visit the schools; hosting visible community-wide events; responding to a wide variety of requests from parents and school personnel, which demonstrates both our value and our willingness to be a partner; and providing regular updates and site visits for our own board of trustees. In addition, CAS played a primary role in founding the Coalition for Community Schools, which addresses national constituency building as one of its main strategies. The Coalition cosponsored the community schools Ad Council campaign with CAS.

Advocacy

Since the beginning of its community schools work, CAS has harnessed the power of its long-standing relationships with local, state, and national political leaders to advocate for increased public support for community schools. CAS staff members have testified at government-sponsored hearings; participated in government-organized planning meetings; prepared public comments in response to *Federal Register* announcements; responded to invitations to review drafts of federal and state Requests for Proposals; taught and organized parents (and even grandparents) to lobby for increased funding for after-school and related community school programs; and collaborated with colleagues from TASC, the New York State After-School Network, the Coalition for After-School Funding, the After-School Alliance, Boys & Girls Clubs, and the YMCA in city and state advocacy campaigns.

Corporate Partnerships: A Multifaceted Approach to Sustaining Community Schools

For CAS the cornerstone that sustains our national community schools work is a partnership with Citigroup, the global banking and financial corporation. The Citigroup Foundation has provided core support for the CAS National Technical Assistance Center for Community Schools (NTACCS) since

1999. This support, which from 1999 through 2003 totaled more than $1 million, underwrites many of the center's basic functions, including publication of 15,000 copies of a manual entitled *Building a Community School*, coordination of approximately 500 site visits per year to our New York City community schools, training conferences, presentations, and telephone consultations. Having this kind of support allows staff members to offer free services to school and community leaders who want to learn about community schools but cannot afford to pay for needed training and technical assistance; and it provides a stable leg to the multipronged funding base that also includes fees for services and private foundation grants.

But the relationship with Citigroup goes beyond funding. For example, Citigroup hosted a national training event for community school adaptation sites at its corporate headquarters in New York City in November 2003. In exchange, CAS has provided significant visibility for Citigroup by acknowledging its sponsorship of publications and events. For example, *Building a Community School* prominently notes Citigroup's generosity in a front-cover credit line.

Another model of a corporate partnership can be found in Newark, New Jersey, where the Prudential Insurance Company sponsors the Quitman Street Community School in a long-term and multitiered relationship. The partnership got its start in 1996 when Don Mann, then chairman of the Prudential Foundation and an executive vice president with the Prudential Insurance Company, served as "principal for a day" at Quitman. Mann became so interested in the school's work and well-being that he enlisted the assistance of his company, including its foundation.

Since then, Prudential has provided more than $5 million in financial support that underwrites a comprehensive array of services, including medical, dental, and mental health care, after-school and summer programs, parent involvement, and teacher development. These services are provided by several community partners, including the Community Agencies Corporation of New Jersey, Beth Israel Medical Center of New Jersey, and the Bank Street College of Education. Prudential employees provide tutoring and mentoring on a regular basis, and they also participate in special events and projects, such as rebuilding the Quitman school playground. In 2003 Prudential published a monograph that describes the history, philosophy, approach, and lessons learned from its partnership with the Quitman Street Community School, with a view to increasing the number of community schools in New Jersey and encouraging other corporations to forge similar long-term alliances with public schools.[3]

Corporate partnerships represent an important strategy for sustaining community schools nationwide. They offer significant win-win possibilities by providing financial and human resources needed by every community school, as well as excellent visibility, goodwill, and meaningful community involvement for businesses that want to be good corporate citizens while also seeing that their philanthropic dollars are well spent.

Sustaining Community Schools:
Key Lessons and Principles

Starting from the premise that sustainability requires a long-term strategy and dozens of shorter-term tactics, here are 10 key lessons learned thus far from the CAS experience in building and sustaining its local community schools work.

1. *Assess your existing resources (financial, capital, and human) to see how they can support community schools.* CAS decided to sell underutilized property and valuable air rights in order to generate endowment and program dollars that could seed and support its original community schools. The underlying idea here was to begin building a pool of controllable and sustainable resources.

2. *For external fundraising, especially seed money, start with your friends.* This path-of-least-resistance strategy worked very effectively for CAS at the beginning, and it continues to be successful. Funders known to CAS—including private foundations, corporations, individuals, and our local United Way—were willing to take a risk by underwriting the early stages of this new work, and many have sustained their funding because they have been pleased with the results.

3. *Assess and share your successes regularly (and share the credit for them).* From the outset, CAS established both internal and external assessment mechanisms to learn from and improve our work. As we learned, we put a lot of effort into keeping funders informed of our progress through written reports, newsletters, and site visits, and we regularly seek to cultivate new donors by hosting events (such as site visits or media forums) that are designed to acquaint potential donors with our work. We are careful to share credit with our funders, whom we view as partners in a collective social-change and service-delivery-improvement enterprise.

4. *In fundraising, there is no substitute for hard work.* Although fundraising is not the only element of CAS's sustainability planning, it is an ongoing core component. In addition, it is a shared responsibility, involving several board members and key staff at all levels of the organization—executive, development, and program. For CAS, successful fundraising involves consistent prospecting and networking.

5. *Be aggressive but realistic in fundraising.* Conduct research continuously to unearth funding possibilities, but do not expect to find a fit everywhere. Assess your chances of success before investing a lot of time in meetings and proposal writing. As an example, CAS decided in 2003 not to apply for new funding through the Federal Substance Abuse and Mental Health Services Administration after assessing the high level of competition (only 12 grants were expected to be made

nationally) and the less-than-optimal level of fit between the funder's priorities and ours (these grants were geared more toward research than direct service).

6. *Be persistent if the fit is a good one.* The initial Community School District 6/CAS application to the federal 21st Century Community Learning Centers in 1998 was not successful, but the reapplication one year later was. This persistence paid off handsomely; the federal funding increased from $40 million in 1998 to $200 million in 1999, and many of the individual grant awards in 1999 were much larger than in the previous year.

7. *Consult with education colleagues to co-construct your sustainability plan, making sure that you are tapping into available education as well as human services dollars.* Developing synergy in the partnership between a school and community-based organization includes educating one another about the complexities of funding sources available to each partner. School personnel often have deep knowledge about creative ways to use major education funding sources (for example, using Title I funds to support parent involvement and after-school programs), while community-based organizations often have equally deep knowledge of United Way, private foundations, corporations, and individuals. In New York City, CAS partnered with the Board of Education's director of funded programs to plan the successful application to the 21st Century Community Learning Centers (and CAS actually prepared the application).

8. *In doing your funding research, look broadly.* CAS and others have tapped into a wide variety of public resources, not only from education sources but also from juvenile justice, substance abuse prevention, child care, summer youth employment, and violence reduction funding streams. In some states newer sources that are supporting community school and after-school programs include TANF (Temporary Assistance to Needy Families) and tobacco settlement dollars.

9. *Because public funds are categorical and spotty, make sure you generate some flexible private resources.* Basic fundraising theory talks about the importance of the "three-legged stool" in order to ensure stability, coherence, and adequacy. This theory is very relevant to community schools, because the major public resources available to support our work are often incomplete: they may not arrive when we need them; they are often targeted toward expansion of existing programs rather than core support of current services; and they may not underwrite all of the components we consider essential. Flexible private resources can help to address these challenges. Although CAS rarely charges fees for the direct service work conducted in our community schools, fees-for-service have turned out to be a highly flexible source of funds for our national training and technical assis-

tance work and now represent about a third of the income needed to underwrite these efforts.

10. *Always make contingency plans.* In fundraising, nothing is guaranteed and almost nothing lasts forever. CAS (along with many others) has had the experience of seeing funders' priorities change, even after a written commitment was made. For example, an early three-year federal commitment for community schools ended after one year because of congressional action that shifted the priorities of the sponsoring federal agency.

In summary, the overarching strategy in sustaining our community schools work might be this: think long-term while acting short-term. Long-term sustainability depends on a series of directed and strategic day-by-day efforts that ultimately—with hard work, intelligence, and persistence—add up to success.

NOTES

1. Many of these ideas are outlined, in an expanded form, in Finance Project, *Sustainability Planning Workbook* (Washington, D.C.: Finance Project, 2003).
2. Finance Project, *Sustaining Comprehensive Community Initiatives: Key Elements for Success* (Washington, D.C.: Finance Project, 2002).
3. Prudential Foundation, *The Quitman Street Community School: Five Year Report, 1998–2003* (Newark, N.J.: Prudential Foundation, 2003).

Evaluation of Children's Aid Society Community Schools

HELÉNE CLARK AND CLAREANN GRIMALDI
Director, ActKnowledge, and Vice President, CitySpan Technologies

Evaluation has been a central part of the Children's Aid Society (CAS) community schools work since the opening of the first school. From 1993 through 1999, a collaborative team from Fordham University's Schools of Education and Social Services conducted process and outcome evaluations of the CAS work, with a focus on the first two schools, Intermediate School (IS) 218 and Primary School (PS) 5. Subsequently, CAS hired ActKnowledge, an independent research firm affiliated with the Center for Human Environments at the Graduate Center of the City University of New York (CUNY), to continue the evaluative work by building on the Fordham findings while using a different (theory of change) approach. Concurrent with the hiring of ActKnowledge, CAS contracted with a technical group called CitySpan Technologies to provide a data management system designed to organize accurate and current information for both program improvement and evaluation. This chapter will review the approach and findings of the earlier Fordham evaluation and then describe the current community schools evaluation, with a focus on its data management system and theory of change approach.

Evaluation at Two CAS Community Schools

CAS began evaluation at the start of implementation because they believed then, as now, that community schools are a model for education reform and that sustainability depended on learning lessons from the start. Three evaluations were carried out from 1993 through 1999:

Formative Evaluations

- *An Interim Evaluative Report Concerning a Collaboration between The Children's Aid Society, New York City Board of Education, Community School District 6 and the I.S. 218 Salomé Ureña de Henriquez School,* 1993, by Esther Robison, Ph.D., Fordham University Graduate School of Social Service
- *A Formative Evaluation of P.S. 5: A Children's Aid Society/Board of Education Community School,* 1996, by Ellen Brickman, Ph.D., Fordham University Graduate School of Social Service

Three-Part Impact Evaluation

- *Washington Heights Community Schools Evaluation: First Year Findings,* 1997, by Ellen Brickman, Ph.D., Fordham University Graduate School of Social Service, and Anthony Cancelli, Ed.D., Fordham University Graduate School of Education
- *The Children's Aid Society/Board of Education Community Schools: Second-Year Evaluation Report,* 1998, by Ellen Brickman, Ph.D., Fordham University Graduate School of Social Service; Anthony Cancelli, Ed.D., Fordham University Graduate School of Education; and Arturo Sanchez, M.S., and Glenda Rivera, Fordham University Graduate School of Social Service
- *The Children's Aid Society/Board of Education Community Schools: Third-Year Evaluation Report,* 1999, by Anthony Cancelli, Ed.D., Fordham University Graduate School of Education; and Ellen Brickman, Ph.D., Arturo Sanchez, M.S., and Glenda Rivera, Fordham University Graduate School of Social Service

To differentiate between the two distinct phases of evaluation, this summary will refer to the first two as the formative evaluations (1993 and 1996) and the second, three-part, report as the impact evaluation (1996–1999).

The focus of the two formative evaluations differed to some extent. The main objective of the first one, completed in 1993, was to provide "an account of program initiation and implementation, impediments and facilitators, structural components, and key elements"; it studied implementation only at the first community school, IS 218, during the school's first year of operation. The second evaluation, completed in 1996, focused on implementation of the model at PS 5. Five program components were evaluated, as well as the structure of collaboration within the school. At the time of the evaluation, PS 5 had been open for two years. Both of these first two evaluations also compared test scores and attendance of students at the community schools and of students at two demographically appropriate comparison schools, IS 52 and PS 152.

Following these two evaluations describing early implementation, the three-year impact evaluation focused primarily on student outcomes in terms of academic achievement and psychosocial characteristics and on parent involvement, though it also examined implementation issues. During the first of the three years (1997), baseline data were collected. During the second year (1998), the emphasis was on parent involvement and teachers' views of the collaboration. The final year (1999) reported changes in students' psychosocial characteristics and compared reading and math test scores, as well as the psychosocial characteristics, with those of students from two comparison schools. Major support for these evaluations was provided by the Charles Stewart Mott Foundation and Atlantic Philanthropies.

Formative Evaluations, 1993–1996

The first formative evaluation of the implementation of the community school model at IS 218 looked at how the collaboration worked by examining four program components. This first look at implementation found the following lessons:

- Obtaining full commitment from the Board of Education and the district superintendent, identifying expected problem areas in the collaboration with the Board of Education, and seeing the collaboration as an iterative process were critical to early success.
- Full involvement by CAS, including the dedication of senior staff to securing commitments and getting programs underway, was also critical.
- Teachers and CAS staff members, despite a guiding philosophy of having a seamless program, operated from two different cultures, and activities to overcome teachers' circumscribed views of social workers were necessary.

**Table 13.1 Percent of PS 5 Students Reading at Grade Level,
for Students Who Were Third Graders in 1993**

Grade and year	Reading	Math
Third grade (1993—year school opened)	10.4	23.3
Fourth grade (1994)	16.2	32.1
Fifth grade (1995)	35.4	56.0

Credit: The Children's Aid Society.

This first evaluation also found that students in IS 218 were doing better than counterparts at a comparison school. IS 218 students had mean scores of 79.3% on an eighth-grade Preliminary Competency Test in Writing, compared to 64.2% for students at the comparison school; attendance was reported at approximately 90% for IS 218 students, compared to 85% at the comparison school. In addition, key informants (such as the district superintendent, the principal, and an assistant principal) observed positive changes in students' attitudes and demeanor, reflected in "no graffiti, no truancy, and no destruction of property," and commented that "children are happy and are comfortable in the school . . . the children say this school is better. They like the way people treat them."[1]

As noted in the evaluation, these indicators were measures taken less than five months after students first enrolled in the community school. Therefore, differences cannot necessarily be attributed to the new school experience. However, statements about the climate of the school and the students' attitudes toward it support an interpretation that the indicators result, at least in part, from participation in a community school. Also, there were no preselection criteria for students to enter IS 218, except for the math, science, and technology academy, so students were not initially different from those at the comparison school.

The 1996 formative evaluation of the community school model at PS 5 reflected the state of the collaboration during the first three years (1993–1995). The first thing noted by the evaluator was the school's atmosphere, which conveyed a sense of busyness, and the cheerfulness of the physical environment. Student indicators were reading and math scores, which were examined from the opening of the school in 1993 through 1995. In both reading and math, the third graders of 1993 had improved enormously by fifth grade in 1995 (see Table 13.1). However, no tests were made for statistical significance, and no comparison to other schools was included. Nonetheless, the improvements were impressive and consistent with other observations about the climate and motivation at the school.

Impact Evaluation (1996–1999)

After the two early evaluations, Fordham University researchers conducted a much more extensive three-year study from 1996 through 1999, also focusing on IS 218 and PS 5. They continued to use IS 52 and PS 152 as comparison schools and followed a cohort in each school. At PS 5 they followed third graders for three years, through fifth grade, and at IS 218 they followed sixth graders through eighth grade. By the third year of evaluation, the comparison schools had some similar programs to those of the community school, making them no longer appropriate subjects. In fact, by 1999, all schools in District 6 had some special programs, and many had extended-day programs. PS 152, the comparison elementary school, became a CAS community school in 1999.

This three-year evaluation was designed to continue the process evaluation and to look at different categories in each of the three years. The first year provided a descriptive picture of PS 5 and IS 218 and a history of reading and math scores for students from 1995 through 1997. The second year focused on parent involvement and teacher attitudes, and the final year focused on students' changes on psychosocial measures and in academic achievement between the first and final years of the study. A summary of the major findings follows.

Student Outcomes

Students at both PS 5 and IS 218 showed improvement in math and reading scores. This was true for students who graduated in 1997 and for the cohort followed between 1996 and 1999, although 1998–1999 test scores were not examined. There was some evidence that participation in extended-day programs correlated with improved test scores, but this was not fully investigated. Students' self-perception ratings improved in both schools; self-ratings of appearance and behavior were particularly strong at PS 5. Attitudes toward school were more positive among community school students than among students at the comparison schools. Specific findings included:

- Student reading and math scores improved in both schools between 1995 and 1997.
- Reading and math scores for PS 5 students increased dramatically between third and fourth grade but dropped slightly in fifth grade.
- Reading and math scores improved somewhat for students at IS 218.
- Community school students' academic improvement followed a similar pattern to that of students in the comparison schools.
- Academic achievement positively correlated in the second year of the study with the number of days students attended extended-day programs.
- Students who attended extended-day programs with the goal of improving academic performance also needed help with emotional issues.
- Students at PS 5 improved significantly more than the comparison group on some aspects of self-concept (perceived appearance and behavioral conduct).
- Students at IS 218 showed improvement in all aspects of self-concept, but no more so than the comparison group.

- At both PS 5 and IS 218, students had lower internal intellectual lo-cus-of-control (they were less likely to attribute academic success to internal factors) than the comparison students in the first year, but those differences disappeared by the third year.
- Students at PS 5 and IS 218 had more positive attitudes toward school than the comparison students (but attitudes at IS 218 were less posi-tive in the third year than in the first year of study).

School Environment

Interviews and observations consistently revealed that the schools themselves were different in ambience from traditional school buildings and that par-ents and students felt welcome. Specific findings included:

- The community schools' environment definitely felt different from that in traditional schools; community schools felt cheerful, busy, and welcoming.
- The community schools exhibited little or no violence or graffiti.
- Teachers, students, and parents considered the schools "special" and felt they were safe places for children to be.
- Teachers in the community schools spent more time on class prepa-ration and working with students than teachers in the comparison schools.
- Attendance rates were slightly higher at PS 5 and much higher at IS 218 than was average for elementary and middle schools.
- Teachers had better attendance rates at community schools than at comparison schools and comparable city schools.

Parent Involvement

According to the Fordham researchers, the dramatic levels of parent in-volvement were among the most significant findings. Parents were more in-volved, took more responsibility for their children's schoolwork, felt more welcome, and were observed to be a greater presence in the schools than were parents in the comparison schools. Parents also received many social services, attended adult education workshops, and received medical services. Specific findings included:

- Parent involvement was significantly higher in the community schools than in the comparison schools—78% higher at PS 5 and 147% higher at IS 218.
- Parents were involved in many ways throughout the school, not just in their children's classrooms.
- Parents had a significant and noticeable presence in the community schools, according to staff and evaluator observations.

- Parents of students in the community schools felt a strong sense of responsibility for their children's schooling.
- Parents who spoke Spanish primarily were more likely to have a positive perception and feel welcome at the schools than English speakers.
- Teachers rated parent involvement as an asset (but one that needed improvement).

Implementation

Overall, the evaluations found many programs serving hundreds of children and families, as well as a strong partnership model that owed much of its success to the sustained attention from all levels of CAS. Nonetheless, with literally hundreds of programs and services offered and many levels of staff and bureaucracy involved, the evaluations found that not all programs were fully developed and that fully integrating programs into an existing educational setting was difficult. Specific findings included:

- Large numbers of children and families received health and mental health services and other social services.
- Hundreds of students attended extended-day, summer, and weekend programs.
- The partnership between CAS and the principals, teachers, district administrators, and Board of Education needed constant proactive attention, particularly as staffing changes occurred and new staff members at all levels needed to become oriented to the philosophy and approach of community schools.
- CAS was able to achieve a high level of success by employing specific strategies to address partnership issues at these multiple levels—for example, getting written resolutions from both the central Board of Education and community-school district in support of the partnership and participating regularly in community-school district board meetings.
- Teachers were unclear about the priorities in the community school.
- Programs were not all fully implemented and did not necessarily have year-to-year continuity.
- The context in which the community schools operated was constantly changing, as new programs and policies were implemented by the Board of Education, as other schools changed, and as the community changed.
- A culture gap persisted between the philosophy of the community schools and some teachers.

Summary of Lessons Learned from the Early Evaluations

Although the formative evaluations done in 1993 and 1996 were conducted near the beginning of the lives of IS 218 and PS 5 and had a different focus from that of the three-year impact evaluation of 1996–1999, some findings were consistent across time or became recurring themes or issues. These are:

- Full involvement by CAS is critical, both initially and over time, to the success of partnerships and programs and to the comprehensiveness of the experience in the school for students and parents.
- Commitment from the Board of Education, the district superintendent, and the school principal is essential.
- Bridging the cultural gap between education and social service staff requires well-thought-out and specific steps. The discrepancy between the philosophy of community schools and some teachers' attitudes was notable in all years of evaluation and should therefore be seen as a significant ongoing issue.
- Uncontrollable events involving the Board of Education, the physical plant of the school, staffing, or community conflicts are definitely going to happen and will affect the community school's functioning. For example, issues such as an asbestos crisis, a departing principal, and conflicts over building use came up almost immediately when a community school opened.
- It is necessary to look beyond standardized test scores to understand the impact of community schools.
- There are many levels at which changes are hypothesized to occur as a result of community schools—schools are transformed as institutions, students do better, families do better, the community views the school as an important local institution for services and events—and these levels are interrelated and affect each other.
- Parents' perception and use of the schools may differ based on language or other cultural differences.

Moving to a Second Phase of Assessment and Evaluation

Upon completion of the Fordham studies, CAS reassessed both its evaluation needs and its data collection approaches. The Fordham studies had provided useful information about partnership and program implementation issues and showed promising results related to student achievement, parental involvement, school climate, and other outcomes of interest to all of the partners. This first set of studies also illustrated that community schools are complex systems making fundamental institutional changes, and this means that effects occur in many ways and on many levels.

In moving to a second phase of assessment and evaluation, CAS and its advisors agreed that the tasks of future research would be to elucidate the pathways to change and to help members of the program staff determine what outcomes their programs can achieve and under what conditions. The importance of giving as much weight to the process of change as to the effects produced was a lesson derived from the first set of studies; it pointed to the need to integrate organizational issues, strategic planning, partnership, and communication with research efforts.

After numerous internal conversations, discussions with school partners, and consultations with an external evaluation advisory group,[2] CAS contracted with a San Francisco–based firm, CitySpan Technologies, to customize a Web-based management information system called YouthServices.net to its specific needs. CAS also contracted with ActKnowledge to develop and implement a new evaluation approach that would build on the Fordham findings while answering an emerging set of questions.

Increased Capacity to Collect and Examine Data

CAS staff research determined that a data management system developed for the San Francisco Beacon schools closely matched its own needs.[3] The advantage of this system is that it can track participation at the individual student level as well as at the program level. This means that, for evaluative purposes, CAS can examine the progress of individual children and correlate results with the frequency, duration, and type of program participation. The YouthServices.net system had other advantages: it was simple and user-friendly; it could accommodate various computer systems and user competency levels; it was scalable and could therefore accommodate program expansion over time; it was flexible enough for a variety of programs and services; it was accessible locally and remotely; and it offered multiple security measures. Finally, the system has the ability to address basic, intermediate, and advanced data needs, all of which existed in the CAS community schools.

Basic Data Needs—Standard Data Collection

In terms of basic data needs, every program needs to know who is participating and what services are provided. While the CAS community schools have always collected this information, their data efforts across sites were inconsistent and not easily aggregated with existing paper systems. The solution offered by YouthServices.net provided staff members with the means to collect, review, and report data on each participating student, while also monitoring daily program schedules and attendance statistics.

Mandatory student registration forms include basic demographics, contact information, signed consents, and medical information. (See appendix to this chapter.) Generally, this information is collected at the beginning of the school year. Parents or guardians are responsible for completing and returning the forms, and the program staff is responsible for entering the information into the system. In most circumstances, an administrative assistant monitors the collection and entering of data, with help during peak periods of data entry, such as the beginning of the fall program, from two or three additional staff members, parent volunteers, or college students. Each child's information takes two to three minutes to enter.

Despite the increased initial work in entering data into the system, the ease of the data entry process has helped garner support for the system. Also, such features as the ability to generate participant lists, activity schedules, and attendance sheets showed administrative assistants that the system could facilitate their daily work by allowing them to generate parent-contact sheets, take attendance, and calculate attendance rates more efficiently.

The community schools provide a wide array of programs and services for children, families, and community members throughout the school year and during summers and holidays. Administrative assistants are responsible for tracking the complex schedules and for providing staff members with a means to collect attendance for some 200–400 youth or adult participants using system-generated attendance sheets. Daily attendance figures are collected by the activity leaders and then given to the program office for data entry either daily or once a week.

A critical factor in securing staff buy-in is providing ongoing training and open communication for all levels of staff. CAS provides technology training on-site and through group workshops to support the technology use and to help staff members learn how to analyze the resulting data for program improvement purposes. In addition, CitySpan Technologies provides a toll-free help desk and an electronic bulletin board, which allow staff members to ask questions and to support colleagues in other locations. The most frequent users of the help desk are administrative assistants, who access the system daily and often provide the technical team with the best suggestions for system enhancements. For example, one assistant reported spending eight to ten hours typing out file folder labels at the beginning of each program year. A simple adjustment to the software now allows staff members to generate file folder and mailing labels at the press of a button.

Intermediate Data Needs—Basic Program Analysis

Having these basic data in one place, program managers are more apt to make best use of the information they have and to think about what additional information they need in order to run efficient and effective programs. One advantage of this system is that it can generate missing data reports, such as missing registration data, consent forms, and attendance information. Analysis of such reports can quickly identify gaps in the system (such as failure of individual staff members to complete their data submission tasks).

The system can also inform managers about program utilization, which helps them better accommodate children and families who are on waiting lists. For example, staff members can run absence reports that list the names and contact information for participants who have been absent a certain number of times within a designated time frame, indicating that they have moved or have left the program. Such information allows staff members to ensure maximum program utilization by moving children from waiting lists into open program slots.

An important priority for program managers is accountability to funders. Despite differences in reporting requirements, all of CAS's community school funders want information on program attendance and participation. Youth-Services.net allows program managers to organize their data to provide an accurate picture of their program by group or subgroup and to demonstrate users' interest in various programs through attendance rates by program or type of activity.

Advanced Data Needs—Making the Case for Programs

All 10 CAS community school programs are using this system, and central CAS administrative staff members often review the data for internal and external purposes. Through a Web-based console, administrative staff members have access to the system and can review site-specific program data as well as aggregate reports. They incorporate these reviews into their monthly management meetings and produce reports to set program-specific targets and budgets based on the cumulative data. These data are accessible in real time, providing up-to-the-minute information on program populations, services, and attendance rates for CAS's executive staff, the Board of Trustees, and funders. Table 13.2 shows the kinds of reports the system can produce.

Most important, accurate reports of who is attending which programs, how often they attend, and what services they are using are particularly useful for program planning purposes. For example, in 2002–2003 CAS administrators reviewed programs in three neighboring Washington Heights community schools that operated during school holidays and vacations to maintain consistent youth services for working parents. Review of participation data revealed lower-than-expected attendance at each of these program sites, leading CAS administrators to merge the three programs into a single-campus model. The YouthServices.net data collected at all three sites informed this decision; as opposed to eliminating the holiday program at all sites, setting up a shared program maintained the services for families who needed them.

This multifaceted data management system serves multiple purposes for CAS, most especially program planning and management and program evaluation. In addition, it is well suited to data collection and management for the second-level evaluation design and approach described below.

The Theory-of-Change Approach to Evaluation

Evaluating community schools is complex, because the schools have many goals and many different strategies designed to meet them. With so many moving parts, all of which work together, a crucial evaluation question is that of attribution. How can we tell that each component of the community school adds value? Even more difficult, how can we tell which components are contributing most to the overall impact? Often, change is attributed to

**Table 13.2 The Children's Aid Society Community Schools
Information System (CSIS) Management and Data Analysis Reports**

Management Reports

Single-Day Attendance Sheet: Creates PDF file of daily attendance for an individual program with space for notes

Multiday Attendance Sheet: Creates data sheet outlining attendance per participant in an individual program across multiple days

Absentee Roster: Creates data sheet outlining absences per participant per program across multiple dates and programs

Lists and Labels: Creates mailing lists and labels using participant demographic data

Missing Demographics Summary: Creates data sheet with missing basic demographic information per participant based on enrollment records

Missing TASC Required Data Summary: Creates data sheet showing missing information per participant required by The After-School Corporation for participant and attendance tracking

Service Status Report: Creates data sheet showing basic attendance and enrollment records per program over a selected time frame

Data Analysis Reports

Average Daily Attendance: Captures average attendance across program categories over a selected time frame

Attendance by Date: Captures attendance per person per date of service offered across program categories

Missing Attendance Summary: Creates data sheet detailing absence rate per program over a selected time frame

Service Summary: Creates report of all programs at specified site, name of person who maintains each program, average attendance, participant level, and program time

Units of Service Summary: Creates report breaking down service hours per session for each specific program across all categories

Demographic Summary: Creates report showing all demographic information for participants entered into the system per site, based on percentages

Query Tool: Tool used in demographic reports used to narrow fields of inquiry or base results only on specified factors

Report Builder: Tool used to create specific reports based on user or administrator need, using fields and search parameters from various other reports

Credit: The Children's Aid Society.

---

a given intervention if an appropriate comparison site without the intervention did not change in the same ways. However, for many of the community school initiatives, there are no appropriate comparison sites.

Given the complexity of a community school, the multiple goals, and the frequent lack of a comparison, a theory-driven evaluation offers many advantages. In a theory-driven approach, relevant stakeholders are asked to articulate what they believe happens, and how it happens, before an evaluation is designed. For example, most community school designers make statements like "a good school climate is necessary for parents and students to feel welcome in the school" or "good communication is a must between the service providers in the school, teachers, administrators, and parents if the program is to be well coordinated." It is easy to get stakeholders to state many such beliefs. Youth development and education literature also provides a base of knowledge about what youth need in order to do well in school and in life. By weaving together this field-based knowledge and the program-design ideas and intentions, the evaluator and the stakeholders can begin to develop a sequence of conditions that are needed to reach the long-term goals envisioned by the community school designers.

Once a basic model of the beliefs (or theory) of the stakeholders is constructed, details are added to fill out the story. What assumptions do the stakeholders make about the context in which they operate, or the people they serve, or themselves? What specific interventions are offered that could plausibly bring about the intended outcomes? And what would success for each outcome look like? When these questions are answered, the initiative has its own "theory of change," which can be simply defined as a theory of how and why an initiative works.

The participation of all partners and stakeholders—not just the program designers—in developing the theory to be evaluated helps ensure that all relevant information and perspectives are incorporated. Facts known only to long-term school administrators or community circumstances best explained by residents will not be left out of the theory-building process. Such participation can also help create a sense of ownership among all the stakeholders. Participants who have a vested interest in *whether* and *how* changes occur, and who fully understand what is being researched and why, are much more likely to share information and less likely to feel threatened by an evaluation.

How does the process of developing a theory of change work? Before beginning, those in charge of the initiative (and usually paying for the evaluation) must work with the evaluator to identify and agree on who will participate and in what way. Then the first step in developing an initiative's theory is to agree on a well-defined long-term goal—for example, "Students will be successful in school," where the definition of "successful" is agreed upon by the stakeholders as something specific about test scores, community involvement, social behaviors, or whatever may constitute "success" for that group. Next, the stakeholders ask themselves, "What do students need in order to be successful in the way we defined success?" They may decide that a strong curriculum, good attendance rates, and student-centered teachers are necessary in order for students to achieve success. They continue asking, "What is needed for this to happen?" until they have worked backwards to the earliest steps needed for the initiative (such as an agreement for collaboration between a service provider and school district). This "backwards mapping" results in a "pathway" encompassing shorter- through longer-term outcomes that all major stakeholders agree on.[4]

The next key step is identifying an indicator of success for every outcome. Although resources may not permit each outcome to be tested, the stakeholders need to know what success would look like. The evaluator, the funders, and the stakeholders must decide which outcomes will be included in the evaluation. Because outcomes are expected to occur at different stages, long-term evaluations can be designed to look first at early capacity-building outcomes, then at interim outcomes such as school climate and attitudes, and finally at academic outcomes after the earlier outcomes are in place.

Once all of the goals and indicators for success (for the collaboration, for the school, for the community, for the parents, and for the students) have been identified and it is clear what has to happen first, interventions (activities undertaken in the community school, such as after-school programs, health services, or parent workshops) are added wherever needed to reach an outcome. This provides an explicit link between process and outcomes.

With the theory on which the program is based in hand, the measurement and data-collection elements of the evaluation process will be facilitated. An evaluation based on a theory identifies what to measure—ultimate and interim outcomes and the implementation of activities intended to achieve these outcomes—and helps guide choices about when and how to measure. The theory should also guide the evaluator in determining what is "good enough." For example, if an indicator of the outcome "improved academic performance" is grades or test scores, the stakeholders are asked to decide what grades or what score will be considered good enough; must students be able to read at grade level, or must they show a 10% improvement in test scores over the course of a school year? Whatever the measure is, the evaluator will have clear guidelines as to what the stakeholders expect to achieve.

CAS Evaluation Efforts Using a Theory-of-Change Approach

Beginning in 2000, researchers from ActKnowledge began working with the CAS staff to develop a theory of change about how the community schools work and a new evaluation plan based on that theory. The ActKnowledge team conducted interviews at all levels of the community schools—CAS leadership, community school administrative staff, community school directors and principals, parents, and students. The resulting document shows both the complexity of the community school intervention and the multiple reinforcements within this comprehensive model; Figure 13.1 is a summary of its major pathways and outcomes.

The theory-of-change document is the basis for the design of a major evaluation, as well as for a series of smaller studies that were subsequently commissioned by CAS:

- A study examining the type and extent of parent involvement in five of the community schools as that component expanded and matured
- A study of the process and outcomes of a health-oriented adaptation of the basic community school model (at PS 50 in East Harlem)
- A study of the process and outcomes of two new community schools in the South Bronx (a neighborhood that is demographically different from Washington Heights, the site of the original community schools)

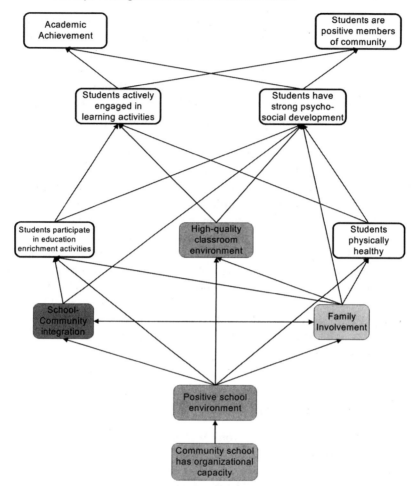

Figure 13.1. Summary of Outcomes Pathway from Community Schools Theory of Change. *Credit:* Prepared by ActKnowledge for The Children's Aid Society.

Although it is too early to have long-term outcome results from these smaller studies, the ActKnowledge team has gathered substantial data at each site, both as baseline information and on the achievement of early outcomes. This will allow realistic evaluation of long-term outcomes, since they are expected to be met only if early outcomes are satisfactorily achieved.

Conclusion

The future of community school evaluation is exciting because there is so much still to learn about what works in what contexts and because it is truly a national movement in which evaluation results can make real contributions to future adaptations of community school models. A participatory, theory-driven approach to evaluation can make that learning an integral part of the community school experience and can also help us sort out the complexities that make community schools both so rich and so difficult to evaluate in traditional ways.

NOTES

1. Esther Robison, *An Interim Evaluative Report Concerning a Collaboration between The Children's Aid Society, New York City Board of Education, Community School District 6, and the I.S. 218 Salomé Ureña de Henriquez School* (New York: Fordham University, Graduate School of Social Service, March 1993), p. 28.
2. Members of this group included Thomas Brock, Manpower Demonstration Research Corporation; Joy Dryfoos, independent researcher; Andres Henriquez, Education Development Center (initially) and Carnegie Corporation of New York (subsequently); Karen Mapp, Institute for Responsive Education; Harold Richman, Chapin Hall Center for Children; and Heather Weiss, Harvard Family Research Project.
3. Since 1996, this Web-based management information system has been in development and currently serves over 1,000 individual program sites, including The After-School Corporation (186 programs), the State of New Jersey Department of Human Services (55 school-based programs), the City of San Francisco (220 youth-serving programs), the DC Children and Youth Investment Trust (150 youth programs), San Francisco Beacons (8 programs), and the Milton S. Eisenhower Foundation (7 full-service schools). This system also serves an array of 21st Century Community Learning Centers, state and citywide programs, and community programs spanning fields of education, youth development, mental health, and adult and community education.
4. "Backwards mapping" is a theory of change term that describes the process of starting where you want to go (the long-term goal) and working back from that to all the preconditions needed to get there.

Appendix: Student Data Form for Evaluation of CAS Community Schools

STUDENT

First Name:* _____ Middle Initial: _____

Last Name:* _____

BOE ID-OSIS:* _____ Current Grade:* _____

Status: Active □   Inactive □

Street Address: _____

City: _____ State: _____ Zip: _____

Gender: Male □   Female □   Birth Date: _____

Home Language: Unspecified □   English □   Spanish □   Other □

Other Specify: _____

Parents' English Fluency: Yes □   No □

Child's Race/Ethnicity: Hispanic □   Black/African American □   Other □

White □   Asian/Pacific Islander □   Native American □

If Hispanic, Specify: Dominican □   Puerto Rican □   Mexican □

Cuban □   South American □   Central American □   Unspecified □

Other □

Home Room: _____   Program Admission Date (Month/Year) _____

FAMILY INFORMATION

Parent/Guardian (1)

First Name:* _____ Middle Initial: _____

Last Name:* _____

Relation: Mother □   Father □   Grandparent □   Aunt/Uncle □

Godparent □   Sibling □   Guardian □   Other □

Street Address: _____

City: _____ State: _____ Zip: _____

Home Phone: _____

Employer: _____

Business Phone: _____

Parent/Guardian (2)

First Name:* _____ Middle Initial: _____

Last Name:* _____

Relation: Mother □   Father □   Grandparent □   Aunt/Uncle □

Godparent □   Sibling □   Guardian □   Other □

Street Address: _____

City: _____ State: _____ Zip: _____

Home Phone: _____

Employer: _____

Business Phone: _____

EMERGENCY CONTACTS

Emergency Contact (1)

First Name:* _____ Middle Initial: _____

Last Name:* _____

Relation: Mother ☐   Father ☐   Grandparent ☐   Aunt/Uncle ☐
Godparent ☐   Sibling ☐   Guardian ☐   Other ☐

Home Phone: _____

Business Phone: _____

Other Phone: _____

Emergency Contact (2)

First Name:* _____ Middle Initial: _____

Last Name:* _____

Relation: Mother ☐   Father ☐   Grandparent ☐   Aunt/Uncle ☐
Godparent ☐   Sibling ☐   Guardian ☐   Other ☐

Home Phone: _____

Business Phone: _____

Other Phone: _____

RELEASE OF CHILD

Permission to Walk Home Alone: Yes ☐   No ☐

Child May Be Picked Up by Following Individuals:

Name: _____

Relation: Mother ☐   Father ☐   Grandparent ☐   Aunt/Uncle ☐
Godparent ☐   Sibling ☐   Guardian ☐   Other ☐

Home Phone: _____

Name: _____

Relation: Mother ☐   Father ☐   Grandparent ☐   Aunt/Uncle ☐
Godparent ☐   Sibling ☐   Guardian ☐   Other ☐

Home Phone: _____

Child May *Not Be* Picked Up by Following Individuals

Name: _____

Relation: Mother ☐   Father ☐   Grandparent ☐   Aunt/Uncle ☐
Godparent ☐   Sibling ☐   Guardian ☐   Other ☐

Home Phone: _____

Name: _____

Relation: Mother ☐   Father ☐   Grandparent ☐   Aunt/Uncle ☐
Godparent ☐   Sibling ☐   Guardian ☐   Other ☐

Home Phone: _____

GENERAL INFORMATION

What primary services would you like your child to receive?

Academic Support ☐   Athletics ☐

Arts Education ☐   Child Care ☐

Technology ☐   Social/Recreation ☐

Holiday Programs ☐   Summer Camp ☐

Other: _____

Adults in Household? (1–15) _____

Children in Household? (1–15) _____

Sibling(s) in Program?   Yes ☐   No ☐

If Yes, Specify: _____

Parent Marital: Single ☐ Married ☐ Widowed ☐ Divorced ☐

Partners ☐ Separated ☐

Highest Grade P/G Comp?

Elementary ☐   Some High School ☐

Received GED ☐   Received High School Diploma ☐

Some College ☐   Completed College ☐

Some Graduate ☐   Graduate Degree ☐

Child Lunch: Free Lunch ☐   Reduced Price Lunch ☐   Full Price ☐

Child's Country of Birth: _____

Year Entered United States: _____

No. Moves in Last 2 Years: 0 Times ☐   1 Time ☐   2 Times ☐

3 Times or More ☐

Do you or your child receive the following ☐

Public Assistance	Yes ☐	No ☐
BEGIN	Yes ☐	No ☐
Food Stamps	Yes ☐	No ☐
Summer in the City	Yes ☐	No ☐
WEP	Yes ☐	No ☐
Medicaid	Yes ☐	No ☐
Family Health Plus	Yes ☐	No ☐

Is participant a WIA-TASC Fellow?   Yes ☐   No ☐

CONSENT

Parent/Guardian:* Yes ☐ No ☐

Date: _____

Evaluation:* Yes ☐ No ☐

Date: _____

Photo/Video/Interview:*   Yes ☐   No ☐

Date: _____

Trips: Yes ☐ No ☐

Date: _____

Food: Yes ☐ No ☐

Date: _____

Food Allergies/Restrictions: _____

_____

_____

MEDICAL CARE

Emergency medical care on file* Yes ☐   No ☐

Health record on file*   Yes ☐   No ☐

Medications authorization on file Yes ☐ No ☐

PERMISSION TO REQUEST HRA/ACD FUNDS

P/G Signature Yes ☐ No ☐

Date: _____

P/G Soc. Security #: _____

P/G HRA Case #: _____

*Required

PART FOUR

National Implications

Introduction

JOY G. DRYFOOS

All of the contributors to this book are clearly in favor of community schools. We would like to see this movement grow rapidly or, as we often say, "go to scale." This would mean that communities with high needs and low performance would be assisted in transforming their schools.

The Children's Aid Society (CAS) work is one of the streams that have come together to create a new field of full-service community schools. The CAS model has been strengthened by many adaptations throughout the country and overseas. A National Technical Assistance Center for Community Schools has been set up at Intermediate School (IS) 218 with facilities for orientation and training. More than 6,000 policy makers and practitioners from all over the world have taken the tour and observed the rich climate at this pilot school.

The concepts of community schools do not necessarily sink in at first encounter; it sometimes takes a while for people to "get it." The question often arises: Do you really expect the schools to do all of that? It is not well understood that the idea behind the community school movement is for schools to do *less*, not *more*! Partners such as CAS come into the building and take responsibility for health, social services, extended hours, and parent and community involvement. However, some school superintendents do get it; Thomas Payzant is a good example (see ch. 15 in this volume). Arne Duncan, head of the Chicago Public Schools, is another strong advocate: "We started with 20 community [school] centers this year [and] we want to add 20 each of the next five years so we will get up to 100 over five years. . . . [T]he Chicago School System cannot do this alone. . . . We have universes, local Boys & Girls Clubs, the YMCA's, Jane Addams' Hull House . . . helping to run our program with us."[1]

The quest for appropriate space within schools for the core components is being addressed in large new school building initiatives around the country. Plans are being developed that incorporate the necessary facilities for schools to become neighborhood hubs. Some of the widely differing design approaches are discussed and considered in this part.

We started this book with an account of the beginnings of the Coalition for Community Schools. Today that group has a membership of 170 national, state, and local organizations who are stakeholders in this movement. It is important to have a strong base in Washington, D.C., and to be affiliated with the Institute for Educational Leadership.

NOTE

1. Arne Duncan, press briefing by the Coalition for Community Schools, Washington, D.C., May 13, 2003.

Gerard van de Burgwal

National and International Adaptations of the Children's Aid Society Model

JANICE CHU-ZHU

Community Schools Consultant, National Technical Assistance
Center for Community Schools, The Children's Aid Society

When the CAS community schools first opened in New York City in 1992, they attracted many visitors interested in learning about and adapting our model. In response CAS created its National Technical Assistance Center for Community Schools (NTACCS) in 1994 to handle the increasing number of requests for information, coordinate the large number of visitors to the schools, and provide technical assistance in the process and operations involved in creating a community school. People who wish to adapt our model can now tour the various components of our program and meet with our staff to ask questions and learn about the implementation of our program.

This chapter will explore the core components of the CAS model and how adaptation sites in the United States and other countries have been able to incorporate elements that represent their signature style and reflect the needs of their individual communities.

Replication versus Adaptation

An immediate dilemma occurs when program planners seek to learn from the experience of others—should they try to replicate the model precisely or should they try to adapt it to their own local circumstances? Replicators often speak of the importance of "program fidelity," while adaptors talk about differing needs among various communities and populations. The National Institute of Mental Health (NIMH) astutely assesses the dilemma: "While individual tailoring may account for success at a given location, there is pressing need for theoretically grounded interventions that will be effective in a wide range of communities. Therein lies a challenge. On the one hand, 'replication' implies fidelity to the original while, on the other hand, 'community-based and culturally sensitive' implies expectation of variation and sensitivity to that variation. The need to vary interventions is widely accepted, but systematically developed and articulated only occasionally."[1]

The NIMH study found two key components that improved the effectiveness of HIV prevention programs as they were implemented in multiple sites around the country. One component was that they were "community-based," designed with the input and skills of the particular communities in which they were implemented. The second was that the programs were "culturally sensitive"—that is, they reflected the needs and cultures of the individuals expected to participate in the intervention and used media and messages relevant to those individuals and their lives.[2]

In working nationally and internationally, CAS has always emphasized that communities should focus on the adaptation of our model and not the replication of our work. Therefore, in the early phases of adapting the CAS model, we encourage the school and community agency to develop surveys, conduct focus groups, gather information, produce a resource inventory of the school's current services, and create a profile of the surrounding community. In addition, all the dimensions of diversity represented in the community—racial and ethnic backgrounds, religious affiliations, immigration status, family composition, and socioeconomic and educational levels—must be considered.

The great strength of the CAS model is that it is a strategy for change. Its core philosophy of wrapping comprehensive services around children helps promote change in a variety of contexts (with families and communities, in school-day and after-school programs, and others). It is the model's flexibility that has led to the development of more than 150 adaptations of the CAS model as of 2003.[3]

Motivators for Change

Motivations for wanting to adapt the CAS model vary widely and are often based on specific social or academic concerns. For example, a violent incident at a school in Japan prompted several of their mental health and university practitioners to visit CAS and learn about the integration of mental health services in our school-based wellness centers. A visitor from Shanghai, China, came to explore ways to work with juvenile delinquents and to prevent an increase in school dropouts. Visitors from Italy had a similar concern; many young people were choosing to drop out of school at age 16, though they lacked the skills needed for good jobs. When a group of principals from the Netherlands visited, the coordinator said, "The group is focused on schools with inner-city problems like in The Hague (multicultural population, sometimes children living in poor housing and/or deprived areas, children from broken families, etc.). . . . I know that one of the effective solutions is community schools."[4]

Though the CAS community schools are located in urban environments, the same kinds of needs that originally inspired our work exist in other parts of this country, as well as abroad. For example, a principal in rural Vermont described the "struggle and turmoil" she saw in her students' families that led her to create a community school.[5] A superintendent of schools from Australia commented, "The issues facing communities under stress from poor services and social dislocation are no different in the metropolitan or the rural areas."[6]

In the United States, schools face the issue of high-stakes testing and the pressures involved in complying with the "No Child Left Behind" legislation. Other concerns include the enormous numbers of schools that fail to meet academic goals, increasing referrals to special education, and the widening achievement gap between whites and black and Latino students. These issues contribute to the problem summed up by Intermediate School (IS) 218 Principal Luis Malavé's maxim, "You can't teach if you can't reach," and constitute powerful motivators for change.

National Technical Assistance Center for Community Schools

As the national arm of CAS's community schools division, NTACCS provides technical assistance for those interested in adapting the CAS model. Its initial work was underwritten with support from the Carnegie Corporation of New York; subsequently, CAS generated major financial support from the Citigroup Foundation as well as from fee-for-service contracts with national organizations (such as Boys & Girls Clubs of America, the Milton S. Eisenhower Foundation, and the Public Education Network).

NTACCS has provided technical assistance on all aspects of planning, implementation, and ongoing development of initiatives to create community schools. The topics that colleagues want help with include: needs assessment; partnership building; getting started; program development; parent and community engagement; responding to the needs of immigrant groups; facility construction planning; sustainability; and evaluation, including establishing realistic outcomes. NTACCS offers a variety of services, including hosting site visits to our New York schools; making presentations at professional conferences and meetings; conducting seminars and training programs; preparing publications; providing information and ideas through telephone consultations; and providing individualized on-site consultations.

Our work draws on current research that supports the explicit components of the CAS model, as well as on the daily operation of our own community schools in New York City in partnership with the Department of Education. It is the actual day-to-day operations and experiences of the CAS community schools that have had immeasurable value to adaptors. The opportunities to consult with peers and to observe a community school program in action facilitate understanding of community school concepts and processes. In turn, the lessons and experiences of our adaptations have added to the pool of information about our model's flexibility and adaptability in other settings.

Components of Successful Adaptations

Comprehensive Framework

It is essential to look at what a "quality program" is and what it truly means to "serve the whole child." The program and services incorporated in this model are responses to the comprehensive needs of youth in all their developmental domains (cognitive, social, moral, physical, and psychological). A balanced program meets all of these needs and also provides services that help reduce or eliminate barriers to learning while providing the competencies and skills necessary for healthy development.

Fertile Ground

Readiness and capacity are key ingredients for successful community schools. There is no substitute for leadership from the principal, who can commit to providing the necessary resources and supports for partner agencies to make their maximum contributions in the school. To generate such commitment, principals should be involved at the earliest stage of an initiative so that they are informed of the expectations, the level of commitment, and the role they will need to play as the initiative grows. Unlike other services that are added to schools without needing much more than the principal's signature, a community school benefits from a collaborative relationship between the principal and lead agency.

Lead Agency Capacity

The CAS model has been referred to as the quintessential model of community schools, not only in integration and comprehensiveness but also in commitment made to each initiative. Inherent in our commitment as a lead agency is the full-time presence we provide, not just in one but in many components of our model. Integration throughout the model is an important factor in the change that occurs in school culture as the partnership grows. All the partners come together and work together in the name of children. This starts at the top, where the CAS community school director and the principal are partners, and it permeates all the systems, operations, and programs in the school.

Agencies can use various indicators of readiness as self-evaluation tools to determine their own capacity to take on and sustain this model. An example of such indicators is the agency's commitment to the long-term financial sustainability of the initiative. Many adaptation sites have continued to build their capacity while they assumed the lead role in an initiative to create a community school. They selected a natural point of entry; for example, they started with an after-school program and eventually built in other components, working up to full-service capacity.

Clear, Written Agreements or Memoranda of Understanding

Once the partners have been identified, it is imperative that the stakeholders come to agreement about their respective roles and responsibilities. A memorandum of understanding (MOU) clearly describes each party's commitment and the roles, responsibilities, and expectations for all participating organizations before the initiative begins. The agreements should include, but are not limited to, agreements between funder and school district, school and lead agency, funder and lead agency, and technical assistance provider and lead agency. There may be subsequent MOUs between the lead agency and other collaborating agencies that come into the initiative, such as health services or program specialists for the extended-day program.

As in any partnership, agreements between the school system and the agency should be in writing; verbal agreements too often lead to erroneous expectations. They should also be constructed between the organizations so they are not dependent on the participation or vision of any single individual. NTACCS recommends that at the highest level, a resolution be passed by the Board of Education (or other equivalent entity) that formally designates a lead agency to work on-site at a specific public school.

Keeping the Focus on the Child

Though the school and the lead agency bring different professional disciplines to community school initiatives, it is important for all parties to agree that the goal is to serve children and families. That focus can help resolve any conflicts arising from private agendas, territorial issues, control issues, and reluctance to commit services or resources to the initiative. Community agencies generally offer a youth development or family systems perspective and need to learn about educational systems and structures as they work at school sites. The reverse also takes place as educators learn about the agency's perspective in working with children and families. By focusing on the child and sharing our collective knowledge, we embrace both disciplines' benefits.

Intentionality

Developing and building up the capacity for community school initiatives includes a strategic emphasis on being intentional in the work. For example, a youth development framework is incorporated and linkages to education are maintained as the extended-day program is designed; parent involvement is included in all aspects of program planning and implementation. More general examples of this emphasis that the adaptations have found beneficial include staying focused on educational achievement as a desired outcome, keeping the child at the center of our attention, and recognizing and honoring the value of active parent/family involvement (see Méndez, ch. 4 in this volume). We strive to develop programs and services whose purpose is to serve, and improve the outcomes for, all children and families, rather than complying with some prerequisite or meeting criteria for particular funding sources.

Balancing Vision and Reality

At the beginning and throughout the partnership, it is important to establish boundaries and point out unrealistic expectations of either partner. Early on in many initiatives, in order to get buy-in and support, unrealistic verbal promises are made that cannot be kept. This leads to mistrust and creates hurdles that must be overcome if the initiative is to progress. It is best to promise only what is within each partner's capacity to provide and build from there.

Coordinated Efforts, Joint Planning, and Integration

As Francis Ianni's research shows, children's development is enhanced when the adults in their lives deliver consistent messages about the importance of education and about behavioral expectations and when the services provided are well coordinated and consistent with these messages.[7] As CAS works with initiatives in the United States and abroad, it is evident that coordination and joint planning lead to better youth and organizational outcomes. However, envisioning and achieving such collaborative approaches is always more difficult than simply implementing a shared activity. It requires much more investment from the partners in working closely together, being purposeful, and involving other stakeholders in the work, but the partners, the youth, and the initiative all benefit greatly when this is achieved.

Stages of Organizational Development in a Community School Model

Many visitors doubt that they can achieve the same outcomes as the CAS schools. It is important to realize that the process by its very nature takes time and that a mature site is not created within a year just because there are new programs at the school. It is even more important to acknowledge the accomplishments achieved at each stage and, at the same time, to recognize that there is no "being done" when one goal is accomplished; rather, we urge our colleagues to think about continuous improvement and to constantly ask What's the next step? Each initiative must also think about its development with regard to each of the following important components of success:

- *Management and Governance:* Some adaptation sites do not have an established school-based support team. As an alternative, they have implemented a leadership team, an advisory group, or a consortium of partners to govern the direction of their initiative. In some schools the principals delegate their partner role to a designated liaison. However, if the liaison does not have decision-making power, waiting for the principal's approval can affect the ability to move forward with the initiative. The partnership must reflect an equal sharing of power between the agency's site director and the school's principal or designated liaison. It is also imperative to have other bodies of governance that include parents and community members.
- *Staffing:* The number of staff members for each initiative will depend on its organizational capacity, program needs, and financial resources. Adaptation sites have employed such options as using volunteers and part-time staff and working with corporations that have employee volunteer programs. In such cases, because of the linkage between the school-day and the after-school programs, provisions must be made for appropriate coverage, back-up, security, and contingency planning when regular staff is not available.
- *Extended-Day Programs and Services:* Some communities may need a high level of services, including weekend, holiday, and summer programs for students or a teen program for youth in the community. Other schools and communities do not require so many hours of services because other

resources are available in their area. These decisions should reflect and respond to the needs of individual schools and communities.

- *Full-Service Components:* A single agency may not have the capacity to provide all the needed services for a school. Many adaptation sites must seek additional partners, establish subcontracts, or work with existing programs that provide other services.

- *Enrichment Activities:* Programs offered before and after school, on weekends, and during the summer should not supplant or duplicate what is already available during the regular school day. Yet the opportunity to link to the school day by infusing academic enrichment through the activities offered establishes a more cohesive link between the partners. Many adaptations have accomplished this kind of enrichment and linkage by incorporating research-based curricula designed for after-school programs that enhance skills such as math, science, and reading.

The appendix to this chapter contains further information on key components and stages of development of community schools.

Individuals' Development in Community Schools

Individuals as well as organizations grow, change, and expand their own capacity as partners in a community school. Much of this growth arises from the cross-disciplinary work that often occurs in these initiatives, especially when partners can adapt, blend, and provide cohesion in mutually beneficial working relationships. Developing these relationships takes time as well as openness to change, continuous effort toward improvement, and commitment to serving children and families.

Challenges in Adapting the Community School Model

Resistance

Resistance to a community school initiative can come in many forms, both overt and covert. For example, in one community that enlisted NTACCS's aid, health services emerged as a need for the children. Despite attempts to provide services in the school, there were substantial delays and hesitation. Later, it was revealed that many teachers had told the principal that they did not want "those sick people" in their building; this overt resistance to addressing documented needs was coupled with the failure of the principal to lead the community school initiative. In other instances the resistance may be less obvious, manifesting itself in excuses or delays in getting tasks accomplished or continuous failure to attend meetings or fulfill responsibilities. Whether overt or covert, resistance impedes the progress of the initiative and may require the intervention of a higher-level administrator, such as the district superintendent.

Organizational Capacity

Visitors often comment that in their areas there is no agency comparable to CAS; they express concern that their agency does not have the capacity and expertise to provide the wide range and comprehensiveness of services that CAS offers, including medical, dental, and mental health programs, extended-day programs, and financial and human resources. Anyone who plans to adapt the full-service model must consider what partnerships or collaborations are available to provide the identified needed services.

Institutional and Systemic Support

Visitors are intrigued by the intensive relationship CAS has built with New York City's Board (now Department) of Education partners, including chancellors, district superintendents, and, most important, principals and staff in the schools. Building, maintaining, and strengthening relationships at all levels of the public education system is a core component of our ongoing local work because, without such institutional and systemic support, our community schools at the building level would surely founder.

Financial Resources

Finding the financial resources to develop a community school is a challenge for most of our visitors. In working with them, we emphasize broadening the focus and looking at the combined resources available through the school, the community, parents, and partnerships with community-based organizations. Many successful adaptations have found creative ways to finance and sustain their community schools. At the Quitman School in Newark, New Jersey, the community partner (Community Agencies Corporation of New Jersey) hired a retired school administrator as business manager in order to tap into his deep knowledge of public education funding streams.

Case Studies of National and International Adaptations

There are more than 150 adaptations of the CAS model in the United States and around the world. The following section describes a few unique examples.

National Adaptations

Working with Special Education: Alliance for Inclusion and Prevention, Boston, Massachusetts

The Alliance for Inclusion and Prevention, Inc. (AIP), has partnered with the Boston Public Schools at the Washington Irving Middle School since 1995.[8]

AIP provides expertise in working with special education services for emotionally and behaviorally troubled students, as well as extensive mental health services through its Inclusion Program. In addition, AIP has experience in operating both therapeutic after-school programming for students exhibiting at-risk behaviors and a broad array of enrichment programs for all students.

One of AIP's major accomplishments was establishing deep working relationships with teachers who were initially resistant to including behaviorally troubled students in mainstream classrooms. By providing teacher training and additional support services for students, AIP helped generate a key result—many students were able to leave "designated behavior classrooms" and reintegrate into less restrictive settings. Through its after-school program, AIP provides services to more than 400 of the 800 students at the school. In addition, it serves all the school's parents through its Family Involvement Program, which sponsors newsletters, parent nights, and parent education workshops. AIP also provides professional development opportunities for the teachers.

Another important accomplishment was redirecting public school special education monies (generally earmarked for high-end emotionally and behaviorally disturbed youth) into extensive new prevention services for all students by means of a deep public-private partnership and demonstrating successful outcomes for all students at the school through the reallocation of these special education dollars.

Multiagency Partnership: Community Agencies Corporation of New Jersey, Newark, New Jersey

The Community Agencies Corporation of New Jersey (CAC of NJ) has served as the lead agency for the Quitman Community School in Newark since 1998.[9] As a lead agency, CAC of NJ is unique in being made up of a group of local youth and family agencies: the Friendly Fuld Neighborhood Centers, Protestant Community Centers, Inc., Cross Counters, Inc., Student Partner Alliances, and Habitat for Humanity-Newark, Inc. This multiagency partnership provides a variety of services to the community, including infant/early childhood services, job training, tutoring and mentoring, after-school/summer and teen youth programs, parent support, leadership and service, and youth residential housing.

CAC of NJ also partners with other organizations to provide needed services for Quitman's students. The Children's Hospital of New Jersey at Newark Beth Israel staffs and runs the school-based health clinic that provides health, dental, and mental health services. A long-term relationship with Bank Street College brings the New Beginnings program to the after-school program and also provides teacher development and support. Because the school's focus was on arts education, CAC of NJ worked to bring in partners to enhance the arts programs offered to the students.

Given the multitude of partners, CAC of NJ's site director must work closely with the school and all the partners to coordinate and integrate services. The business consultant mentioned earlier helps monitor and unify the budget to provide the needed resources. As a result, the Quitman Community School has been able to serve the entire student body through its health clinic and to provide a daily after-school program for about a third of the school's population. Through CAC of NJ's close partnership with the school staff, the level of parent and community involvement increased, leading to a solid pool of volunteers and advocates for the school. Other outcomes include increased student performance in the arts and increases in their academic scores (math and writing).

Change Agents Working within a School District: Achievement Plus, Saint Paul, Minnesota

In spring 1997 Achievement Plus began a year of development and planning at two public schools in Saint Paul—Dayton's Bluff Achievement Plus Elementary School (kindergarten through grade 6) and Monroe Achievement Plus Community School (kindergarten through grade 8).[10] With financial and technical support from the Amherst Wilder Foundation, Achievement Plus, along with the Saint Paul Public Schools, conducted substantial physical renovations and expansions in these buildings to allow proper implementation of the Achievement Plus reform initiatives. These reforms include a standards-based curriculum that draws heavily on ideas developed by the National Center on Education and the Economy; an extensive set of learning supports for students and families modeled on ideas developed by the University of California–Los Angeles Center for Mental Health in Schools (crisis intervention and prevention, classroom-focused supports, home involvement in schooling, support for student transitions, community outreach and volunteering in schools, mental health counseling, dental clinic, nurse practitioners, and health education classes); and extended learning opportunities, including before- and after-school programs that are directly linked to the standards-based curriculum used during the regular school day.

A third school, John A. Johnson Achievement Plus Elementary School (kindergarten through grade 6), opened in the fall of 2000. A former high school, the building was completely redesigned to serve as the Achievement Plus demonstration school for the entire Saint Paul school district. This school represents a unique partnership with the Saint Paul YMCA, which built a full fitness center adjacent to (and used by) the school and which shares in the implementation of the Achievement Plus programs.

An unusual aspect of the Achievement Plus initiative is that its director, Maria Lamb, serves as both chief education officer of the Saint Paul Public Schools and executive director of Achievement Plus. In this dual role, she leads the initiative and brings the lessons learned from Achievement Plus to reform efforts across the city's schools.

Going to Scale: YMCA of Greater Long Beach, California

The goal of the Stevenson-YMCA Community School (S-YCS), which was established in 1997, was to enhance the academic, social, and career development of youth through active partnerships among students, parents (caregivers), school, and community resources to provide an array of school-site activities. A key additional partner from the outset was the School of Social Work at the California State University of Long Beach. S-YCS pursues four objectives in order to meet its overarching goal: to increase parental involvement; to increase communication among youth, parents, and school staff; to provide a wide range of activities after school and on weekends; and to promote seamless school-day and extended-day programming.

Based on its early success, which included positive evaluation data generated by its university partner as well as district support from then-superintendent Carl Cohn, S-YCS was selected by the James Irvine Foundation to serve as the Long Beach model for Irvine's Communities Organizing Resources to Advance Learning Initiative (CORAL), a 10-year community-based learning initiative designed to boost the achievement of children and youth through out-of-school programs.[11] Launched in 1999, the CORAL initiative works in five cities—Fresno, Long Beach, Pasadena, Sacramento, and San Jose. With the infusion of Irvine Foundation funding, the Long Beach site was able to expand to five additional elementary schools and to increase and sustain the work at S-YCS. Based on its accomplishments at S-YCS, the YMCA of Greater Long Beach was selected as CORAL's lead agency and a former YMCA staff member, Ralph Hurtado, was named the first executive director of CORAL Long Beach. Hurtado's experience at Stevenson convinced him that "schools can become the hub of the community."[12]

International Adaptations
Role of an Intermediary: Community Schools in the Netherlands

In the 1990s various Dutch organizations contacted CAS to learn more about its community schools. Led by consultant Dr. Gerard van de Burgwal, the Netherlands adaptation process included organizing groups of educational administrators, school personnel, and community agency staff to visit the CAS community schools in New York and translating the CAS publication *Building a Community School* into Dutch.[13]

The Netherlands community schools got under way in 1995 in Groningen, whose education policy at the time was deemed a failure because investments in education and related services had not resulted in sufficient and sustainable improvements for children and families. The city's solution was to design facilities in which children and families had access to services at the moment they needed them. The city board, in collaboration with various school boards, created *vensterscholen* ("window schools") in every neighborhood of the city; the goal was to set up 10 facilities, each with an elementary school at its center. According to the needs of the neighborhood, different services were brought together either in one building or in a network of services. Making a commitment to support the project for 10 years, the city provided money for facilities and for an "integration manager" or director of programs who would serve as the principal's partner. These concepts were based on the CAS model, which views the school as the center of the community and which requires a full-time director who partners with the principal and coordinates a variety of programs.

Another Dutch adaptation site is the Community School Amsterdam de Pijp. The school has many similarities to CAS's New York City schools: the programs provide a variety of services for children ages two to twelve and extend activities for adults and seniors in the evenings; the education director (paid by the Board of Education) and the director of social programs (funded by a community agency) share governance and management responsibilities; and the school population includes many students whose families have recently moved to the Netherlands from northern Africa. Their struggles mirror those of the Washington Heights Dominican community—children and families are required to learn a new language and customs, and parents have to secure housing, employment, and child care. Dr. van de Burgwal notes that some educators still find this model of partnership difficult to accept.

Despite some resistance, the community school movement in the Netherlands has gained significant momentum in recent years. In 2003 two of every three local authorities in the Netherlands had such programs or were on their way to creating them.[14] However, the actual number of community schools varies by location. In The Hague, 86 out of 190 elementary schools call themselves community schools, while in Amsterdam only 22 of 200 elementary schools are in the development stage, although several have a full-service model.[15] It is expected that by 2012, 300 of the 500 local authorities will have such schools and programs.[16] But community schools are not yet a part of Dutch national educational policy. According to Dr. van de Burgwal, there is no legislation to establish them and little money for research, although there is considerable verbal support and a lot of freedom at the local level to move in this direction.

Private Industry Serving as Catalyst and Lead Funder: Community Schools in Bogotá, Colombia

In October 1999 the Bogotá Electric Company decided to work to improve the quality of life in the 23 municipalities in the states of Cundinmarca and Meta, where its infrastructure towers are located. The company's goal was "to contribute to the long term socio-economic development of the most deprived communities in these municipalities."[17] In the first phase of the project, designed to last three years, the goals were to initiate programs that would benefit families and youth through the provision of community activities, educational opportunities, employment and entrepreneurial opportunities, and electric power to remote rural areas.

By 2002 the project reported progress in all of these categories. The community activities have involved more than 61,000 adults and youth. Rural electrification was provided to 657 families, with 500 more families targeted for 2003. In employment, the company supported the creation of 26 microbusinesses and 15 cooperatives. In education, CAS's full-service model was adapted in five schools. The company's 2003 newsletter announced that the schools would be open to the community from 7 A.M. to 10 P.M. and would offer a variety of programs and services. As in CAS schools, through strategic partnerships the schools provide enrichment, cultural and adult education opportunities, vocational training, health services, sports programs, and parent involvement activities.

The electric company's leadership role in this adaptation has included establishing strategic alliances with universities, banks, community organizations, and other for-profit companies that have contributed U.S.$1.5 million to the initiative. Additional financial support, in the area of community development, comes from the scholarships offered by the electric company to top students at these schools who will pursue careers that will benefit their region; the students commit to three years' work in those designated regions. This program has provided a great incentive for students to continue their studies. The company has also provided resources not only for the five community schools but for other schools, including 37,000 notebooks, 25,000 pencils, and 60 computers, as well as trips for 3,000 rural students to museums, universities, and historic places.

Elsewhere, community agencies have partnered with private industry as a source of funding and other resources, such as volunteers. In Colombia's unique adaptation, the electric company itself has assumed a dual role: generating community development as a private company through the education of its young people. As with any initiative of this nature, the company faces the daunting task of coming up with funding to sustain it.

A Government-Sponsored Initiative:
New Community Schools in Scotland

Scotland's community school initiative is unique in that a national government is committed to this philosophy and provides financial backing. The New Community Schools (NCS) initiative began in November 1998 and included 150 schools in its first phase; by 2002 more than 400 schools were involved. The initiative's Web site describes its philosophy and approach:

> New Community Schools are at the leading edge of this Government's radical strategy to promote social inclusion and to raise educational standards. The wider barriers to learning that can prevent children from realizing their potential have not always been addressed in a properly co-ordinated fashion. Access to the necessary support has not been available when and where it is needed. New Community Schools will embody the fundamental principle that the potential of all children can be realized only by addressing their needs in the round—and that this requires an integrated approach by all those involved. Barriers to learning must be identified at the earliest stage, and intervention must be focused, planned and sustained. A range of services is necessary to assist children [to] over-

come the barriers to learning and positive development—family support, family learning and health improvement. New Community Schools will ensure that such expert advice and support is at hand—not at the end of a referral chain to other agencies.[18]

It is no accident that much of this official language echoes key concepts developed and promoted by CAS. The Scottish Executive (the government) has adapted our model on the largest scale imaginable. The structural and creative collaboration takes place at the top: the country's minister of education, chief of social services, chief medical officer, and other high-level officials oversee the progress of the initiative. The wide canvas provides an opportunity to roll out projects to large groups of schools (for example, all elementary schools that feed into a particular middle school).

In one city, Stirling, integration across services has been a shared policy aim of all partner agencies. Overall responsibility for NCS development in the Stirling Council area (53 schools) rests with the Children's Services Community Planning Group, made up of senior managers from Children's Services, community services, health services, and police, as well as representatives from all the local Executive Groups, which are based on secondary school catchment areas. This body sets the budgets for local Executive Groups, reviews progress against local outcome targets, and oversees staff development.

The day-to-day operation of Stirling's NCS and the management of devolved budgets is the responsibility of the Executive Groups, which include representatives from health, community services, social work, schools, nurseries, voluntary agencies, and the police. The Executive Groups must:

- Consult with service providers and with the community in order to draw up an annual Action Plan for NCS developments, which must include proposed outcomes, and to allocate funding to the plan
- Gather data to show progress toward outcomes in an annual report
- Engage with the community to set specific targets and consider what activities to support. Executive Groups promote community involvement in NCS through links with community groups and special interest groups such as school boards, Parent-Teacher Associations, and the Parent's Forum, which advises the education authority.[19]

No initiatives in the United States compare in scale to Scotland's countrywide program. In 2003 the initiative was renamed Integrated Community Schools; Scotland's education minister pledged to extend the concept to every school by 2007 and is providing the financial capital to support this commitment.

Public Education Support: Community Schools in England

England's nationwide effort to implement community schools began in 2002.[20] As in Scotland, funding comes only from the government or the public education system. This major difference from the CAS model, as well as support from the minister of education, means that the British initiative can move more quickly and become more extensive.

A change agent supporting the community school model in England is the Community Education Development Centre (CEDC), a charitable trust whose purpose is to promote family education and community schools. CEDC's excellent publications are used in classrooms and at home with children and parents; its outreach in community education goes to more than 600 schools in the United Kingdom and is growing rapidly.[21] The CEDC's Community Schools Network has members all over England, including schools, community centers, local education authorities, and individuals, who understand the linkage between school improvement and community engagement. The Network itself consists of 2,000 schools representing all types and stages of community school development.

The Education Act of 2002 specifically names "Extended Schools"—that is, schools that offer complementary activities to children, families, and the wider community—as a key national school improvement strategy. The Local Government Association welcomed the central government's plans to develop Extended Schools. In 2002 the community school model was piloted in seven locations; soon the initiative was extended to 18 more local education authorities.[22] In 2003 the minister of education supported the idea that at least one school in every English education authority would provide a full range of community services by 2006. She also offered a three-year plan to turn 240 primary schools into Extended Schools with child care, health and social services, lifelong and family learning, parenting training, study supports, arts programs, and computer access. Economically disadvantaged areas would be the first to benefit from this plan.[23]

England, like Scotland, is attempting a rapid expansion of its community schools initiative. The pressure to create full-service schools so quickly may not afford schools enough time to build relationships and go through the necessary stages of growth. Much will depend on the actual supports and resources the education system provides to local education authorities and on the generation of support from other stakeholders such as schools, families, and communities.

Conclusion

As these brief case studies illustrate, one of the real strengths of the community schools strategy is that many kinds of leaders can understand and support its adaptation and implementation—private foundations, intermediate organizations, social service organizations, government entities, and private industry. The wide range of adaptations in very diverse settings bears witness to the central ideas of responsiveness to local needs and the integration of local resources around public schools serving as the hubs of their communities.

We expect continuing demand for technical assistance, both in the United States and overseas. As in the Netherlands, educators and social service workers are finding common goals and are pushing school systems to "go to scale." The rapidity of the movement's growth in some countries is remarkable. We in the United States would do well to emulate the pace of development. Of course, our school and support systems are both decentralized and fragmented, so that "going to scale" in the United States would demand the participation of 50 states, if not each of the 15,000 school districts. Until recently the NTACCS has been working mainly with one or a few schools at a time. Now the demand is beginning to come from citywide coalitions and state governments. As this movement grows, we can look forward to the development of more technical assistance capacity in universities, city and state governments, and, if legislation favoring community schools goes forward, even in the federal government.

Our experience tells us that planning, implementing, and sustaining community schools are not simple matters. Practitioners need a lot of help at every stage. As the concept becomes better known, the NTACCS and others in the emerging field must be ready to provide consistent, sustained, and knowledgeable assistance.

NOTES

1. National Institute of Child Health and Human Development and National Institute of Mental Health, "Replication of Community-Based HIV Interventions for Youth RFA," 1998, http://0-grants.nih.gov.spartan270.nsu.edu/grants/guide/rfa-files/RFA-HD-98-015.html (accessed 2003).

2. Ibid.

3. The Children's Aid Society National Technical Assistance Center for Community Schools, year-end report, 2002.

4. Toon Dykstra, letter to CAS, March 3, 2001.

5. Joy Dryfoos and Sue McGuire, *Inside Full-Service Community Schools* (Thousand Oaks, Calif.: Corwin Press, 2002), p. 6.

6. Ian Wilson, letter to CAS, January 18, 2003.

7. Francis A. J. Ianni, "Meeting Youth Needs with Community Programs," Dec. 1992, ERIC Clearinghouse on Urban Education, New York, N.Y., ERIC, ED 356291, http://www.ericfacility.net/ericdigests/ed356291.html (accessed March 12, 2003).

8. The source for this section is an organizational profile submitted by Robert Kilkenny, Executive Director, Alliance for Inclusion and Prevention, Inc., to the Children's Aid Society Practicum in New York City on November 5–7, 2003.

9. The source for this section is an organizational profile submitted by Dorothy J. Knauer, Deputy Director, Community Agencies Corp. of New Jersey, to the Children's Aid Society Practicum in New York City on November 5–7, 2003.

10. The source for this section is *Achievement Plus,* 2003, http://www.achievement-plus.org/origins/index.php (accessed February 18, 2003).

11. James Irvine Foundation, 2004, http://www.irvine.org/frameset_cp.htm (accessed 2003).

12. James Irvine Foundation, *Five Cities, One Vision—CORAL: Linking Communities, Children and Learning* (Los Angeles: James Irvine Foundation, 2001).

13. *Bouwen aan een Community School,* trans. Gerard van de Burgwal et al. (Utrecht: Dutch Institute for Care and Welfare, 1998).

14. Gerard van de Burgwal, *Community Schools in the Netherlands,* report prepared for CAS, received May 11, 2003. In 2001 the first year report on this development was published in the Netherlands. The development will be monitored over the next few years.

15. OOG Educational Services in Amsterdam, under the leadership of Dr. van de Burgwal, conducted a quick scan in November 2001 in preparation for the first conference on community school development in Amsterdam.

16. Oberon, cited in *Community Schools in the Netherlands.*

17. Eberth Artunduaga, "Bogotá Electric Company's Social Development Project," trans. Hersilia Méndez, report prepared for CAS, received May 10, 2002.

18. Donald Dewar, foreword to "Prospectus," *New Community Schools,* 1998, http://www. scotland.gov.uk/education/newcommunityschools/pros.htm (accessed December 11, 2003).

19. These obligations are itemized in an unpublished report prepared for CAS and submitted by Margaret Doran, Head of Schools, Children's Services, Stirling, Scotland, received August 29, 2003.

20. Tony Gelsthorpe and John West-Burnham, eds., *Educational Leadership and the Community: Strategies for School Improvement through Community Engagement* (London: Pearson Education Limited, 2003).

21. Alice Dodge Berkeley, report prepared for CAS, received April 24, 2002.

22. "England's Community Schools Pilot To Be Extended," November 1, 2002, *National Literacy Trust,* http://www.literacytrust.org.uk/database/community.html (accessed December 11, 2003).

23. "Every LEA in England To Have at Least One Community Access School," March 14, 2003, *National Literacy Trust,* http://www.literacytrust.org.uk/database/community.html (accessed December 11, 2003).

Appendix: Stages of Development of a CAS Community School

Management and Governance

Organizing Principles		Stages		
	Exploring	Emerging	Maturing	Excelling
Defining characteristics	Principal as sole manager of the school/programs	Formal management structure of the partnership, mission, and objectives are defined	Early integration of leadership and management of services—establishing protocols, policy, and procedures	Integrated leadership team; parents, staff and community seen as key stakeholders
Key activities	Recognize that schools are most effective when their primary role is that of instructional leader	Decide to select a Lead agency to manage partnerships Develop criteria and selection; clarify roles and responsibilities of CBO and school Establish operational issues (space, services, hours of operation) but revisit needs periodically	Recognize both principal and site director as authorities/leaders in the school Site director to establish sufficient trust and credibility to be the authority in the absence of the principal	Establish efficient communication processes and mutually agreed-on policies and procedures Re: succession planning for either principal or site director, both can voice their criteria to select the best candidate
Leadership	Principal as the sole manager of the school	Lead agency is selected to serve as manager and leader for support services in the school	High level of accountability by the CBO to school, parents, and community	Collaborative leadership of school by both school administration and CBO
Formal structures	Existing school governance structures (i.e., Pupil Personnel, School Leadership Team, PTA, etc.)	Establish decision making and communication processes between school and lead agency; some sites may convene regular meetings of key stakeholders Establish formal partnership agreements (e.g., Memorandum of Understanding)	Regular meetings between principal and site director Some sites may establish governance bodies such as advisory boards, partners forum/board, to monitor program quality, impact, and relevance Formal agreements with the school system to further establish the initiative	Regularly scheduled meetings keep decision makers informed and engaged
Informal structures	Network of staff and/or parents working to improve the school	Informal parent, student, staff, and community leaders who influence the design and delivery of programs	Informal "grapevine" or phone tree to communicate with parents and community about urgent events	The governance structure and process are established and well-known Strong communication between school and CBO staff to assess gains and respond proactively to needs

(continued)

Appendix: Stages of Development of a CAS Community School (*Continued*)

Management and Governance

Organizing Principles	Exploring	Emerging	Maturing	Excelling
			Stages	
Integration	Varying degrees, primarily in district-mandated governance structures (i.e., school leadership team, local school restructuring team, etc.)	Lead agency/school leadership jointly develop a shared vision, strategic plan, service priorities, target groups	Lead agency serves as an umbrella agency for other service providers in the school, without compromising the integrity and autonomy of the school and other partners	Consistent integration in both administrative and operational activities CBO serves on the school's leadership team and is integrated into the school fabric; principal may serve on governance team of CBO
Objectives	Establish a formal statement of interest by the school district to establish the community school	Establish formal structures (e.g., MOUs with the school district)	Have established agreements with all partners, reflecting a deepened commitment from the school district; established operating protocols and procedures	Have established agreements that reflect a deepened commitment with the school district to further institutionalize the model

Staffing

Organizing Principles	Exploring	Emerging	Maturing	Excelling
			Stages	
Defining characteristics	Some thought is given to staffing, though not linked to a formal budget	At least one key lead agency staff person is on site and very accessible/visible to staff, parents, students, and the community Staff working long hours with more responsibility than delineated in their job descriptions	Moving towards full staffing of programs and services Staff is sometimes overextended as they take on multiple tasks unrelated to their primary duties	Full complement of qualified, dedicated staff Staff has more consistency between job descriptions and actual duties
Key activities	Generate preliminary ideas about staff, skills, roles, and responsibilities	Preliminary considerations are made to re-deploy staff and commence services in the CS Establish staffing needs/position but	Begin succession planning for key positions in the school, lead agency and support programs As operational needs change, position	Planned succession at all levels; core of experienced, skilled and committed staff provides stability during transitions Site directors transition to administrative

	remain flexible to respond to actual program needs Lead agency may contract (as opposed to permanent hire) with urgently needed staff to fill gaps Hire site director and other staff, recruit volunteers	descriptions and skill sets also may change Clarification of the staff and skill sets needed for the job; formal termination policies for staff Expand opportunities for professional development and career advancement	positions; seasoned staff contribute to process improvement Staff is more attentive to and cognizant of implications of school, local, state, and federal policy	
Leadership	Principal has control over staffing	Full-time site director is hired to work closely with the principal and share management of the school	Capable, innovative site director and principal responsible for their respective staff Director manages all the community school staffing issues Non-lead agency staff is accountable to the director and organizational lead, even when not directly supervised by the site director	Director manages multidisciplinary and multigenerational staff. Is trusted with oversight of the school when principal and senior administrators absent. Seasoned staff are able to discern and influence changes in school climate and attitudes toward the community school
Formal structures	School staff operates a district-funded after-school program	Position descriptions; salary and benefit compensations; policy and procedures to govern the school, lead agency and/or partner organizations Specific opportunities to celebrate staff gains/program successes	Policies around leave and vacation times Training and monitoring staff around observance of mandated professional practice on issues such as child abuse and neglect, etc. Performance reviews Strategic plans with stated outcomes; guided in part by conditions of the grant	Established structures for career-pathing, professional development, and succession planning Staff use expertise in providing technical assistance by hosting site visits, presenting at professional conferences Joint intra- and interdisciplinary professional development activities
Informal structures	At-will volunteers	Some school staff may be employed by both the school and lead agency; various celebratory events, morale boosters, are organized for the staff	Celebrations, affirmations and relationship building between the lead agency and school (i.e., jointly sponsored retreats and parties with the school) Staff makes program and staffing/volunteer recommendations based on observations and interactions with others	Staff creates informal support and learning networks for their own nurturing and for quality service

(continued)

Appendix: Stages of Development of a CAS Community School (Continued)

Staffing

Organizing Principles	Stages			
	Exploring	Emerging	Maturing	Excelling
Integration		Challenge of creating a shared culture, of integrating culture of school, lead agency, and other partner organizations The unifier is the co-creation of a shared vision, mission, and initial goals and objectives	More intentional work with school staff and lead agency focusing on their shared goals Staff begins to deliver services in collaborative fashion—clients are unable to distinguish who works for lead agency or for school Principal and site director have regular meetings; site director is included in principal cabinet meetings and school leadership team	Staff delivers services in collaborative fashion; school administered through shared leadership of principal and site director New staff acculturated in collaborative model; school internal and external communications include both principal and director as leaders of the school
Objectives		To co-create a shared vision and culture	To operationalize the shared vision and culture	To maintain a high level of integration in all areas

Programs and Services

Organizing Principles	Stages			
	Exploring	Emerging	Maturing	Excelling
Defining characteristics	Awareness of service needs No formal integrated programs/services	Initial program start-up targeting a small portion of the community Staggered rollout based on space, funding, and urgency of need	Service plans are established but flexible according to changing needs and best practices Some signature programs emerge/are established	Quality programs are fully integrated into the school Broad menu of services Many signature programs
Key activities	Brainstorm ideas to meet service needs Conduct an informal assessment of current available resources	Conduct a comprehensive needs/asset assessment including all stakeholders	Provide services that are consistent with core competencies of partnering agencies Use data to analyze utilization	Establish a clear and uniform process for referral and accessing of services and support staff

Leadership	A combination of any of the following may provide leadership: individuals, school staff, parents, and/or the community	The principal and lead agency Some funders may choose to be active and visible at this stage A site director and/or program co-ordinator is usually on site, leading program implementation	Program coordinator responsible for programs/services; reports directly to the site director Principal and site director work closely to develop menu of services based on needs assessment	Principal and site director work closely to ensure the services remain responsive to the needs of the school and community Site director and principal co-design programs where funds are co-mingled
Formal structures	PTA/PTO; school strategic plan; in some cases, there are no formal structures	Established menu of service, staffing needs, program policies, space commitments, referral process Grant goals determine who will be served and how Program/service attendance/utilization records	One or more of the CS activities may be formally integrated into the school day and become part of the daily schedule or academic requirement Enrollment, disciplinary, and termination policies for students	Program calendar; formal program/service evaluation Referrals for services come from both users and providers
Informal structures	Individuals/small groups of parents, staff, community organizations advocating for school improvements	Groups of parents, teachers, and community organizations advocate for services Students self-referring for services	Maintaining an open door for program graduates to return as employees, volunteers, or clients	Parents and teachers offer to instruct classes they are skilled and interested in; students request specific classes or programs Annual celebratory events
Integration	There may be willingness to align and integrate isolated activities, but not on a programmatic level	Parallel, extended-day programming develops to complement existing school-day programs Content and staff from the day school are included in after-school Early attempts to align EDP content with standards	Referral for services through existing school structures, such as Pupil Personnel Teams Services are linked to the school's priority outcomes Programs from other providers are coordinated under the lead agency umbrella Limited services integrated in day school hours (e.g., parent involvement, medical, dental, mental health)	Strong alignment between the services and the targets established for the school, with clear goals, objectives and outcomes School day includes before-, during- and after-school programs One orientation event and registration form for all extended day programs
Objectives	Fill the service gap with available resources, look for new resources	Expand programs and services, integrate data of needs/assets and current best practices and research	Focus efforts on issues of quality (i.e., frequency and intensity, timely delivery, staff competencies)	Modify programs according to shifting needs (data), best practices, and research

(continued)

Appendix: Stages of Development of a CAS Community School (*Continued*)

Parental Involvement

Organizing Principles	Stages			
	Exploring	Emerging	Maturing	Excelling
Defining characteristics	Awareness that parental involvement is directly correlated to children's academic success	Strong outreach to engage parents as advocates of quality education for their children, the school and the CS model	Parents are more connected and invested in their children's education	Parents are more informed about and skilled in addressing educational issues such as academic standards and how to secure quality education for children Strong presence in the school as staff, advocates, volunteers, PTA/PTO representatives, and on appropriate governance structures in the school Many parents also have formal and informal leadership roles in the community
Key activities	Investigate ways to expand/facilitate parental involvement	Develop a critical mass of parents who are actively committed to the establishment of the CS	Empower parents to *use* the CS as an engine of change to improve the quality of life for their children and families	Facilitate active parental engagement in the education and development of their children; encourage speaking out and taking initiative around pertinent school and community issues Parents become active change agents to improve the quality of life for themselves, their children, families, and communities
Leadership	Informal identification of parent leaders who are most solicited/involved in school change	Hire parent coordinator to manage parental involvement activities Work to empower and develop elected and informal parent leaders, as well as expand cadre of leaders	Parent leaders may have leadership positions in the school, PTA/PTO, or community Some informal leaders may become resources for other parents—informing them of their rights and directing them to appropriate service providers in the school or community	Established cadre of parent leaders in the school that share knowledge, mentor other parents, and serve as advocates for/with others Parent leadership and activism is carried over into the community to address critical issues impacting them such as safety and quality of life

Organizing Principles				
Formal structures	PTA/PTO	Accessible space dedicated for parents or family resource center staffed by a parent coordinator	Formal and informal leaders may serve as advocates for their children and community in various public forums Coordinator serves as facilitator for parents	PTA and other parent involvement bodies work closely with the community schools to keep parents informed and engaged
Informal structures	Groups naturally formed around commonalties such as same neighborhood, children in same class, or grandparents	Opportunities are created to affirm, utilize, highlight, celebrate, and enhance the strengths of parental partnership	Parents create their own network of supports, identify resources and trainings needed; recruit participants for special events	More seasoned parents direct new parents to available resources, help new parents acculturate and serve as mentors to others
Integration	Not defined	Parents are included in community schools planning and governance structure	Parents in school as volunteers or employees	Parents assume roles as advocates and change agents
Objectives	To get parents involved	Have dedicated staff to plan and coordinate activities with and for parents Develop formal and informal parent leaders; have accessible, dedicated space for parents to meet Promote parent involvement and education around their child's education	Lead agency staff facilitate parent involvement with parent leaders taking more active roles in recruitment, programming Involve parents in support and advocacy of quality education Integrate parents into governance structures in the school	Encourage parents to be more proactive about child's education and successful advocates for their children Allow parents to demonstrate a commitment to their personal development and understand its importance to their child's school success Foster development of parent-led support networks

Community Involvement

Organizing Principles	Stages			
	Exploring	Emerging	Maturing	Excelling
Defining characteristics	Acknowledgement that a community school will be an asset for the entire community School looking to build upon community needs	Community becomes educated about and embraces the idea of community schools to support students, families, and communities	Increased visibility within the community and responsiveness to its changing needs	CS as an important community pillar; delivering quality services with the well-being of the community as a priority

(continued)

Appendix: Stages of Development of a CAS Community School (*Continued*)

Community Involvement

Organizing Principles	Exploring	Emerging	Maturing	Excelling
			Stages	
Key activities	Preliminary awareness of community concerns/needs	Host strategic community activities to build interest and support of the CS Conduct needs and assets assessment of and with the community Develop communication plan to keep community apprised of progress (i.e., standing community and school district meetings)	Host events and celebrations open to the public Based on capacity, lead agency commits a percentage of service for the community (e.g., it provides summer camp physicals to siblings of its students) CS representatives attend community meetings, stay abreast of relevant policy and climate changes Selectively serve on committees that are planning/implementing community-wide events consistent with its core competencies and values (e.g., community health fair or back to school kick-off events)	CS joins community efforts in areas where there is alignment between its goals and priorities and those of the larger community Partners with other credible community organizations to jointly pursue funding to address shared priorities CS is strategic in maintaining high levels of visibility, relevance and value to the community CS develops and manages relationships with powerful community organizations, without alienating itself from other groups
Leadership		Principal and CBO share responsibility	CBO and school actively encourage parent and youth leaders to become change agents in the community, through membership in various community organizations	The principal and CBO continue to provide leadership, while retaining autonomy
Formal structures		The CS partnership may have community members on its governance bodies or school leadership teams Strong public education campaign and a clear communication plan to keep the community engaged in the CS process CS may establish contracts or MOU with community organizations providing services at the school	Communication plan to keep community informed and engaged	CS and other community providers serve on influential committees and governance structures within the community

	Exploring	Emerging	Maturing	Excelling
Informal structures	Relationships with leaders concerned about healthy youth development		Strong relationships with leaders and key influencers in the community	The CBO has established viable relationships with key legislators, civic and faith leaders, and government entities within the community, city, and state
Integration	Not defined	Community is involved in the CS process from planning stages and thereafter	Community members may serve on governance structures for school, the CS partnership; Other community organizations may deliver services through the CS partnership	CBO and other community organizations may jointly apply for funding, participate in advocacy and outreach activities for critical school and community issues; The CBO may have office space at the local school district office
Objectives	To deliver services to students	Include community in planning, needs and resource assessment, and implementation processes; Garner strong community support	To partner with other community organizations for more holistic and comprehensive family interventions; Find ways to include influential community organizations in the CS process	To find ways to partner and combine core competencies to deliver comprehensive services and supports to students, families, and the community

Evaluation

Organizing Principles	Stages			
	Exploring	Emerging	Maturing	Excelling
Defining characteristics	Acknowledgment that there needs to be a way to measure program impact/effectiveness; Some intimidation by the high cost of evaluation	Desire to document and evaluate the process of becoming a CS; Data collection begins to establish baselines, and measure progress on goals	Process evaluation underway or completed; baselines established; Outcomes evaluation begins	First formative evaluation completed and outcome evaluation in process
Key activities	Identify preliminary program objectives	Establish criteria for and selection of evaluator, as well as parameters of the evaluation; Discuss/decide upon the design, period to be covered, and budget of evaluation; Use preliminary data collection to demonstrate a correlation between program utilization and documented need	Adjust program quality, intensity, frequency, and timeliness of interventions to produce the desired outcomes; Identify outcome evaluation components; Establish consistent data collection processes	Data continues to influence program design, policies, and procedures

(continued)

Appendix: Stages of Development of a CAS Community School (Continued)

Evaluation

Organizing Principles	Stages			
	Exploring	Emerging	Maturing	Excelling
Leadership	Not defined	CBO and principal and evaluator/evaluation team	CBO and principal and evaluator/evaluation team	CBO and principal and evaluator/evaluation team Evaluators take leadership roles in documenting results, analyzing and helping to interpret the data
Formal structures	None or not defined	Contract with evaluator Grant goals and objectives Information gathering instruments (consent forms) and evaluation requirements	Contract with evaluator Grant goals and objectives Information gathering instruments (consent forms) and evaluation requirements	Contract with evaluator Grant goals and objectives Information gathering instruments (consent forms) and evaluation requirements
Informal structures	Observations by staff and others	Schedules of time, space, and participants for evaluation activities	Collection of anecdotal reports of program impact on students/families; informal discipline or team discussions involved in action research—reflecting on the variables that most influence student success or lack of it	Teams and disciplines reflecting on the evaluation data and the implication for their work Teams also discussing outcomes they are observing that may not be part of the evaluation design
Integration		Program objectives aligned with evaluation goals	Evaluation examines the impact of the integrated service design	Relevant data and analysis are shared with the school on an ongoing basis to help inform its instructional service delivery
Objectives	Identify goals and objectives	Select evaluator based on established criteria that were identified Define parameters of evaluation design Establish evaluation goals; conduct process evaluation Establish data collection processes for baseline data	Complete process evaluation Apply learnings from evaluation to process improvement Begin outcome evaluation	Continue outcome evaluation, while adjusting program and process based on evaluation data Share data with school

Sustainability

Organizing Principles	Stages			
	Exploring	Emerging	Maturing	Excelling
Defining characteristics	Awareness that additional programs will require more money Optimism that "there is enough money out there"	Commitment to secure funding is determined by the urgency for services being offered and program size	Funds for current implementation Signature programs attract specific funding sources Critical mass of diverse supporters developed Diverse public and private funding streams identified	Lead agency develops and implements a comprehensive sustainability strategy that includes financial and succession planning to maintain and expand programs The CS has individuals or organizations who champion its work and generate funds for it
Key activities	Research both public and private funds as viable options	Identify funders to underwrite needs assessment, planning and early implementation (1–3 years) Establish process for keeping funders informed of progress and changes Become part of networks with similar target groups or mission for advocacy purposes Based on client demographics, identify various public-funding streams that it may tap into to underwrite services provided to students (e.g., Medicaid, Head Start, etc.) Begin to develop 3–5 year sustainability plan	Develop a strong public engagement campaign to educate about the CS and develop a critical mass of supporters within the school and externally Use existing public, organization or school funding streams to pay for some programs Develop partnerships with organizations with independent funding, which share common mission or guiding values or the CS target groups Inform funders of progress Approach the school district to explore what in-kind or monetary support can be contributed to strengthen the partnership Implement the 3–5 year plan, while receiving some funding, adjusting plan as needed Identify and share powerful success stories	Developer/grant writer on staff Lead agency establishes credibility within funding community through high levels of accountability, quality programming and positive impact on clients' lives Lead agency is part of network of organizations that actively advocate for appropriate public funding; is on many databases to receive RFP funding CBO works collaboratively with school and school district or community organizations to pursue funding such as 21st Century, Department of Justice Lead agency reviews trends in public education, funding, identifies strategic opportunities consistent with its core competencies and pursues emerging or available funding
Leadership	Not defined	Lead agency initiates and manages all activities in this area; principal consulted and appraised of funding, and helps determine how funds are used	Lead agency continues to be primary fundraiser; helps school to look creatively at how its funds can be maximized	Lead agency organizes fundraising events, public relations activities, and visits to the school to generate funding

(continued)

Appendix: Stages of Development of a CAS Community School (*Continued*)

Sustainability

Organizing Principles	Stages			
	Exploring	Emerging	Maturing	Excelling
Formal structures	Not defined	Lead agency boards or governance and decision making structures influence or direct sustainability direction Funding requirements as outlined in grant contract (e.g., funder may give matching grant which warrants specific level of fund raising in specified time frames)	Sustainability plan; established accountability structures or benchmarks to ensure that conditions of funders are satisfied CBO boards or governance and decision making entities who influence or direct sustainability issues; funder's requirements—grant document (e.g., funder may give matching grant which warrants specific level of fundraising in specified time frames)	Development staff; goals and objectives and reporting requirements of the funder Sustainability plan; CBO boards or governance and decision-making entities who influence or direct sustainability issues; funder's requirements—grant document (e.g., funder may give matching grant which warrants specific level of fund raising in specified time frames)
Informal structures	Almost all the processes and activities here are informal	Cultivating relationships with organizations with independent funding who may partner in the initiative	An intentional effort to build a strong constituency, advocates and champions who can speak compellingly about the initiative and raise support Consistent attention to accountability to funders	Site visits for potential champions and funders; professional opportunities at conferences and local and state meetings/events are strategies to cultivate long-term interest in and funding for the initiative Lead agency implements process of continuous improvement as accountability measure; signature programs attract funding and champions
Integration		Dialogues with school and school system about directing discretionary funds to CS	School and CBO funds are combined for special programming	CBO approaches school district to see what in kind or monetary support it can contribute to institutionalize the partnership
Objectives	Have enough money to keep programs going	Receive substantial funding for at least 3 years for planning and implementation Partner with organizations with independent funding; develop critical mass of supporters Pursue additional funding	Demonstrate high levels of accountability, deepen the confidence and support of current funder Implement sustainability plan Be awarded funding Develop signature programs to attract funding	Implement aggressive sustainability plan with developer/grant writer Involve champions and advocates in development activities Secure committed funding for upcoming 2–3 years Pursue emerging trends and their funding streams when consistent with lead agency's core competencies and mission

Boston Public Schools

Extended-Service Schools
as a District-Wide Strategy

THOMAS W. PAYZANT
Superintendent, Boston Public Schools

Approaches to education reform rarely follow a simple, linear path. Rather than pursuing one approach single-mindedly over an extended period of years, school reform—informed by research, changes in public policy, and differences in the dynamic needs of students from changing communities—tends to be characterized by continuous change and sometimes seems to recycle approaches that have been tried before.

For those of us who have worked toward education reform throughout our careers, this process of change does not betray a lack of consistency or

219

commitment but constitutes a necessary response to the continually changing conditions in which public schools must operate. The demographics of
our schools are dynamic, particularly because of escalating numbers of immigrants from around the world. Our fiscal circumstances are in continual
flux. Community expectations of what schools should provide are subject to
change as well, often through a growing national awareness of the connection between the quality of America's schools and the character of our democratic institutions.

Focused Service or Extended Service?

Two of the most significant reform strategies to emerge during the past
decade may seem contradictory: on the one hand, those strategies that concentrate relentlessly on instructional improvement, and, on the other hand,
those that seek to establish the school as a community centerpiece for addressing a broad range of personal, social, and family needs that relate
to the health of the community as a whole. At first glance these two
strategies—a narrow focus on teaching and learning contrasted with a wider
focus through what are called extended-service or full-service schools—
appear to be at cross-purposes.

Poor student performance, particularly when combined with difficult economic times, gives rise to a set of tough questions that all educational leaders sooner or later must confront: Can schools be all things to all people?
Are educators being asked to take on too much? Can schools be expected to
solve all of society's problems with very limited resources? Is it not better for
schools to do a few things well, rather than taking on too much and risking
superficial results?

The flip side of these very reasonable questions is the reality that children in ever growing numbers are coming to school unprepared for academic
learning at a time when nearly every school is expected to set high standards
for all students and the public expects accountability for results based on assessment of student achievement. Students' noneducational realities, such
as nutritional deficiencies, medical problems, safety concerns, even daily
hunger, are daunting barriers that can obstruct even the most flexible educational program.

It is urgently essential that educators find a sensible and effective way to
balance the competing demands of basic skills and basic human needs. In
an era when resources on both sides of this equation—schooling and family services—are in short supply, the only possible solution is for schools to
find new and powerful ways to make use of all the resources available to
them. Much more thoughtful and persistent work must be done to strengthen
and streamline the connections for families between the classroom and the
providers and funders of extended services. Without these connections, the
struggles that schools and families face will only intensify.

Boston's Focus on Children

Since 1996 most of the public schools in Boston have wrestled with this challenge. The highest priority of the Boston Public Schools' comprehensive plan for school reform issued in July 1996, *Focus on Children,* was improvements in teaching and learning in order for students to reach high academic standards. *Focus on Children* also established engagement with the community as a necessary means of addressing nonacademic barriers to achievement. Since then it has become increasingly clear that many schools will be able to focus on teaching and learning only if other organizations and individuals work aggressively with the schools in stronger and more focused collaborations.

The primary challenge now being addressed in Boston's public schools is taking the teaching and learning reforms described in *Focus on Children* to scale, which includes improved student achievement in all schools, in every classroom, for every child. The difficulty of meeting this challenge, especially in a stringent economic climate, underscores the need for schools to collaborate closely with external partners, rather than trying to accomplish too much on their own. If schools are focused in addressing their teaching and learning challenges and are open and ready to engage with the community in carefully articulated partnerships, the extended-service school model can begin to take hold.

Partnerships in the Boston Public Schools

Partnerships between schools and external organizations have been a mainstay of Boston's public schools since the emergence of the Boston Compact in 1982. The Compact was originally conceived as a quid pro quo between the Boston Public Schools and the city's business community: the agreement set measurable goals for school improvement in return for measurable increases in school support and youth employment opportunities from participating businesses. The Compact had a five-year sunset provision, so that every five years a new Compact agreement could be negotiated. Partners, no longer limited to businesses, now include local colleges and universities, the Boston Teachers Union, cultural institutions, and community-based organizations.

By the mid-1990s, the momentum for partnership development in Boston was so strong that schools were becoming distracted from their primary mission of teaching and learning. *Focus on Children* in 1996 called for an end to "projectitis," defined as the proliferation of discrete programs that provided small numbers of students with experiences that were not connected to instruction. In 2000 the Boston Compact Steering Committee called for partnerships that had specific connections to the instructional plans in every school and that were designed to have an impact on large rather than small numbers of participants.

For businesses the focus of partnership activity has been a successful set of career development programs. For universities the focus has largely been on curriculum, teacher training, and professional development. For community-based organizations the focus has been on bringing more support services to students and families.

Collaboration in Boston between a school and its community has sometimes been difficult, because the population of students served by most Boston schools does not come entirely from the contiguous community. One legacy of court-ordered desegregation in Boston is that most of the city's schools draw from neighborhoods other than their own, in some cases for a majority of their students. This is somewhat less true in elementary schools and more the case in high schools, with middle schools somewhere in between. The differences between where students live and where they go to school are not the result of jury-rigged student assignment zones; they result largely from providing parents with as much choice as possible, which has been a very high priority for Boston parents since the mid-1970s. Creating a student assignment plan that gives parents more choice has meant that nearly every Boston school draws upon a catchment area that extends well beyond its natural neighborhood and into several other areas of the city.

The trade-off for giving parents more choice has been that many Boston schools have not enjoyed the natural constituency of their surrounding community. Many nonprofit community-based agencies historically have been funded to support children and families based on residence, which creates mismatches between schools and the service areas of support agencies. If students attend school in one area of the city and then return to their home neighborhoods or to other locations chosen by parents for after-school programs, connections between schools and after-school academic services are more difficult to maintain.

In this context schools have sometimes been wary of external forces that, because of potentially conflicting demands, might have a divisive effect and create a drain on limited resources needed for teaching and learning. *Focus on Children* aimed to challenge this way of thinking about external relationships and give schools strong encouragement to find meaningful connections with their communities, even if exactly what constituted a community for a school might need careful deliberation.

The Gardner School and Its Partners

One of the Boston schools that took this encouragement to heart was the Thomas A. Gardner Elementary School, located in the large and diverse Allston-Brighton neighborhood. Allston-Brighton is the home of one major institution of higher education, Boston University, and the immediate neighbor of another, Boston College. Allston-Brighton constitutes one of the

Boston Public Schools' nine clusters—groups of elementary and middle schools in a given neighborhood where some feeder patterns are possible even within the guidelines of broader parental school choice. Cluster 5 consists of 12 schools, including Gardner elementary, along with Brighton High School (all high schools in Boston are citywide for purposes of student assignment).

In 1996 the Gardner School embarked upon a partnership with Boston College and several Allston-Brighton community organizations that was unique, even for a city rich in partnerships of all imaginable permutations. It is significant that this effort began with a request for help from the principal, Catalina Montes, because it demonstrated a recognition within the school that help from the external community was sorely needed. Like most Boston schools, the Gardner School was struggling with the prospect of high-stakes testing (the Massachusetts Comprehensive Assessment System, which would institutionalize graduation standards by 2003), as well as the problems attendant upon a growing population of new arrivals to Boston who were settling in the Allston-Brighton area and choosing the Gardner School. Ms. Montes first approached Professor Mary E. Walsh of Boston College's Lynch School of Education; this initial request set in motion a sequence of conversations, meetings, connections, agreements, and relationships that resulted in the evolution of the Gardner School from a traditional elementary program into an extended-service school.

The partnership that evolved at the Gardner School was modeled on the highly successful program developed by The Children's Aid Society (CAS) in New York City, in which various institutions including schools, universities, and community organizations come together to provide integrated support services to children and their families. Boston College has a long history of successful projects linking the college and a number of Boston's public schools and has been a seminal member of the Boston Higher Education Partnership since its founding in 1983. But the partnership envisioned by the planners for the Gardner initiative would be both deeper and broader than previous school-college partnerships in Boston. Early in the planning process, a goal was established—that the program could, if successful at Gardner, be extended to schools throughout Cluster 5.

Underwritten by the DeWitt Wallace-Reader's Digest Fund, the initiative at the 500-student, kindergarten–grade 5 Gardner School was planned jointly by the school, Boston College, and the Allston-Brighton Healthy Boston Neighborhood Coalition. Its key elements were described by its leading planners—Mary E. Walsh, Mary M. Brabeck, Kimberly A. Howard, and Francine T. Sherman from Boston College; Catalina Montes from the Gardner School; and Timothy J. Garvin from the Allston-Brighton Family YMCA:

> The extended service school . . . (a) developed programs for children (before school, after school, and summer), (b) arranged for new or expanded school-based or school-linked services (dental and medical care, mental health, and social services), (c) developed

evening programs for parents and other adults (ESL, GED, immigration counseling, housing, access, and health education), and (d)
raised matching funds. The Steering Committee . . . comprised of
representatives from the four institutional partners (school, university, community agencies, and the community coalition) continues to meet on a regular basis and is being evaluated by both internal (university-based) and external evaluators. The university has
also provided a cadre of "coaches" (Boston College faculty and staff)
to the school to assist with implementation of new curriculum standards, frameworks, and teaching methods and has provided faculty
to work with school staff in developing new models of student support to address the nonacademic barriers to learning.[1]

The Gardner School now provides a base for the university's continuing
research on communities and schools. On its side Boston College, particularly the Lynch School of Education, which provides intern teachers and social workers to the Gardner School and other Boston schools, has broadened
its approach to educational research in order to deepen its commitment to
the practice as well as the theory of education.

Cluster 5: Taking the Extended-Service
School Model to Scale

The community partners engaged in developing the extended-service school
at Gardner elementary began planning expansion to other schools in the cluster soon after the project was operational. A planning grant to examine the
feasibility of expansion, to raise funds, and to organize the work was provided anonymously by a foundation based in Boston, and soon a major grant
was awarded to the steering committee by the Charles Hayden Foundation.
Additional funders included the Herman and Frieda L. Miller Foundation,
Verizon, and the Collaborative Fellows Program. The goal was to create an
effective student support model in every school in the cluster that wanted
one and was ready to do the work.

The emerging program, which now includes nearly all of the Cluster 5
schools, employs an executive director, school-based coordinators at each
school, and parent liaisons, and it operates a family instructional support
center to identify and coordinate connections to health and social service
providers for students and their families. The coordinators provide case management services for students, coordinating whole-school programming and
out-of-school activities. The Community Resource Coordinating Council,
which includes the school, university, community agency, and medical
providers, supplies services to families and promotes connections with city
and state agencies and the business community.

One potentially problematic issue that was dealt with early on in the expansion of Cluster 5 was whether community organizations could serve children who were not from the Allston-Brighton community. Many community-

based agencies have a defined mission that limits them to serving youth and families within a target neighborhood. Because of the impact of parental choice, many students come into the Allston-Brighton cluster from other neighborhoods in the city. The steering committee partners decided to serve all children in the school regardless of where they lived; this may sound like a simple decision, but it is one that required a genuine stretch for neighborhood nonprofits.

Patrice DeNatale, principal of the Horace Mann School for the Deaf and Hard of Hearing and cluster leader for Cluster 5, has been an active participant in implementing the rollout of the extended-service model in her school as well as across the cluster. She said,

> A major challenge for everyone involved in the program has been to always keep our focus on reaching all the children who need help. The community agencies all have their own missions, and their own service base, and each school has its instructional program to manage and its own Resource Advisory Council to convene. So the mutual interest of working collaboratively has to be carefully and supportively defined, and a big part of the work has to be a sustained commitment on the part of all the engaged organizations to work through any interagency tensions and challenges that may emerge.[2]

The challenges the program faces seem fairly typical of any expansion effort that moves from one to multiple sites. The level of implementation varies from one school to another; as the Gardner School demonstrates continuing refinements, other Cluster 5 schools run the spectrum from fully engaged to still struggling with start-up issues. Other challenges are the continuing shortage of seats in after-school programs for students who need them and the high cost of transportation for after-school activities.

Funding

Not surprisingly, the greatest obstacle to long-term successful conversion from traditional schools to extended-service schools is funding. As with all new ideas and innovative practices, it is easier to create initiatives than it is to institutionalize them into long-term systemic operations. While the extended-service schools have been resourceful in capturing funds from a variety of sources, most of these sources sooner or later will reach their point of sunset.

When the economy is robust, as it was during the late 1990s, public institutions at the local, state, and federal level can be pursued as revenue sources to support innovation. In times of declining revenue when the economy has slowed, even the philanthropic community, whose portfolios depend to some extent on the investment marketplace, experiences shortfalls and tightens its purse strings. For school districts and individual schools, when budgets grow tight, funding the basic instructional program comes first, and other services may soon be perceived as extras that are someone else's responsibility.

Yet, once a school has undergone the transformation from traditional program to extended-service operation, it is extremely difficult, even painful, to imagine retreating to a singular focus on what takes place inside the classroom. Fortunately for Cluster 5, as of mid-2003, the private grants had yet to run their course and funds were still available. What happens, however, when the funding cycles are completed? Is it a reasonable systemic strategy to have successful innovation continue to be dependent on a patchwork of private external funds cobbled and re-cobbled together each year? Conversely, can a school district in the midst of teacher layoffs and massive cuts in personnel manage to pick up even part of the difference?

Boston: Changing the District to Improve Services in All Schools

Reorganization of Services

An important part of solving the problem of funding extended-service schools throughout a district comes from rethinking the way services are organized throughout the system. In 1999 the Boston Public Schools initiated a major reorganization of special education, counseling, and support services into a new team designed to provide a full continuum of support services for students, with or without disabilities. While no reorganization in and of itself can substitute for the expertise, resources, and perspectives that external organizations can provide to schools, the Unified Student Services Team was created with the goal of providing extensive support to the reform agenda outlined in *Focus on Children* and serving as a means for eliminating administrative redundancies and improving management and delivery of services to every school.

In 1999 almost 14,000 of the nearly 64,000 students in Boston's public schools were identified through the special education evaluation process; this translated into an egregiously disproportionate percentage (almost 22%) of children in special education. Part of the reason was the legacy of Massachusetts law on special education, which used a much broader and more literal definition of disabilities than the federal definition. For many years, special education in Massachusetts had been seen as the only option for acquiring services for students who may not have had an actual disability but who were for a wide variety of reasons underachieving. The high cost of serving children in special education, many of whom did not have disabilities, drained resources that could have been used to serve *all* children more effectively.

The Unified Student Services Team brought together in one operation the related services of student support, school counseling, health and medical services, alternative education, and special education. The focus also changed: rather than being seen as a separate system within a system, special education services were now viewed as part of a continuum of services, aimed at helping schools connect all students to the best possible programs to support their growth, safety, and academic achievement. These connections include identifying students for, and enrolling them in, after-hours programs; this is based upon the recognition, learned in part from the experience of extended-service schools in Boston and New York, that when after-hours services are brokered and coordinated directly by schools and school people, the educational and social dividends of the extended day can be significantly amplified.

One benefit of the reorganization of services into the Unified Student Services Team was that as services within Boston improved, the disproportionate number of out-of-district placements declined and more funds were used for Boston schools rather than for out-of-district programs. The differential between the more expensive private placements and the more cost-effective placements within the Boston Public Schools has been directed into the schools, creating a modest but important revenue stream.

At each Boston school, school-level Student Support Teams serve as the focal point for discussion of students' academic and nonacademic needs. The agenda for these teams includes special education, alternative education, physical health, mental health, and external partnerships. The mission of the Unified Student Services Team includes serving as the catalyst to connect schools and external agencies and partners to help steer students and their families to appropriate services.

Focus on Literacy

Another reason for the historically high levels of students referred to special education in Boston was the lack of a focused literacy plan throughout the district. Without a systematic approach to basic skills achievement, in math as well as English, students with a lack of reading progress for many years were placed in special needs classrooms for individualized literacy instruction. Thus, the lack of a focused literacy plan not only caused more referrals to special education but also limited the district's ability to deal with diverse literacy needs; too few safety net programs and too few prereferral interventions were available. Simply put, a student's inability to read became a license for referral to special education, rather than an impetus to analyze the teaching part of teaching and learning and make better instructional decisions to help the student to read.

The implementation of *Focus on Children* changed this practice, and it has been further refined and sharpened with the development of *Focus on Children II* in 2001. Literacy across the curriculum and an intensive program in mathematics, from the elementary level through high school, have been the district's primary goal since 2001. The emphasis on literacy creates an educational program in which community-based programs, business partners, after-school programs run by the City of Boston, and volunteer organizations can have a more effective role. Read Boston, a citywide literacy initiative created and sponsored jointly by city, school, and private institutions, now provides a means by which community organizations, families, and schools can address literacy challenges both during and after school hours.

The greater concentration on literacy and mathematics has also helped schools prepare students to meet the high standards of the Massachusetts Comprehensive Assessment System (MCAS) tests, while encouraging them to find ways to connect partners to this effort. An example of the community's expanding role is the Summer of Work and Learning program established by the Private Industry Council in 2001. Concerned about high MCAS failure rates, several major corporations in Boston (Gillette, Verizon, and the Federal Reserve Bank) that participate in the Private Industry Council's Boston Summer Jobs Program agreed to free their Boston summer teenage workforce for 90 minutes a day of literacy training designed to help them prepare for the MCAS tests. Boston teachers conducted the teaching, while the Private Industry Council identified tenth and eleventh grade students who had already failed MCAS to work at the participating firms. The results after the first year were salutary, and the program expanded the following year. In the summer of 2003, over 80% of the students, all of whom had previously failed MCAS several times, managed to pass the retests. The Private Industry Council plans to expand the program further, involving more corporations and including students from earlier grades.

Funding

Connections between schools and the community are greatly enhanced by a systematic program of literacy and mathematics and a unified approach to support services. Yet such district-level changes are not in and of themselves enough to provide a structure that can take the place of the network of extended-service schools now operating in Cluster 5. When the grant funding is no longer available, there will still be costs for services, including after-school programming, in-school coaching, student support personnel to case-manage services, and for the all-important elements of convening, staffing, and connecting the community-university-school advisory committees so that the partners are fully engaged in the work and can have routine access to the school, the students, and their families in order to provide their services.

In Boston after-school programs have been enhanced and coordinated by the establishment of Mayor Thomas Menino's 2 to 6 initiative, which is aimed at increasing the number, quality, and educational connections of after-school programs. Funding has been provided by business and philanthropic grants as well as by the city of Boston, while funds for middle-school programs have been provided through federal sources such as the 21st Century Community Learning Centers program.

Like teaching in a classroom, coordinating all the elements of an extended-service school is labor-intensive work. The Boston Public Schools, through its reorganization of services and its focus on literacy, provides a greatly improved platform for the connections and relationships that an extended-service school can make. The most critical issue that schools and community partners must wrestle with in order to avoid having valuable services be considered "add-ons" is *alignment*: Is the work outside the classroom aligned with the goals of the child? The answer to the concern expressed by many school-based people— Are schools expected to do too much?—is that if services are closely aligned with the educational mission, the child benefits directly. Without this alignment, children and families can feel as if they are pulled in multiple directions, caught amid a variety of agencies and services that are not working together, especially at a time when resources are disappearing.

One potential revenue stream available to communities for funding some of the work of extended-service schools is Medicaid reimbursements. Boston, like most major cities around the nation, has made effective use of Medicaid reimbursements to pay for aspects of medical care for special needs students. Because Boston has so many major hospitals and schools of medicine, the public schools attract families with medically fragile children who can receive high-quality medical care as part of their Individual Education Plans. Most of Boston's public high schools now have school-based health clinics, and several middle schools now have them as well. These clinics work closely with the city's network of community health centers, which are vehicles for providing mental health counseling for students in the context of providing support for families.

School-based direct services, such as occupational therapy, physical therapy, speech therapy, and adaptive physical education therapy, are all reimbursable under Medicaid. School districts also may qualify for Medicaid reimbursements for transportation of special needs children on days when they receive medical services and for administrative activities such as time spent processing referrals to medical care. Some capital claims are also eligible for reimbursement, including the use of school rooms such as nurses' offices or physical therapy rooms and use of other school spaces to provide medical care. In extended-service schools such as those in Cluster 5, Medicaid reimbursements may be a means of paying for services now paid for out of their school budgets.

This funding source, however, is also an example of the problems that can arise for schools and school districts when the alignment is inadequate between federal and state levels. In Massachusetts a school district that follows state Department of Education regulations regarding special education services may soon find itself out of alignment with the federal Division of Medical Assistance, which oversees reimbursements for Medicaid. School districts are forced to become experts in complying with state and federal auditing procedures in order to provide medical care to students with special needs and be properly reimbursed for them. This failure of alignment may occur between different state agencies as well as between state and federal agencies. Nevertheless, tenacious schools and school districts whose record keeping is in good order can use Medicaid as a source of support for children who need these services.

To meet the long-term funding challenges, the most compelling question may be, Who *should* pay for these services? The answer relates to the organization, practices, and funding mechanisms of public services and institutions whose mandates are beyond the control of any school district but whose missions are—or should be—intimately connected with them.

The Long-Term Challenge: Changing Institutions to Improve Public Services

As a person who manages a large and complex public institution, I am mindful of the reality that any organization operating on public funds must deal with an enormous knot of mandates, laws, and bureaucratic requirements that can have an impact on how its customers feel about the institution itself. Spending the public's money *should* require a lot of public accountability. Yet in most cities throughout the United States, similarities among public services and among the populations these services are designed to help has led to too many agencies doing the same things for the same people. The result is that the neediest families in our cities are the ones who are most often caught up in the tangled web of our social service systems.

The issue with major public service agencies is not that they are clumsily operated but that their missions often overlap. In Massachusetts there are separate departments for mental health, hospitals, social services, youth services, and children's services, and all of them are operated without any formal or institutional liaison with the public school districts. These are primarily state-level agencies, and they are in most cases connected to comparable federal departments and agencies. Their number and mandates reflect the complexities in state and federal policy, and their services, while often addressing the needs of the same families, are funded by different federal and state revenue streams. Massachusetts is not unique; virtually every state has multiple departments with overlapping purposes, which mirror the federal agencies and the revenue streams that fuel them. Many students served in every city are "multiagency-involved kids" whose families must deal with many different public agencies in order to receive basic services. This complexity can be daunting. A major purpose of case management services in extended-service schools is to use the considerable knowledge that schools develop about individual children to help families cope with these complex relationships and demands.

In order for schools to deal effectively with nonacademic barriers to education, they need to know how to access services such as psychological counseling, family therapy, immigration assistance, translator services, probation oversight, drug testing, and medical insurance. Finding the right professional help outside of a school is not an easy task. Accessing these services often means that school staff must deal with a different public agency for each one and, often, with multiple divisions within each public agency.

While the solution may seem obvious—streamline them all!—in fact it is not just administrative or even budgetary entanglements but also redundancies of policy and of law at both the federal and state level that create the predicaments for communities, schools, and families. The dilemma that social service advocates have faced for years is that when some form of agency streamlining or realignment is accomplished, it often has the undesirable consequence of creating a call for reducing funding allocations.

Follow the Child

The model for connecting and rationalizing different services that is being used in extended-service schools might offer a solution to this labyrinth of policy, practice, and expense. Most extended-service schools use a team approach, such as Boston's Student Support Teams, to address students' multiple needs; it is modeled on the educational team concept that has been the hallmark of special education for nearly three decades. School districts may be able to use this same child-centered approach by convening the respective public agencies serving a city's families, identifying problems on a case-study basis, and case-managing services in ways that cut across institutional identities and cut through red tape.

This will only happen to any significant extent if public agency funding follows the child. This funding approach is not new in education: special education funds have followed the education plans of children on an individual basis for decades; charter school funding in Massachusetts follows the student (although the formula needs refining so that it does not disadvantage public school systems). Boston Public Schools has been looking seriously at a wholly different approach to school budgeting, based on the model now used by the school district's network of Pilot Schools, which operate like in-district charter schools. The budgets of Pilot Schools are student-centered, rather than school-centered, and are driven by a pupil allocation rather than a staff or school allocation. The same approach could be put in place for state-level agencies that serve families and children. Instead of carving up the annual state revenue into departmental entitlements that grow or shrink depending on the economy and legislative priorities, departments would receive their operating budgets as reimbursements for the people they actually serve, with premiums built in to assure that agencies work collaboratively with one another to combine services instead of competing for families and schools.

For some this approach—funding that follows the child—may encourage comparison with voucher programs. Voucher programs are designed to provide a source of funds for parents that enables them to widen their choices among schools. There are important differences, however. The problem with voucher programs is not that the concept of earmarking funds for individual students is wrong but that voucher systems are not based on a level playing field. Most educational voucher programs provide only partial funding for a child's schooling, which means that parents with greater financial resources have more choices than those who must depend on public funds for schooling. Voucher programs are largely intended to fund educational seats in private and parochial schools, which are not accountable to the public for educational results as public schools are. They are premised on the myth that there are enough attractive choices for all children, when in fact there are limited seats available; in addition, most of the available seats are in schools whose entrance criteria limit access while skewing enrollment in favor of families with higher incomes and students with higher academic entry skills.

The concept of funding the child, rather than the state agency or department, would still allow for the high level of fiscal accountability that the public can reasonably demand from its governmental institutions. If the result were that families would be able to look to their schools and their local community providers rather than to a complex system of bureaucratic agencies, this would be an enormous dividend.

Looking to the Future

The development of more extended-service schools and new funding approaches to providing services to children will require long-term, community-based strategic planning. To that end, Boston in 2001 convened an informal group of Boston Public Schools educators, full-service-school providers, city and state administrators, and advocates to develop a long-term strategy for increasing the number of full-service schools throughout the city. Now known as the Boston Full Service Schools Roundtable, the group has been working on plans to provide schools, community organizations, funders, public agencies, and the public with up-to-date information and technical assistance on aligning schools and services and on identifying potential funding sources to expand the work to more schools and to involve more partner organizations.

The only way for schools to improve their educational mission for children is to engage with the children in the communities where they live. To do this requires a commitment from everyone in a school to the whole child, as well as a recognition that the instructional program within the school must be connected to a program of health and well-being in the community and family. The policies, guidelines, and implementation strategies of state departments and public agencies that serve children and families must be much better aligned in order to avoid a tangled knot of onerous bureaucratic requirements for schools, families, and local agencies that serve them. For community partners, there are requirements as well: that the valuable services agencies and professionals provide must wherever appropriate be informed by and aligned with the child's educational program, so that children and families are not pulled apart by conflicting social services and agendas. The extended-service school movement, as it grows in Boston and throughout the nation, is premised upon the hope that if good people work together, the systems serving us all will be enhanced and made more accessible to everyone.

NOTES

1. Mary E. Walsh et al., "The Boston College–Allston-Brighton Partnership: Description and Challenges," *Peabody Journal of Education* 75, no. 3 (2000): 6–32.
2. Patrice DeNatale, interview by author, January 2003.

Bill Foley

Schools as Centers of Community: Planning and Design

STEVEN BINGLER
President, Concordia LLC

The Challenge

As we stand at the beginning of the twenty-first century, we face a national challenge in planning and designing learning environments that meet the needs of all learners. Throughout the country, elementary and high school districts are spending unprecedented amounts of money to renovate existing school facilities or build new ones. In 2001 alone roughly $27 billion worth of kindergarten through grade 12 construction projects were approved and funded, a trend that is likely to continue for several years.

In 2000 public and private kindergarten through grade 12 school enrollment reached a record 53 million students. The Department of Education projects that 55 million children will enroll in 2020 and 60 million in 2030.[1] By 2100 the pattern of steady growth is expected to result in a total of 94 million school-age children, an increase of 41 million students over the century. It is also projected that diversity will increase, with most of the growth among Hispanic children. They represented about 15% of the public school population in 2000; that proportion is expected to grow to 24% by 2020.

This steady increase in the number and diversity of school children, all of whom need and deserve a quality education, suggests that the design of new school facilities and the modernization of old ones will be an ongoing process in communities across the United States. One important component of this challenge is the need to rethink how we plan learning environments to coincide with some new ways of thinking about education. It seems as if such a short time has passed since Howard Gardner introduced the theory of multiple intelligences at a time when other educational strategies, including project-based learning, cooperative learning, primary source learning, real world experiential learning, and their many variations, were enjoying a renaissance or were in the developmental stages.[2] Many of these teaching and learning strategies have found their way into the mainstream as powerful tools that help to create more meaning-centered and personalized learning for students and educators alike. This new group of educational strategies is more diverse, more integrated, and, perhaps, more compelling than their more predictable predecessors.

More than a new trend in education, this shift to more integrated learning models tracks a parallel mode of thought that has been evolving nationally at all levels of planning and design. Emerging from the failure of the isolated planning and development strategies in public education, public housing, public health, social welfare, and other community need domains that negatively impacted our nation's quality of life in the twentieth century, this new wave of thought is moving us closer to more integrative and participatory strategies in the planning and design of learning environments. We want to rid ourselves of the duplicated efforts of governments and planning bodies and involve a wide array of participants in the process. This movement fits right into the full-service community school conceptual framework.

Innovative Strategies

The factory model of education is finally being properly examined and admonished for its failure to address the individual needs of children and families, especially those in low-income rural and inner city neighborhoods, who are in search of effective learning opportunities. Large classes and large schools, once seen as the panacea for increasing curriculum options and financial efficiency, have become the subject of serious scrutiny, and a new movement toward smaller and more intimate learning settings has emerged with unprecedented speed. A similar consensus seems to be building around the long-held suspicion that large school districts may also be too cumbersome to manage the more intimate and urgent needs of neighborhoods and small communities.

In the meantime, innovative learning environments are being planned and developed, including new and smaller designs for school sites. Another category of design focuses on the integration of community needs, such as community health clinics, recreation, and adult education, into the learning environment. Still other innovative solutions abandon the traditional stand-alone school site altogether and co-locate learning environments with a wide range of the community's physical, cultural, social, economic, organizational, and educational resources, such as shopping centers, museums, and zoos.

To date the development of a strategy for integrating learning and community programming has been executed largely through the development of stand-alone models rather than system-wide initiatives. These models represent different degrees of integration among community and educational needs.

Examples

Primary School 5

The Ellen Lurie School, Primary School (PS) 5, a Children's Aid Society (CAS) community school, opened in 1993 (see Moses, ch. 2 in this volume). It was the CAS model with the most intentional community school design. A large, urban elementary school serving prekindergarten through grade 5, PS 5 is located in the northern Manhattan neighborhood of Washington Heights in New York City and serves a community comprised primarily of recently arrived immigrants from the Dominican Republic.

Because it was specifically designed to be a full-service community school, PS 5 offers many school-design features, as listed below, that support its programmatic emphasis.

- The exterior of the school is decorated in primary colors (passersby often refer to PS 5 as the "Lego School")
- The interior of the school is equally cheerful and offers students a stimulating print-rich environment
- There are special classrooms, entrances, and playgrounds for the school's early childhood programs
- The medical and dental clinic has colorful, age-appropriate space on the ground floor of the school
- A family resource room or "family room," also centrally located, provides parents and other family members with a place to meet, socialize, and participate in workshops

- The principal (employed by the New York City Department of Education) and the community school director (employed by CAS) have offices right next to each other to facilitate joint planning
- Brightly lit hallways are lined with bulletin boards and built-in glass showcases displaying students' short stories, vocabulary lessons, and other exercises

In this school student transitions are eased by the comprehensiveness of the program at PS 5 and by the school's design. One of the key concepts is integration of school and support mechanisms. Kindergarten classrooms situated just down the hall from the Head Start rooms let students become familiar with the staff and the building from an early age. The family resource center helps to make the school a friendly and welcoming place for parents and the community. Operated by CAS and school staff, parents, and volunteers, it offers a space for parents to learn about the full range of school activities and programs available to them and their children and serves as a gathering place for parents to socialize and network.

Tenderloin School

The Tenderloin School in downtown San Francisco is a new school designed to support interaction among school and community needs. This kindergarten through grade 5 facility is augmented by a children's center for three- and four-year-olds. The Tenderloin community is composed largely of recent immigrants from Southeast Asia. The school district wanted an efficient, secure kindergarten through grade 5 elementary school; the community wanted a school, a child development center, and on-site services for children and their families, including medical and dental facilities, counseling rooms, adult education facilities, family resource center, community garden, and community kitchen. The architectural planning and design accommodates all of the above, including a parking garage and open rooftop playgrounds on a highly visible and very compact site.

The Tenderloin's new community school enables parents to participate in their children's education—something previously denied them because of the distance their children were bused to school. Challenging traditional notions of school as a closed fortress, the school—in its diverse program, strong community influence, and physical design—opens its doors to express the innovation and learning that is happening within.

Downtown School

The Inter-district Downtown School in Minneapolis, Minnesota, is also a new facility that integrates learning and community needs. Designed for a maximum of 600 students, the five-story, 102,500-square-foot building emerged from collaborative effort that included 10 school districts. On the upper levels are instructional houses for six multiage groups of 100 students each, while the street level has shared whole-school and community-use space. The whole-school space and instructional houses provide environments for students to learn while doing, with flexible groupings for different teaching and learning styles.

Rather than isolating students from the surrounding environment, this multicultural magnet kindergarten through grade 12 school also leverages its location to fully integrate educational programs and architecture with the downtown neighborhood. Through partnerships with many local organizations, agencies, and businesses, the learning environment is extended into the larger urban fabric of programs and facilities. The nearby Orchestra Hall serves as the auditorium, the YMCA as the gymnasium, Loring Park as open space, and the Downtown Library as an adjunct to expand the resources of the on-site collection. The result is a learning environment that costs less money to build and operate, conserves natural resources, and provides enriching real world experiences for learners and educators in a setting that is more authentic and compelling than more traditional stand-alone counterparts.

MET Center

The MET Center in Providence, Rhode Island, was developed by the Big Picture Company, a leading innovator in best learning practices; the center consists of a system of small public high schools (grades 9–12) serving an economically and socially diverse student population. The Big Picture Company's philosophy is to educate one student at a time, with each student's curriculum reflecting his or her unique interests, background, and learning style.[3] As a part of their learning plan, students at the MET spend three days each week at their small, self-contained "home base" learning center, where overall enrollment is limited to approximately 120 students; they participate in extended learning experiences for a minimum of two days each week at an outside community-based learning site, such as a hospital, professional office, governmental institution, restaurant, or other similar venue. At these extended-learning sites, they follow an innovative and highly personalized learning-through-internship model, in which the student, advisor, and parent collaborate to support the student's learning through an integrated curriculum based on real-world experiences. In the MET "teachers" are replaced by "advisors" whose responsibility is to facilitate and assess each student's learning plan in his or her "advisory." An advisory, which contains a maximum of 14 students, starts in the ninth grade and remains together until graduation. The trust that is developed during this period between advisor and students helps optimize students' motivation and investment in their own learning.

The Big Picture Company believes that the physical design of a learning environment shapes learning. All aspects of each individual school are designed for personalization. The MET Center's first community-based learning environment began operations in two inner-city home base campuses in Providence, one in an existing downtown office building and the other in a stand-alone facility. A third new campus, located in a challenging inner-city neighborhood in South Providence, adds four independent, stand-alone small schools, along with shared community facilities that include a fitness center, performing arts center, health center, media center, and outdoor recreational spaces. In addition to accommodating the school's fitness and athletic programs, the outdoor spaces double as a community "town square" in the evenings and on weekends. With "parking streets" that crisscross the site, rather than large parking lots, and a notable lack of fences, the school is clearly open to and supportive of the community that it serves.

Taconic Hills Kindergarten through Grade 12

The new Taconic Hills Central School in Craryville, New York, is the culmination of an effort begun more than 30 years ago when two rural districts merged to resolve problems of overcrowding and deteriorated school buildings.[4] After 11 unsuccessful referenda, a new alternative was developed and approved that called for the creation of a new kindergarten through grade 12 building at a central site. This building provides the students and communities with a wide range of resources and also offers the opportunity to generate revenue through community use of the facility.

The property encompasses a state-of-the art performing arts center that opens to an outdoor amphitheater, an aquatic/fitness center, two technology-rich media centers, and three subdividable gyms. The building is designed as two schools and a community center within a single building.

The Abbott Decision

The possibilities for constructing new community schools or remodeling old buildings have been greatly enhanced by some state efforts. One of the most far-reaching initiatives can be found in New Jersey. Beginning in 1985, in a remarkable series of seven major decisions known as *Abbott v. Burke,* the New Jersey Supreme Court ordered a comprehensive set of programs and reforms to close the achievement gap between urban and suburban students. The Education Law Center in Newark, New Jersey, was the prime mover behind all of these cases.

The decisions call for "parity": per-pupil funding for poor districts equal to the state average (about $10,000 in 2002–2003). As of 2003, 30 communities were eligible to become Abbott Districts because of high levels of poverty and disadvantage. Each selected district, with funds provided by the state, must introduce Whole School Reform (WSR) as well as supplemental services to compensate for student disadvantage. High-quality preschool for three- and four-year-olds must be included. Of particular interest here is the fact that the state must support new and rehabilitated facilities to house all programs, relieve overcrowding, and eliminate building violations. In 2000 New Jersey's state legislature enacted the Educational Facilities Construction and Financing Act authorizing the state to finance and implement $6 billion of Abbott school-facilities improvements.

Abbott-supported facilities must be healthy and safe, have reasonable class size (21 for kindergarten–grade 3, 23 for grades 4–5, and 24 for grades

---

Box 16.1 Press Release Announcing a New Abbott-Supported School

October 22, 2002: Union City, New Jersey

Governor James E. McGreevey today celebrated the groundbreaking of a new middle school in Union City which will not only serve the educational needs of 6th, 7th, and 8th graders, but will include a library for residents and health center for the 11,000 students in the community.

"This new middle school is an example of a successful partnership between the State of New Jersey and Union City to provide our children with quality educational facilities," said McGreevey. "The State's full funding of this school construction project—$24.7 million—is not only being used to provide 6th, 7th, and 8th graders with a 21st Century school, but to provide the community with a new library and all of Union City's students with access to healthcare. The State's funding of this project is also providing $24.7 million in property tax relief to Union City's residents."

Superintendent Thomas Highton emphasized the importance of the community features of the new facility: "The architect and the community worked closely together to come up with a design that will serve this neighborhood around-the-clock," said Highton. "We will have great new classroom space for our students, and a public library and health care facility, as well."

The new school will also include 27 new classrooms, 11 special education/small group learning classrooms, 6 science and technology labs, music rooms (including practice rooms), a cafetorium with full-size stage, a full-size gymnasium suite, a library/media center, a health center, a computer lab, an "applied technology" lab, an interior courtyard, and a football/soccer field and softball field.

Source: State of New Jersey, office of James E. McGreevey, Governor, "McGreevey Breaks Ground in New Middle School in Union City, October 22, 2002," press release, http://www.state.nj.us/egi-bin/governor/njnewsline/view-article.pl?id=894.

6–12), have adequate space both for enhanced curricula and specialized needs, and provide space in schools or community agencies for preschool children year round. The process starts with a district-initiated Long Range Facilities Plan that must be approved by the state. The New Jersey Economic Development Authority is responsible for funding, design, and construction. See Box 16.1 for a description of an Abbott-supported facility.

New Planning Concepts: The Community Engagement Process

In order to move schools to the center of the community, a wide range of participants must be involved. This community engagement process requires a broad cross-section of community constituents to assemble at regular intervals to review data, investigate options, and make firm recommendations to the elected bodies responsible for carrying out the collective will of their constituents. In this model elected officials receive clear input and direction about their constituents' wants and needs as well as community ownership and buy-in. Although the engagement model is sometimes considered expensive and time consuming, its format of open dialogue usually means that issues are more thoroughly reviewed and resolved without protracted and costly delays resulting from infighting and lack of information and trust.

Another benefit of broad-based community engagement is that recommendations are often more systemic, incorporating a broad range of the community's physical, cultural, social, economic, organizational, and educational domains into elegant, cohesive, and efficient solutions. The community's resource domains are listed below.

- Physical resources, encompassing the total of the community's built assets, including buildings, bridges, highways, and telecommunications infrastructure, as well as natural resources such as parks and other outdoor recreation areas
- Cultural resources, encompassing programs and artifacts related to the expression of individual and communal values and aesthetics, including social, ethnic, and religious diversity
- Social resources, encompassing public health, public housing, social welfare, and other agencies and programs that deliver the kinds of support systems that people need to survive, including health care, human services, and housing
- Economic resources, encompassing programs and activities related to financial capital, as well as human and environmental capital, plus activities ranging from regional and local economic development programs to innovations and initiatives developed by private business and social and environmental entrepreneurs
- Organizational resources, encompassing the various components of community governance, such as the school board, city and county boards of supervisors, Rotary Club, Lions Club, political parties, and a myriad of other civic organizations. This category identifies how decisions made on behalf of the community at large are developed, deliberated, and implemented and helps ensure that the full range of visions, dreams, and desires of community stakeholders is incorporated into the decision-making process.
- Educational resources, encompassing early childhood, prekindergarten to grade 12, community college, university, and adult educational delivery systems, as well as all of the community's civil service training and public and private workforce and skills-development programs

These six domains of community resources encompass a wide cross-section of the community's most vital learning assets. Although individually they are components of every community system, it is the quality of their interactions that contributes most to the community's learning health and well-being. But in order to be effective, the identification, development, and integration of these diverse community assets must be in tune with the heartbeat of the total community organism; this is why they must be developed through the creative input of a wide range of community stakeholders. As in John Dewey's maxim, we need not only education in democracy but also democracy in education.

Examples of the Community Engagement Process

In the Walnut Hills area of Cincinnati, Ohio, the school district had a master plan that located a school in the neighborhood. The community engagement process (including a community inventory and a study of needs) led to the idea that there were better sites for the school; a new proposed location was across the street from a library and adjacent to a park with a YMCA that included a swimming pool on the same piece of property. The community said in essence, "Let's build a school where we can hook into these things."

In Littleton, New Hampshire, the community engagement process led to using the basement of a local business to house a high school economics program. In exchange, the high school's students provided the business owner with computer services. The school then was able to use its empty classroom for a NASA-sponsored geographic information systems program. The basement redesign took two months, with the community raising $500 and donating services to refurbish the space.

An Important Opportunity

In 1997 the U.S. Department of Education sponsored the development and publication of *Schools as Centers of Community—A Citizen's Guide for Planning and Design.*[5] The document, updated in 2003, was a collaboration with professional educators, policy wonks, educational planners, architects, and others in the field. It lays out a strategy and a set of six principles for the planning and design of contemporary environments for learning. These six design principles are predicated on three broadly accepted conditions: (a) learning is a lifelong process; (b) design is always evolving; and (c) resources are limited. (It should be pointed out here that the most energy-efficient and cost-effective building is the one we do not have to build because we can reshape an existing structure.)

The six design principles are relatively straightforward, but together they call for bold action to transform America's schools by asserting that, in order to meet the nation's needs for the twenty-first century, we must design learning environments that:

1. Enhance teaching and learning and accommodate the needs of all learners

2. Serve as centers of the community
3. Result from a planning and design process that involves all interested citizens
4. Provide for health, safety, and security
5. Make effective use of all available resources
6. Allow for flexibility and adaptability to changing needs

The opportunity that now exists to design learning environments that manifest the best practices outlined in current educational research is limited only by our collective imagination. Based on what we know about the benefits of parent and community engagement and the value of more integrated, project-based, and real-world learning experiences, we can see a compelling need to move forward with greater intent to develop more inclusive, extended, and integrated environments for living and learning.

As citizens and communities continue to demand higher levels of participation, the opportunity to engage extensive and diverse input in creating and maintaining community-based learning environments has never been greater.

The shift from a representative form of governance to one in which more voices participate in an authentic and creative dialogue of decision making parallels a long-standing revolution in American ideology that continues to unfold. Over 200 years the basis of our system has evolved from the needs of a small group of founding fathers to a consideration and protection of the civil rights of citizens of every race, gender, and creed. As the revolution continues, the integrative tools and methods of self-governance and civic engagement must continue to be defended, refined, reinvented, and implemented by the citizens, workers, administrators, and civic entrepreneurs of this and future generations.

NOTES

1. Department of Education, *A Back to School Report on the Baby Boom Echo: Growing Pains* (Washington, D.C., August 21, 2000), p. 10.
2. Howard Gardner, *Multiple Intelligence: The Theory in Practice* (New York: Basic Books, 1993).
3. *Big Picture Company,* http://www.bigpicture.org (accessed November 12, 2003).
4. The source for this section is *National Clearinghouse for Educational Facilities,* http://www.edfacilities.org (accessed November 14, 2003).
5. Department of Education, *Schools as Centers of Community—A Citizen's Guide for Planning and Design* (Washington, D.C., 2003), http://www.ed.gov/inits/construction/ctty-centers.html (accessed November 14, 2003).

Reaching Out to Create a Movement

MARTIN J. BLANK
Director, Coalition for Community Schools

If You Build It, They Will Come

In 1997, after their community school concepts received a cold shoulder at a school reform conference, Joy Dryfoos, C. Warren "Pete" Moses, and Ira Harkavy knew it was time for action. All three had been deeply involved in creating new school-community relationships. Joy Dryfoos had helped call national attention to the overlapping needs that put one of every four children at risk; her 1994 book *Full-Service Schools* outlined a community school approach to help meet those needs.[1] As chief operating officer of The Children's Aid Society (CAS), Pete Moses, together with CAS's chief executive officer, Philip Coltoff, had helped bring the resources of one of New York City's oldest child welfare agencies directly into neighborhood schools as part of a comprehensive educational approach. Ira Harkavy, director of the University of Pennsylvania's Center for Community Partnerships, was creating opportunities for University of Pennsylvania students and faculty to work with, and learn from, students and residents in Philadelphia schools, using the community as a resource. All three knew from experience that community schools offered an effective strategy for building strong schools, strong families, and strong communities and that these were essential for learning.

The group began thinking about how to jump-start a community school movement. After a second meeting a few weeks later, they were convinced that more like-minded people needed to be involved. They decided to hold a Community Schools Forum at Fordham University and invited about 30 people they thought would be interested. When 125 participants showed up, they knew they were on to something. This chapter tells how that experience helped launch the Coalition for Community Schools and its drive to put community schools at the center of a twenty-first-century education-reform agenda.

The Past as Prologue

In 1997 a "coalition for community schools" was a new idea, but community schools were not. Part of what drew so many to the Fordham summit was the opportunity to give new voice to time-tested approaches to connecting school and community and, participants hoped, to use them more broadly to address current concerns.

John Dewey, whose ideas helped create community schools, observed that "the true starting point of history is always some present situation with its problems."[2] Solving children's nonacademic problems was certainly a starting point for community schools, beginning with the efforts of Jane Addams and the settlement house movement in the late nineteenth century to bring health and social services to children and families in America's industrialized urban areas.[3] During the twentieth century, community school strategies went well beyond service delivery to help create what the founders of public education knew democracy required: an educated citizenry. Community schools fostered learning by reconnecting schools to their communities.

According to University of California–Los Angeles professor John Rogers, the community school vision has historically connected three ideas: the school as a physical and social center; the community as a source of curriculum; and the importance of engaging school and community partners in new roles. Early community school advocates tended to view each of these threads as part of an organic whole.[4] Nowhere was the connection between school and community demonstrated more clearly than at Benjamin Franklin High School in East Harlem in the 1930s (see Box 17.1).

Box 17.1 A Community School in Action

In the midst of the Depression, New York City's Benjamin Franklin High School was envisioned by principal Leonard Covello and local residents as "an education in social living." Located in a predominantly poor and immigrant East Harlem neighborhood, the school served as a social center, coordinating education and support services from settlement houses and health centers. Working with partners from Columbia and New York universities, as well as from many local agencies, the school developed a curriculum that involved students in community research projects as an integral part of their schooling. By bringing community residents together to address neighborhood issues and take action for positive change, "it challenged the negative stereotypes of East Harlem as an irredeemable slum." By 1942 the school had acquired strong political and public support and national recognition. World War II would soon draw attention away from community concerns to national defense. But for many students and their families, 1,300 new low-rent housing units and a shining new public school building open "every hour of every day of the year" stood as testament to what school and community working together could achieve. It is interesting to note that this school is now a CAS community school—the Manhattan Center for Science and Mathematics.

Source: John Puckett and Michael Johanek, "A Public Place, a Public Purpose: Leonard Covello and the American Community School," manuscript, 2002. See also John S. Rogers, "Community Schools: Lessons for the Past and Present," report to the Charles S. Mott Foundation, 1998.

Community education, developed in the mid-1930s, moved forward interest in community schooling, especially the notion of schools as social centers. In 1934 Frank Manley, a high school teacher from Flint, Michigan, and industrialist Charles Stewart Mott convinced the Flint school board to launch a pilot community education program in five schools. Funded by a $6,000 grant from Mott, the program worked with community members to plan recreation programs after school, on weekends, and during the summer as a way to prevent juvenile delinquency. The Flint approach garnered broad attention, and in 1965 the National Center for Community Education, supported by the Mott Foundation and located in Flint, was launched to provide leadership development and training to thousands of community school practitioners.[5] The center became a focal point for training grantees of the 21st Century Community Learning Centers program in 1998.

Moving toward the Twenty-First Century

Over the decades individual elements of a community school vision continued to influence many schools and practitioners. In the 1970s, for example, there was renewed interest in community schools as opportunities for greater parental control of, and community involvement in, educational decision making. However, integrated efforts to create schools as social centers, use the community as a source of curriculum, and engage the community in new ways were seldom undertaken. Innovations took place, such as Communities in Schools,[6] but were too seldom viewed as integral to the school's academic mission.

By the late 1980s, educators and others concerned about the well-being of children and families were beginning to look seriously at collaborative solutions to the problems of "a nation at risk." A wave of national school-community models emerged, including Beacon Schools, Schools of the Twenty-First Century, University-Assisted Community Schools, and the United Way–sponsored Bridges to Success initiative.[7] Local innovation in the field also flourished.[8]

By 1997 a renaissance in community schools was clearly underway, much of it fueled by reform efforts originating outside the education community. Throughout the twentieth century, the community school movement had ebbed and flowed. If this new movement were to stay on track in the twenty-first century, it would need a comprehensive vision to unite its various models and a vehicle to advance its message.

An Emerging Coalition

The Coalition for Community Schools began to take shape in 1997 in a series of strategy sessions among a small working group. Pat Edwards, associate director of the National Center for Community Education (NCCE) and program officer at the Mott Foundation, joined the original summit leaders. The Institute for Educational Leadership (IEL), based in Washington, D.C., through its president, Michael Usdan, offered to staff the project and to help generate support from major educational organizations. As IEL's director of School/Family/Community Connections, I was then leading a national community schools mapping project and working closely with the United Way on their Extended Services Schools initiative. I stepped up to coordinate the effort, which was originally dubbed the Emerging Coalition for Community Schools (two years and more than 100 partners later, the term "emerging" was formally removed from the name).

Core Assumptions

Several assumptions guided the fledgling Coalition's development. The founders believed that it should promote broad institutional and policy change. They saw the Coalition's defining contribution as its ability to organize under a single umbrella national, state, and local organizations, networks, and funders interested in promoting a community school vision. Therefore, the Coalition would be:

- *A coalition* for, *not* of, *community schools:* The Coalition is more than an association of community schools. In order to develop a strong policy and advocacy capacity, the Coalition aimed to engage organizations that, while not community schools themselves, could advance a national agenda.
- *A coalition of organizations, not individuals:* The National Community Education Association has long provided an important membership group for individual community schools and practitioners. However, with a single exception made for founding partner Joy Dryfoos, an independent researcher, the Coalition involves only organizations that agree to promote the community school vision and have the capacity to do so.
- *A coalition of partners, not members:* This language was intended to communicate the expectation that partner organizations would not merely lend their names but would work, individually and collectively, to vigorously promote the community school vision.
- *A coalition of networks, not individual schools:* The Coalition actively seeks partnerships with networks of schools where there is major school district commitment to community schools or there exists a leadership group of school and community leaders supporting community schools. Individual schools benefit from Coalition activities and participate in Coalition conferences and other events but do not serve formally as partners.

Organizing Strategies

From 1997 through 1999, the Emerging Coalition held a series of individual conversations and major meetings. These were strategically designed to simultaneously build the coalition and clarify its core ideas. The national process began much as local initiatives do—by reaching out to key constituencies with a stake in community schools, building a shared vision, and agreeing on a common purpose. From the outset, major funders—the Mott Foundation, the DeWitt Wallace-Reader's Digest Fund, the Ewing Marion Kauffman Foundation, and the Carnegie Corporation—have provided critical support, not only financially but also through active participation.

Building a Big Tent

Conversations began with major education associations and unions and steadily widened to include leaders of national organizations and government agencies in all of the broad areas promoting community school initiatives from outside the education community: youth development, health and human services, and community development. Within these groups, Coalition organizers hoped to reach leaders connected to such areas as after-school programming, service learning, school facilities planning, health and mental health services, school-to-work efforts, literacy, and family support, among many others.

Special effort was made to involve leaders of all of the major national community school models. Beacon Schools, Community Education, Communities in Schools, Schools of the Twenty-First Century, and Communities in Schools, as well as the CAS and University-Assisted Community Schools, all eventually had representatives on the Coalition's steering committee.

Local and state constituents were also invited in. Given the inherently local nature of community schools work and the fact that many initiatives in the late 1980s and early 1990s were fueled by state funds, it made sense to include state and local actors as well as national players. The participation of local groups would give the Coalition local roots and enable it to tap the experience of local community school leaders. Engaging state initiatives would better position the Coalition to affect community school policy and strategy at the state level.

These early meetings gave potential partners representing many different sectors and perspectives an opportunity to take part in developing a shared vision and to see the benefits of joining forces with like-minded others. The idea was to create a "big tent" inclusive enough to represent the genuinely comprehensive nature of community schools.

Creating a Shared Vision

Crafting language that reflected a united vision was a crucial—and challenging—task. Every event, from large-scale meetings to individual discussions, provided an opportunity for people to clarify their beliefs, challenge assumptions, and search for ways to express common understandings.

As work continued internally, Ernesto Cortez, director of the Southwest Region of the Industrial Areas Foundation, suggested a series of community focus groups. They were designed to further test the viability of the Coalition's approach and strengthen the Coalition's community development perspective. Meetings in 1999–2000 in Birmingham, Houston, Philadelphia, and San Francisco affirmed the value and importance of the Coalition. They also brought tensions and critical issues to light. Many participants were doubtful that public schools, because of their hierarchical and bureaucratic nature, could ever become genuine centers of community and freely share their resources. Participants were also concerned that public school emphasis on academic achievement (even greater since passage of the No Child Left Behind Act) would diminish the importance of youth development strategies in community schools.

The challenges raised in these community forums were echoed in Coalition meetings, setting areas of disagreement among Coalition partners into bold relief. As partners stated their views and questioned assumptions, often many times over, understanding grew. While core debates still exist, a common ground has been found. A formal statement of vision and guiding principles was issued by the Coalition in 2000 (see Box 17.2).

Box 17.2 Vision and Principles: Coalition for Community Schools

Using public schools as a hub, community schools bring together many partners to offer a range of supports and opportunities to children, youth, families, and communities—before, during, and after school, seven days a week. These partners work to achieve the following results:

- Children are ready to learn when they enter school and every day thereafter.
- All students learn and achieve to high standards.
- Young people are well prepared for adult roles in the workplace, as parents and as citizens.
- Families and neighborhoods are safe, supportive, and engaged.
- Parents and community members are involved with the school and their own lifelong learning.

There are many community school models, but they tend to share a core set of operating principles:

- Foster strong partnerships—Partners share their resources and expertise and work together to design community schools and make them work.
- Share accountability for results—Clear, mutually agreed-upon results drive the work of community schools. Data helps partners measure progress toward results. Agreements enable them to hold each other accountable and move beyond "turf battles."
- Set high expectations for all—Community schools are organized to support learning. Children, youth and adults are expected to learn at high standards and be contributing members of their community.
- Build on the community's strengths, Community schools marshal the assets of the entire community, including the people who live and work there, local organizations, and the school.
- Embrace diversity—Community schools know their communities. They work to develop respect and a strong, positive identity for people of diverse backgrounds and are committed to the welfare of the whole community.
- Avoid cookie-cutter solutions—Building on the lessons of others, each community school defines its needs, identifies its assets, and creates its own version of a community school.

Advancing a National Agenda

Influencing the Water Supply

Jane Quinn, one of the Coalition's initial funders as program director for the DeWitt Wallace-Reader's Digest Fund and now assistant executive director for community schools at CAS, often summarizes one of the Coalition's major purposes this way: "It's all about getting the idea of community schools into the water supply." By fulfilling its mission to mobilize the resources and capacity of multiple sectors and creating a united movement, the Coalition can help make community schools a permanent part of the education landscape.

Since its formal inception in June of 1999, the Coalition has focused on four major goals, each with multiple objectives.

- Share information about successful community school policies, programs and practices
- Build broader public understanding and support for community schools
- Inform public- and private-sector policies in order to strengthen community schools
- Develop sustainable sources of funding for community schools

It has used communication, knowledge development, and public-policy strategies to make tangible progress in each area.

Galvanizing Partners across Sectors

The Coalition's effort to build and mobilize a community school network has resulted in a partnership of more than 170 national, state, and local organizations. They cut across a dozen or more sectors, all of which are vital to the long-term development of community schools.

Partners have advanced the work of the Coalition in many ways, often by actively organizing within their own organizations. Many have written about aspects of community schools in their respective journals and hosted presentations on community schools at conferences and symposia. These continuing events greatly multiply the number of people the Coalition is able to reach. Biannual national conferences provide a forum for generating new momentum and celebrating the achievements of community schools. Two hundred people attended the first event in 1998; by 2002 the number had grown to more than 600 participants from 34 states.

Educating Policy Makers, Practitioners, and the Public

In 1998 the Coalition summarized its vision and guiding principles in a brochure for parents, teachers, community members, and policy makers. A companion publication, *Community Schools: Partnerships for Excellence*, provided concrete examples of what community schools look like. Community schools were further showcased by a media campaign, financed by CAS and cosponsored by the Coalition and the national Ad Council, that generated significant inquiries about community schools and helped prepare the ground for expanded community school efforts.

Two other major publications by the Coalition have helped educate the public and added significantly to the movement's knowledge base. In 2000, *Community Schools: Evaluation Findings to Date* by Joy Dryfoos documented 49 school-community initiatives and summarized early research on their ef-

---

Box 17.3 Making the Difference: Broad Findings

- *Student learning:* Community school students show significant and widely evident gains in academic achievement and in essential areas of nonacademic development.
- *Family engagement:* Families of community-school students show increased stability, communication with teachers, and school involvement. Parents demonstrate a greater sense of responsibility for their children's learning success.
- *School effectiveness:* Community schools enjoy stronger parent-teacher relationships, increased teacher satisfaction, a more positive school environment, and greater community support.
- *Community vitality:* Community schools promote better use of school buildings, and their neighborhoods enjoy increased security, heightened community pride, and better rapport among students and residents.

Source: Martin Blank, Atelia Melaville, and Bela Shah, *Making the Difference: Research and Practice in Community Schools* (Washington, D.C.: Coalition for Community Schools, 2003).

---

fectiveness. Building on this work, in 2003 the Coalition published *Making the Difference: Research and Practice in Community Schools,* which outlined for the first time the unique advantages of community schools and the conditions for learning that they make possible.[9] It also reviewed research from the multiple fields, such as early childhood education, parent programs, and health services, on which these conditions are based and reported on evaluation findings from 20 community school initiatives (see Box 17.3). Both publications were designed to help partner organizations and individual schools communicate the effectiveness of community schools to a wide range of potential supporters and to help practitioners see where and how to strengthen their own efforts.

Informing Policy

The Coalition has devoted considerable attention to developing an effective policy framework. This is a complex undertaking because such a framework must demonstrate how to cross many different institutional boundaries and link state and federal funding streams into an inherently local endeavor. Coalition papers have explored key policy issues at both the state and federal level.[10] In 2003 publications and presentations focused on relationships with the Education Commission of the States and the Council of Chief State School Officers and its members, who run state departments of education, as well as with education and local government organizations such as the American Association of School Administrators, the Council of Great City Schools, the National League of Cities, the U.S. Conference of Mayors, and the National Association of Counties. Invitations to speak at national conferences demonstrated the growing interest in the community school vision.

Building Capacity

With a broad base of support across many sectors, the Coalition is well positioned to act as a catalyst for building networks of comprehensive community schools in local communities. The Coalition has used its Web site, on-line newsletter, various positioning documents, major conferences, and numerous presentations to encourage this development. The steering committee and partners meet several times annually to discuss developments in the field, learn about local initiatives, and address key issues. Events that grew out of these meetings, listed below, were specifically designed to bring together partners across different sectors to help build the capacity of community school networks and strengthen a comprehensive community school vision.

- Youth Development and Education Forum: Together with the Institute for Educational Leadership and the National Collaboration for Youth, in 2002, the Coalition sponsored a forum for national education and youth development leaders that led to the publication *Helping Young People Succeed: Strengthening and Sustaining Relationships between Schools and Youth Development Organizations.*[11]
- Fostering Community as a Resource for Curriculum: A comprehensive community school vision views the community as a learning laboratory, a living textbook that helps students use classroom knowledge and skills to solve problems in their own neighborhoods. The Coalition convened leaders from different models (service learning, academically-based community service, environment as an integrating context for learning, place-based education, and school-to-work programs). The dialogue led to an article in the journal *New Directions for Youth Development.*[12]
- Promoting Intermediary Organizations: Intermediary organizations, such as the United Way, Communities in Schools, and local leadership groups, play a valuable role in facilitating community school networks. They can nurture community alliances and foster relationships between schools and a range of other community agencies and institutions. To help convey their importance, the Coalition worked with five national partners to prepare *Local Intermediary Organizations: Connecting the Dots for Children, Youth and Families.*[13]

Meeting Key Challenges

The challenges facing the community school movement today are not fundamentally different from those in the past. Positioning community schools front and center on the education reform agenda requires the Coalition to

---

Box 17.4 Conditions for Learning

- *Condition #1:* The school has a core instructional program with qualified teachers, a challenging curriculum, and high standards and expectations for students.
- *Condition #2:* Students are motivated and engaged in learning—both in school and in community settings, during and after school.
- *Condition #3:* The basic physical, mental, and emotional health needs of young people and their families are recognized and addressed.
- *Condition #4:* There is mutual respect and effective collaboration among parents, families, and school staff.
- *Condition #5:* Community engagement, together with school efforts, promotes a school climate that is safe, supportive, and respectful, and that connects students to a broader learning community.

Source: Martin Blank, Atelia Melaville, and Bela Shah, *Making the Difference: Research and Practice in Community Schools* (Washington, D.C.: Coalition for Community Schools, 2003).

---

give continuing attention to clarifying its message, deepening partner engagement, and increasing financial assistance.

Communicating the Capacity of Community Schools to Do More, Better

Community schools work to counter the dominant idea that "school should play a narrow academic role set apart from local experiences and life."[14] While the Coalition has made significant progress in communicating our message, much more remains to be done. National attention in 2003 appeared focused not on what schools could do but on what many feel they are failing to do.

Such a limited view of education, which historians John Puckett and Michael Johanek call "a lack of imagination," poses a major obstacle to education reform. They argue as well that by failing to think more broadly about the connection between school and society, we lose an important opportunity to address the growing cynicism, distrust of institutions, and political disengagement that threaten not only classrooms but also democratic society itself.[15] Educators wedded to a narrow view of the school's role cannot avoid the problems of the community; they merely remain isolated from the resources and support an engaged community could provide.

We must communicate to a wide audience the capacity of community schools to do more and do it better. The Coalition's 2003 publication, *Making the Difference: Research and Practice in Community Schools*, shows how this is possible. It describes a community school's comprehensive approach in terms of five "conditions for learning" (see Box 17.4). These conditions relate directly to the school's academic mission. By addressing children's social, emotional, and physical development and the well-being of their families, these learning conditions create an environment in which *all* children can learn at high levels.

Community schools can create these conditions and ensure that no child is left behind because they have three important advantages over traditional schools: (1) they garner additional resources for the school and reduce demands on school staff; (2) they provide learning opportunities that develop both academic and nonacademic competencies; and (3) they help young people, families, schools, and community members build networks of social support and increase their engagement in schools and community life. Community schools are a better idea—and one that works. The Coalition's challenge is to continuously refine and communicate this message to a broad audience.

Fostering Coalition Growth, Inside and Out

The challenge of sustaining a vigorous forum in which individual organizational interests are respected and values maintained while working toward a shared vision is never-ending. The Coalition must continue to nurture community schools by working with partners from inside the educational establishment as well as with outside reformers. Active, highly visible champions for community schools are needed across disciplines and sectors.

The No Child Left Behind Act has placed significant pressure on schools to improve academic performance—with minimal new resources to accomplish this task. Many schools and school districts, faced with these challenges, look only inward for solutions. Others, however, are reaching out and seeking help and support where they can find it. Growing numbers of superintendents are realizing that they do not have all the answers. Bart McCandless, superintendent of the Evansville-Vanderburgh School Corporation in Indiana, sees education as shared responsibility. From his perspective, creating that sense of responsibility "takes getting out there in the community, not just being visible, but actively participating."[16]

The Coalition is working to make its case succinctly to educators and education policy makers, reaching them through as many channels as possible. The various national education associations have been a valuable resource in this process, and more activity is underway closer to the ground through state and local networks. Sharing the successful experience of local community schools, especially in districts that have moved beyond pilot projects to incorporate community school strategies system-wide, is another major Coalition tactic.

At the same time, the Coalition must continue to work outside the education establishment. Leaders in a range of different arenas—elective offices, youth development organizations, human service providers, community development and community organizing groups, and business, civic, and faith-based groups—must see themselves not as helpers or another pair of hands doing the schools' bidding but as partners working jointly with educators to transform schools by creating more effective reform strategies. The Coalition, and community schools, find their strength in the combined and diverse resources of many partners.

As with any large constituency, there are primary, secondary, and other stakeholders. Inside the Coalition, people whose work is devoted to community schools are the primary stakeholders. Other organizations whose core missions focus on a particular constituency or issues see community schools as an important strategy to move their agendas forward. The Coalition often speaks openly about "informing, influencing and infiltrating" their agendas so that community schools gradually will become a more and more important priority for them.

Financing Community Schools

In 2003 states faced some of the toughest fiscal times in recent history, forcing close-to-the-bone cutbacks in education, social services, and other supports for children and families. Little was done at the federal level to fill the gap. In fact, advocates had to fight hard to maintain funding levels for 21st Century Community Learning Centers' after-school programs when the Bush administration proposed a $400 million reduction. In virtually every state, dollars evaporated despite authorization of the No Child Left Behind Act, and unemployment and poverty rates were on the rise.

This fiscal climate poses a major challenge to finding financing for the community school movement. Community schools are able to do more than traditional schools in part because they make the best use of resources by combining existing funding streams in ways that maximize their impact. Large-scale implementation of community schools relies on the strategic use of local resources supplemented by state and federal dollars.

In addition, system-wide implementation typically requires a certain amount of "glue" money. While the philanthropic community has made enormous contributions in this regard, the Coalition recognizes that stable sources of core support are needed to institutionalize community schools. In order to work well, community schools need the following kinds of financial assistance.

- *Funding for community school coordinators:* Hired by a community-based organization or a school district, the coordinator mobilizes and integrates community resources at the school. The annual cost of a coordinator is $40,000–$60,000. Coordinators play a pivotal role, but it is generally difficult to convince policy makers to invest in this kind of operational "glue" money.
- *Flexible funding to attract partners and existing resources:* Experience suggests that where limited flexible support is available, partners are

better able to attract an array of funding sources and redirected services from various agencies. This kind of "glue" can help underwrite the
cost of pulling people together and begin to fill small gaps in service.
By signaling the initiative's credibility and external support, flexible
funding encourages others to participate and can help create a band-
wagon effect.

- *Technical assistance and training:* Training and technical assistance are
  essential to forging enduring relationships between schools and community partners and to sustaining successful community schools. However, most technical assistance is attached to specific categorical programs. Since a community school is not a program but rather a strategic
  approach to aligning related efforts, no earmarked funding is available
  to help guide community school planning and implementation efforts.

A national community school movement warrants federal support. However, the Coalition has not yet found the right formula to make the case for
federal investment in financing community schools. One seemingly obvious
solution, creating a block grant in which several funding streams would be
earmarked at their point of origin for community schools, has never been
advocated by the Coalition. First, this solution would risk undermining the
best interests of partners who rely on specific funding streams for their "bread
and butter" support; second, block-granting of funds is unlikely to increase
the amount of funding available overall.

The prevailing focus on academic achievement in the federal No Child
Left Behind legislation also has made it difficult to frame a federal legislative agenda for community schools. As of 2003 we were still seeking the right
pathway toward this goal, while also working to be ready for the request for
reauthorization of the No Child Left Behind Act expected in 2006.

In the meantime, local community school initiatives recognize the long-
term challenge but choose not to make a lack of startup or operational money
an excuse for doing nothing. "We have a lot of partnerships that, like a
phoenix, grew out of the ashes," reports one Indiana school superintendent.
"It's nice to have money, but you can get started even if you don't."[17]

Curriculum and Community

Community schools planners and leaders believe that the community itself
is an important resource for the academic curriculum and that its history,
culture, assets, and challenges should be part of the curriculum's content.
Our experience shows that this approach can help overcome the disconnect
students experience between learning and life and can help motivate them
to learn. Research continues to confirm this. In a 2004 report on high schools
in the United States, a National Academy of Sciences committee found: "The
instruction typical of most urban high schools . . . fails to engage students
cognitively, emotionally or behaviorally. Evidence indicates that when in-

struction draws on students' preexisting understanding, interests, cultures and real work experiences, the curriculum becomes more meaningful to them."[18]

We believe that the growing concern about students' disengagement from learning, particularly that of students who do not do well on high-stakes tests, opens the door to this more participatory learning strategy. The Coalition expects to focus its attention more intensively on this topic in the future.

Staying Focused on the Big Picture

In that initial conversation in 1997, the founding partners of the Coalition looked forward to a day when community schools were recognized as a central and permanent feature of the educational landscape. Without a concerted effort across many sectors, they knew that that day would be a long time in coming.

Since then, scores of partners have come together under the auspices of the Coalition for Community Schools to call attention to community school ideas. Working under the Coalition's umbrella, as well as individually through their own organizations, Coalition partners have used effective communication, research, and knowledge development, as well as public-policy advocacy at state, national, and local levels, to build a strong, national vehicle for community schools. The language of community schools is indeed making its way into the water supply.

The Coalition is now using that strength to build understanding of community schools not just as a good idea but as an essential strategy in educational reform. The emergence of champions of community schools, such as David Cicilline, the mayor of Providence, bodes well for the future. According to Cicilline, "community schools deliver what few, if any, other . . . reforms can: the opportunity for many different partners to participate in a joint venture, to excel in that venture, and to contribute collectively to permanent change in the course of a child's life, or in the life of an entire community."[19]

When CAS writes about its important achievements 10 years from now, the list, no doubt, will be long. At the top should be its role in advancing community schools, both as the developer of a powerful community school model and as a founding member of the Coalition for Community Schools. Helping to transform public schools by expanding opportunities for educational excellence and building a sense of connection to a caring community is an extraordinary contribution to society. We believe that if our children are to flourish—and democracy is to endure—it is a contribution whose time has come.

NOTES

1. Joy Dryfoos, *Full-Service Schools: A Revolution in Health and Social Services for Children, Youth, and Families* (San Francisco: Jossey-Bass, 1994).

2. John Dewey, *Democracy and Education* (1916; reprint, New York: Free Press, 1944), p. 214.

3. Jane Addams, *Twenty Years at Hull House* (New York: Macmillan, 1912).

4. John S. Rogers, "Community Schools: Lessons for the Past and Present," report to the Charles S. Mott Foundation, 1998.

5. The National Center for Community Education remains a vital resource for community education and community schools works. For more information, go to http://www.nccenet.org/.

6. Communities in Schools was originally called Cities in Schools. The official name change occurred in 1996. For information about their current work, go to http://www.cisnet.org/.

7. To learn more about these different approaches to community schools, check the following Web sites: Beacon Schools, http://www.fcny.org/html/youth/; Schools of the Twenty-First Century, http://www.yale.edu/21C/index.html; University-Assisted Community Schools, http://www.upenn.edu/ccp/about.shtml; and Bridges to Success, http://www.bridgestosuccess.org/.

8. For a look at 20 different local, state, and national approaches, see Atelia Melaville, *Learning Together* (Flint, Mich.: Institute for Educational Leadership and Charles Stewart Mott Foundation, 1998).

9. Martin Blank, Atelia Melaville, and Bela P. Shah, *Making the Difference: Research and Practice in Community Schools* (Washington, D.C.: Coalition for Community Schools, 2003), http://www.communityschools.org/mtdhomepage.html.

10. See *A National Policy Approach To Create and Sustain Community Schools: Promoting Policies That Strengthen Schools, Families and Communities, a Work in Progress,* Coalition for Community Schools, 2000, http://www.communityschools.org/POLICYDRAFT5.PDF, and *A Handbook for State Policy Leaders: Community Schools, Improving Student Learning, Strengthening Schools, Families and Communities,* Coalition for Community Schools, 2002.

11. Martin Blank, *Helping Young People Succeed: Strengthening and Sustaining Relationships between Schools and Youth Development Organizations,* Coalition for Community Schools, 2002.

12. Martin J. Blank, Sheri Deboe Johnson, and Bela P. Shah, "Community as Text: Using the Community as a Resource for Learning in Community Schools," *New Directions for Youth Development,* Spring 2003: 107–20.

13. Martin Blank, *Local Intermediary Organizations: Connecting the Dots for Children, Youth and Families,* Coalition for Community Schools, American Youth Policy Forum, Center for Youth Development and Policy Research at the Academy for Educational Development, Finance Project, Jobs for the Future, and New Ways to Work, 2003, http://www.communityschools.org/Intermediaries.pdf.

14. Rogers, "Community Schools," p. 6.

15. John Puckett and Michael Johanek, "A Public Place, a Public Purpose: Leonard Covello and the American Community School," manuscript, 2002.

16. Martin Blank and Dan Cady, "Systems Change through Community Schools," *School Administrator Magazine,* January 2004, p. 28.

17. Bart McCandless, interview by author, June 10, 2003.

18. National Academy of Sciences, *Engaging Schools: Fostering High School Students' Motivation to Learn,* Washington, D.C., 2004.

19. David Cicilline, press briefing for *Making the Difference: Research and Practice in Community Schools,* May 13, 2003, http://www.communityschools.org/DCicilline.pdf (accessed October 17, 2003).

Looking to the Future

JOY G. DRYFOOS AND JANE QUINN

It may seem strange in a chaotic political period to say that the community school movement is alive, well, and growing. Yet such chaos can give rise to collaborative concepts. Out of adversity comes action, and that action is directed toward helping children succeed in an increasingly difficult environment of higher poverty levels, less health insurance, failing schools, more mental health problems, and a widening gap between social classes and races. It is not a pretty picture, but it is a challenging one.

The Children's Aid Society (CAS) is moving forward with its commitment to community schools. Although we thought we would stop at 10 school sites in New York City, during the 2003–2004 academic year we initiated three more—two in the Bronx and one on Staten Island. Our Technical Assistance

Center is in great demand, hosting more than 600 visits in 2003 and responding to more than 500 requests for technical assistance. Also in 2003 we convened representatives from more than 60 of the national and international adaptation sites for a three-day practicum—a training and networking session at which we heard testimonials to success and stories about challenges. Many of the original adaptation sites have moved from one dynamic community school to a cluster of schools within their neighborhoods or districts. And some of these original adaptation sites have matured to the point of providing guidance to other schools that want to emulate their success. There are now more than 200 adaptation sites—community schools based on the CAS model—in the United States and other countries.

We are often asked, "Just how many community schools are there in this country?" We have a reasonable census of CAS sites (13) and adaptations (215), but that is only the beginning of a count. The question is difficult to answer because there are so many versions of other models and so many schools without any of these components that nevertheless call themselves "community schools." We have tried to construct a continuum along which schools can measure themselves.

Phase One: One or two components, such as after-school programs or school-based clinics, offered by outside agencies but not integrated with school.

Phase Two: Three or four components, such as after-school, before-school, clinic, and family resource center, not integrated with school.

Phase Three: Three or four components, such as after-school, before-school, clinic, and family resource center, integrated with one another and with the school curriculum; full-time coordinator from lead agency.

Our best guess is that thousands of schools fall into the first category (1,400 schools have clinics; 7,500 have after-school grants), perhaps 2,000 into the second group, and a couple of hundred into the third. The Coalition for Community Schools in 2004 was in the process of compiling a directory—an essential tool for further program development.

What would it take to "go to scale"? We do not believe that every school needs to become a full-service community school, but certainly those schools that are eligible for Title 1 services have many needy children. About 25% of the 85,000 public schools in the United States (almost 19,000) would fit this definition. The Department of Education, operating under the No Child Left Behind Act, had in early 2004 already identified 8,652 schools that, according to their regulations, were failing. It is clear that the potential for our kind of school reform—one that addresses the academic as well as the nonacademic needs of children—is enormous.

All the ingredients for going to scale are described in this book; the most important is the vision of a full-service community school. Someone in the school system or someone in the community support system has to get turned on to the concept. People have to come together and figure out what their particular school or their whole school system needs in order to help the children and parents overcome barriers to learning. They need to be exposed to the program components and to see how they might fit together. If technical assistance for data gathering and planning were readily available on a large scale (for example, if states had that capacity), this movement could pick up steam very rapidly.

Obviously, funds are needed—about $500 to $1,000 per student per year, depending on the complexity of the needs and the availability of co-located services (existing services that can be moved into a school building). It is time for federal legislation to specifically support community schools. We have carefully built the models, conducted a range of research to show their impact, and learned a lot about implementation. Our friend in Congress, Steny Hoyer of Maryland, has been trying for several years to gain support for the Full-Service Community Schools Act. Although the initial draft legislation calls for only $200 million, it would nevertheless give visibility and credibility to this significant movement.

Between the two of us, we have visited scores of school sites around the country and encountered many heroic individuals. We strongly believe that committed people are the most important ingredient of successful community schools. Not everyone is a born collaborator. Some have to acquire the skills, and others just do not know how or do not want to know how to work intensively with others. Born collaborators keep their eyes on the importance of the outcomes of their efforts and are able to withstand the threats of day-to-day inefficiencies, turf wars, and crises. They work long hours and go to endless meetings.

Training programs can provide help for people who need and want to acquire the necessary skills. A few universities are taking first steps by offering combined graduate degrees in education, social work, and psychology. In our ideal course of studies, we would include public health and business for those interested in pursuing careers as principals or coordinators of community schools. At least one graduate school of social work, the School of Social Service Administration (SSA) at the University of Chicago, is developing a degree program specifically for community school directors. Former SSA dean Edward Lawlor said, "This program will develop an important new professional role for social work in the schools. . . . These leadership roles are complex and demanding, requiring expertise in education, clinical practice and assessment, program development, family support, management, policy, and community development."[1] This new program is designed to prepare graduates to work nationally and locally; the Chicago Public Schools have publicly committed themselves to the development of 100 community schools over the next five years, and the first cohort of 20 such schools has already been selected.

Looking ahead, we see that another issue holding promise for the growth and vitality of community schools is the influx of new Americans coming into the nation's schools. The 2000 Census confirmed what many educators and planners already knew—the United States is experiencing the largest wave of immigration in our nation's history. Many schools are struggling to catch up with this reality, including the facts that more of their students are English language learners, that many of the students' parents may not be literate in their native languages, and that some students are arriving in middle school with no prior formal education. At the institutional level, schools face such challenges as underprepared teachers and staff who are unable to speak the languages of the recent arrivals.

The community schools strategy represents a viable approach for addressing these issues. Many community agencies are skilled at welcoming new Americans and building on their considerable strengths, and they may have more flexibility than schools in hiring community residents who speak the language and understand the culture of their neighbors. Immigration is a key factor in spurring interest in community schools internationally as well as in the United States. CAS has hosted hundreds of international visitors over the past decade, and one of the primary reasons these visitors cite for their interest in the community schools strategy is their search for ways to meet the needs of recent arrivals to their countries.

Another major trend that is creating demand for community schools is the current boom in building for education—by most accounts, the largest in recent memory. Several factors have contributed to this wave of new school construction: policy makers project that by 2008 public school enrollment will climb another 1.4 million, to 48 million; inattention to the physical infrastructure of schools over the past several decades is catching up with many districts; and a spate of court decisions mandating equitable financing of public education has compelled some state governments to make needed investments in their low-income schools, including the physical facilities. As new schools are built in communities across the country, many community-based organizations are exploring joint use agreements and other promising ways to make the best use of public facilities and reach more young people with youth development services.

Based on 12 years of living in, and partnering deeply with, schools, CAS has developed three mantras that guide our daily work:

- It's all about relationships.
- Everything has to be negotiated, all the time.
- To make partnerships really work, you have to have the word "yes" written in your heart.

The future is likely to bring more opportunities for the kinds of partnerships described in this book, as schools and policy makers alike discover that if we are serious about leaving no child behind, our society will have to create more responsive institutions that address children's nonacademic as well as academic needs.

On a recent visit to the Gardner School in Boston, one of the strongest and most mature CAS adaptation sites, we observed that the principal and the coordinator shared an office. This seemed to symbolize the growing togetherness that successful partnerships can bring. It is no longer "my" school or "your" school, but "our" school. Everyone must share the responsibility. Our hope is that the lessons we have propounded here will be used to spread the word and meet that challenge.

NOTE

1. "Bank One Donates $1 Million to Create Community Schools Leadership Program at SSA," *University of Chicago School of Social Service Administration News and Notes,* March 2004: 1.

Index